AF777617

© 2022 World Scientific Publishing Europe Ltd.
https://doi.org/10.1142/9781800610408_fmatter

# Contents

# Dual-Channel Supply Chain Decisions with Risk-Averse Behavior

# Dual-Channel Supply Chain Decisions with Risk-Averse Behavior

*Editors*

**Bo Li**
*Tianjin University, China*

**Dong-Ping Song**
*University of Liverpool, UK*

World Scientific

NEW JERSEY • LONDON • SINGAPORE • BEIJING • SHANGHAI • HONG KONG • TAIPEI • CHENNAI • TOKYO

*Published by*

World Scientific Publishing Europe Ltd.
57 Shelton Street, Covent Garden, London WC2H 9HE
*Head office:* 5 Toh Tuck Link, Singapore 596224
*USA office:* 27 Warren Street, Suite 401-402, Hackensack, NJ 07601

**Library of Congress Cataloging-in-Publication Data**
Names: Song, Dong-Ping, editor. | Li, Bo (Professor of economics), editor.
Title: Dual-channel supply chain decisions with risk-averse behavior /
editors, Bo Li, Tianjin University, China, Dong-Ping Song, University of Liverpool, UK.
Description: New Jersey : World Scientific, [2022] | Includes bibliographical references and index.
Identifiers: LCCN 2021025591 (print) | LCCN 2021025592 (ebook) |
ISBN 9781800610392 (hardcover) | ISBN 9781800610408 (ebook) |
ISBN 9781800610415 (ebook other)
Subjects: LCSH: Business logistics. | Marketing channels.
Classification: LCC HD38.5 .D823 2022 (print) | LCC HD38.5 (ebook) | DDC 658.7--dc23
LC record available at https://lccn.loc.gov/2021025591
LC ebook record available at https://lccn.loc.gov/2021025592

**British Library Cataloguing-in-Publication Data**
A catalogue record for this book is available from the British Library.

Copyright © 2022 by World Scientific Publishing Europe Ltd.

*All rights reserved. This book, or parts thereof, may not be reproduced in any form or by any means, electronic or mechanical, including photocopying, recording or any information storage and retrieval system now known or to be invented, without written permission from the Publisher.*

For photocopying of material in this volume, please pay a copying fee through the Copyright Clearance Center, Inc., 222 Rosewood Drive, Danvers, MA 01923, USA. In this case permission to photocopy is not required from the publisher.

For any available supplementary material, please visit
https://www.worldscientific.com/worldscibooks/10.1142/Q0306#t=suppl

Desk Editors: Jayanthi Muthuswamy/Michael Beale/Shi Ying Koe

Typeset by Stallion Press
Email: enquiries@stallionpress.com

© 2022 World Scientific Publishing Europe Ltd.
https://doi.org/10.1142/9781800610408_fmatter

# Preface

In the era of e-commerce and digitalization, new commercial patterns and opportunities are emerging. For example, in addition to traditional reselling marketing channels, manufacturers can easily open direct channels using a variety of digital marketing strategies. These new marketing channels will cause conflict and competition between manufacturers and resellers. This raises the important question of how to make optimal decisions for multiple players in dual-channel supply chain contexts. Within changing and uncertain operation environments, business enterprises must face tougher challenges than before to survive in competitive markets.

This book aims to address representative decision-making problems in dual-channel supply chains with risk-averse channel members. The most recently developed risk assessment technique, Conditional Value-at-Risk (CVaR), will be adopted as the predominant criterion to measure the risk-averse attitude. Based on game theory, important issues such as channel selection, pricing, order quantity, manufacturer encroachment, greening strategy, consumer return policies, financing strategies, channel coordination, contract design, information asymmetry, and capacity constraint will be modeled and analyzed. This book will help readers better understand operations management in dual-channel supply chain contexts with risk-averse behaviors, and will also provide effective techniques and tools for researchers and offer managerial insights for practitioners.

© 2022 World Scientific Publishing Europe Ltd.
https://doi.org/10.1142/9781800610408_fmatter

# About the Editors

**Bo Li** is a Professor in the College of Management and Economics at Tianjin University. She obtained her PhD degree from Tianjin University. Her research field includes supply chain management and behavior operation management. She is an editorial board member of *Asia-Pacific Journal of Operational Research* and an Executive Director of behavioral operations management branch at Operations Research Institute in China. She has had papers published in journals including *Omega*, *European Journal of Operational Research*, *Transportation Research Part B/E*, *International Journal Production Research, International Journal of Production Economics*, and *International Journal of Electronic Commerce.*

**Dong-Ping Song** is a Professor of Supply Chain Management in Liverpool University Management School. He obtained his PhD at Newcastle University and was a Professor of International Logistics at Plymouth University Business School. He is a Senior Member of IEEE; an Associate Editor for *Transportation Research Part E* and *International Journal of Shipping and Transport Logistics*. He has research expertise in applying mathematical modeling, data analytics, artificial intelligence, and simulation-based tools to various supply chain, logistics and transportation systems, particularly in the area of maritime transport. He has had papers published in journals including *IEEE Transactions on Automatic Control*, *Transportation Research: Part B/E/D*, and *European Journal of Operational Research*.

© 2022 World Scientific Publishing Europe Ltd.
https://doi.org/10.1142/9781800610408_0001

# Chapter 1

# Dual-Channel Supply Chains and Risk-Averse Behaviors

**Bo Li**[*,‡] **and Dong-Ping Song**[†,§]

[*] *College of Management and Economics, Tianjin University, China*
[†] *School of Management, University of Liverpool, Liverpool, UK*
[‡] *libo0410@tju.edu.cn*
[§] *Dongping.Song@liverpool.ac.uk*

## 1.1. Introduction

Over the last decade, e-commerce has grown significantly and become an indispensable business framework in the global retail industry. According to Statista (www.statista.com), e-retail sales worldwide were 1548 billion US$ in 2015 and reached 3535 billion US$ in 2019. In terms of the share of global retail sales, e-commerce accounted for 7.4% in 2015 and reached 14.1% in 2019. It was estimated that about 1.92 billion people purchased goods or services online in 2019 (Clement, 2020). Specifically, the retail e-commerce sales worldwide in billion US$ and its share of total retail sales from 2015 to 2019 are shown in Table 1.1 (based on Clement (2020)).

The outbreak of the COVID-19 pandemic has reshaped our daily life. More consumers tend to do shopping online in greater quantity and frequency. According to the report from IBM's US Retail Index, the department stores are expected to decline by over 60%, whereas e-commerce is estimated to grow by nearly 20% in 2020 (Perez, 2020).

With the rapid development of e-commerce and information communication technology, online direct sales channels have become

Table 1.1. Retail e-commerce sales and share worldwide from 2015 to 2019.

| Year | 2015 | 2016 | 2017 | 2018 | 2019 |
|---|---|---|---|---|---|
| Sales in US$ billion | 1548 | 1845 | 2382 | 2982 | 3535 |
| Share of total retail | 7.4% | 8.6% | 10.4% | 12.2% | 14.1% |

an important marketing channel strategy for manufacturers. Many brand manufacturers, e.g., IBM, HP, Lenovo, Unilever, Heinz, Nike, PepsiCo and Nestle, have been involved in e-commerce. In fact, there have been about 45% of manufacturers selling directly online (Redtechnology, 2020).

The benefits of adopting online sales channels are evident including increasing revenue, reducing costs, expanding reach, influencing the end-users, deepening customer relationships, and gathering insight for product development. However, the direct sales channels also bring about many challenging issues on relationship management along supply chains. In particular, there is a common concern that creating a direct-to-consumer online channel will lead to competitions and conflicts with existing physical offline marketing channel. This phenomenon is sometimes called manufacturer encroachment. Specifically, manufacturer encroachment refers to a practice where the manufacturer in a supply chain introduces a direct channel and competes with the retailer in the traditional wholesale market. A dual-channel supply chain may be defined as a supply chain system consisting of a traditional offline retail channel (i.e., brick-and-mortar channel) and a direct online channel. This book aims to address how to manage and coordinate the decisions of players in such dual-channel supply chain contexts.

Since the dual-channel supply chain is closely related to marketing channel theory and supply chain management (SCM), Sec. 1.2 will describe the marketing channel theory and SCM and their relevance to dual-channel supply chain systems. Section 1.3 explains the concepts of uncertainty, risk and risk attitude, which leads to an important phenomenon of decision makers in supply chain systems, i.e., the risk-averse behaviors. Three most commonly used types of risk assessment techniques including mean–variance, value-at-risk (VaR), and conditional value-at-risk (CVaR) will be explained and contrasted in terms of their relative advantages. Section 1.4 describes typical decision-making problems in dual-channel supply chain systems. Finally, the structure of the book is presented in Sec. 1.5.

## 1.2. Marketing Channel and SCM

This section introduces the relevant concepts in the marketing channel theory first, and then introduces the concept of supply chain management with the discussions of their relevance to the dual-channel SCM.

### 1.2.1. Marketing channel and relevance to dual-channel supply chains

Marketing channel can be defined as "*the external contractual organization that management operates to achieve its distribution objectives*" (Rosenbloom, 2004). Kotler and Keller (2015) indicated that marketing channels are sets of interdependent organizations involved in the process of making a product or service available for use or consumption. From the above definitions, marketing channel emphasizes the contacts with external organizations. Such contacts are mainly associated with negotiatory functions, e.g., buying, selling, transferring title to goods or services. The distribution objectives of marketing channel are to make a product or service available to the customer for use or consumption in an efficient and effective manner.

The basic role of marketing channel is to bridge the gap between the producer of a product and its users. Marketing channel strategies involve the design and management of channel structure. From the managerial perspective, channel structure can be defined as the group of channel members to which a set of distribution tasks has been allocated. In consumer markets, there are a range of channel structures, e.g., direct channel, multi-level indirect structure. The most common channel structure for consumer products is a four-level indirect channel from manufacturer to wholesaler, retailer, and consumers. After a marketing channel has been established, a number of flows emerge among channel members, e.g., product flow, negotiation flow, ownership flow, information flow, promotion flow, and payment flow. More specifically, product flow refers to the actual physical movement of goods from the manufacturer through all of the channel members who physically possess the goods, to final consumers. Negotiation flow refers to the interplay of the buying and selling functions between two channel members concerning the transfer of title to goods and the payment arrangement. Ownership flow refers to the movement of the title to the goods as it is passed along from the manufacturer to final consumers. Information flow refers to the documentation and communications that are exchanged among channel members associated with the negotiation, transaction and physical distribution. Information flow can move up or down among all relevant parties. Promotion flow refers to the flow of persuasive communication from upstream parties to downstream parties in the form of advertising, personal selling, sales promotion, and public relations. Payment flow refers to the fund transactions in the purchase and sale of goods or services, which is the reverse of ownership flow. Broadly speaking, marketing channel strategy involves planning and managing all of the above flows associated with the marketing channel (Rosenbloom, 2004).

In the context of marketing channel, there are three important types of channel behaviors that characterize the channel relationships: competition, conflict, and power. Competition is the behavior in which different parties are working for a goal or object controlled by another party, e.g., competing for customers in the same market. Channel competition occurs when organizations in different marketing channels compete with each other in the convention commercial sense. It is an inter-channel relationship. Conflict is a state of opposition or discord among the organizations comprising a marketing channel. Channel conflict occurs when one channel member perceives that another member's actions impede the attainment of its goals. Hence, channel conflict is an intra-channel relationship. There are seven common causes that lead to channel conflict: role incongruities, resource scarcities, differences of perception, differences of expectation, decision domain disagreements, incompatible goals, and communication difficulties (Rosenbloom, 2004). In the dual-channel context, competition and conflict co-exist because the same two channel members (e.g., manufacturer and retailer) may be located in the same marketing channel in a vertical relationship (traditional offline channel); meanwhile, they may also be located in different marketing channels in a horizontal relationship (offline channel versus online channel).

Channel power is defined as the capacity of one channel member to control or influence the behavior of another channel members, e.g., to get another channel member to do something that might not be done otherwise. There are five typical categories of channel power include reward power, coercive power, expert power, referent power, and legitimate power (Rosenbloom, 2004). Channel conflict often arises because channel members have power relationships. For example, Dell had been selling HP printers for 8 years, which was often bundled with Dell's computers. When HP heard that Dell was considering selling its own line of Dell printers, HP employed coercive power by dropping Dell as a channel member from its marketing channel with the intention to dissuade Dell from implementing its plan (Rosenbloom, 2004). In general, channel members will gain cooperation best if they cultivate the channel power in the order of referent power, expert power, legitimate power, and reward power, and avoid the use of coercive power that may escalate the channel conflict and even lead to the breakdown of the marking channel (Kotler and Keller, 2015). In the dual-channel context, the appropriate use of channel powers may be able to coordinate channel relationships and mitigate the double marginalization phenomenon.

Marketing channel theory focuses on inter-organizational relationships with less attention to intra-organizational issues. Moreover, marketing channel theory has less emphasis on the contact with facilitators or facilitating intermediaries such as raw material suppliers, transport operators, freight forwarders, public warehouse companies, banks, insurance companies, etc. In that sense, the concept of supply chain expands the notion of marketing channel, which will be explained in next subsection.

### 1.2.2. SCM and relevance to dual-channel supply chains

According to the Council of Supply Chain Management Professionals, SCM can be defined as the active management of supply chain activities to maximize customer value and achieve a sustainable competitive advantage. Here the supply chain activities cover everything from product development, sourcing and production to logistics, and the information systems needed to coordinate these activities. It implies that multiple organizations are linked together to form partnerships as the supply chain through physical product flows and information flows [https://cscmp.org].

A few points can be extracted from the definition of SCM. Firstly, SCM encompasses the planning and management of all activities involved in product development, sourcing, procurement, operations, and logistics. Secondly, SCM can include all the relevant organizations such as suppliers, intermediaries, third-party service providers, and customers as channel partners. Thirdly, SCM emphasizes coordination, collaboration and integration internally within an organization and externally across various channel partners with the aim to maximize customer value in the most effective, efficient and sustainable way.

The differences between supply chains and marketing channels may be explained from the following aspects:

- *Activities*: Supply chain involves broader activities. It can span from raw materials, work-in-progress, finished goods, to reverse logistics. Marketing channels mainly focus on the product by bridging the gap between the producer and customers. Hence, marketing channels provide a narrower scope within the supply chain.
- *Entities*: Marketing channels usually involve manufacturer, wholesaler, retailer, and customers as channel members. Supply chain can involve a wider range of entities, not only including those in marketing channels, but also including third-party service providers, logistics agents, supplier's suppliers, and customer's customers.
- *Focal points*: Marketing channel is purely customer-facing with the emphasis on the marketing mix, i.e., product, place, price, promotion. The marketing channel management attempts to address the questions like: Does the product meet customer needs? Will customers be able to find the product where they shop? Will customers consider that the product is priced favorably? Will marketing communications be able to reach customers? On the other hand, SCM focuses on the flow and storage of raw materials, work-in-progress and finished goods along the supply chain by maximizing customer value in the most effective, efficient and sustainable way.

- *Relationships*: Entities in marketing channel are often loosely linked on the basis of an arm's length transaction. Channel conflict and channel power are two important behaviors in marketing channels. SCM emphasizes partnerships. Coordination and collaboration are essential relationships among supply chain members in order to achieve its goal. Supply chain contract can be an effective measure to resolve the channel conflict and channel competition issues arising from dual-channel situations.

From the above discussion, it can be seen that it is more appropriate to discuss the decision-making in the dual-channel context from the SCM perspective. Therefore, this book will use the term dual-channel supply chain, which refers to a supply chain system consisting of a traditional retail channel and a direct online channel.

Supply chain systems face a variety of uncertainties that may exist in supply (e.g., material supply and subcontract order), production (e.g., processing time and resource availability), transport (e.g., delivery delay and equipment availability), demand (e.g., customer orders and demand arrivals), and environmental factors (e.g., market price, exchange rate fluctuation, politic events, natural disasters). Different decision-makers may perceive the impact of uncertainty differently. This leads to the concept of risk attitude, which in turn affects the supply chain members' decision behaviors. Such behavior is an emerging and important phenomenon that will be discussed in the next section.

## 1.3. Risk-Averse Behavior in Dual-Channel Supply Chains

Uncertainty is defined as the state of being uncertain, usually applies to future events that cannot be predicted accurately. Uncertainty may be classified into two types: aleatory uncertainty (due to randomness) and epistemic uncertainty (due to lack of knowledge). Risk can be defined as the negative effect of uncertainty on objectives. It emphasizes on the undesirable outcome caused by the uncertainty.

Risk attitude refers to the decision maker's chosen response to the risk, which is influenced by its perception on the consequence of the uncertainty. Risk attitudes exist on a spectrum covering risk paranoid, risk-averse, risk-neutral, risk seeking, and risk addicted. Nevertheless, the terminologies of risk-averse (risk avoiding), risk-neutral and risk seeking (risk loving) are the most commonly used risk attitudes in practice.

In economics and finance fields, risk aversion is an attitude that an investor prefers lower returns with more certainty (i.e., lower risk). Risk seeking is an attitude that an investor prefers higher returns with less certainty (i.e., higher risk). Risk-neutral is the middle attitude that an investor has an indifferent preference toward risk. In practice, most investors are regarded as risk-averse.

In the last decade, risk attitude, especially, risk-averse behavior, has attracted much attention in SCM. The main reason is that supply chain operations are facing a substantial level of risks that may be caused by various uncertainties existed in the supply chain system and its environment. Note that the same uncertain situation may lead to different risk attitudes from decision makers depending on how they perceive the risk implied by the uncertainty. This drives different behaviors and then affects the decisions. Therefore, it is important to consider the risk attitudes of decision makers in the supply chain systems.

There are three common types of methods to measure a decision-maker's risk attitude: mean–variance model (Chiu and Choi, 2016), VaR (Tapiero, 2005), and CVaR (Li *et al.*, 2014). Each type of risk measures has its own characteristics, which will be briefly introduced in the following subsections.

### 1.3.1. Mean–variance method

Mean–variance is the first analysis method proposed to estimate risk attitude (Markowitz, 1959). The idea of the mean–variance method is to consider both the expected payoff (i.e., mean) and the variation of payoff (i.e., variance). The variance of the payoff represents the risk associated with the investment decision-making problem. Intuitively, the variance of payoff reflects the level of uncertainty. A risk-averse investor would avoid the high variance of the payoff.

Mathematically, let $\pi$ denote the profit of the decision maker. Under the mean–variance criterion, the utility function can be defined as:

$$U = E(\pi) - \lambda \cdot V(\pi), \tag{1.1}$$

where $E(\cdot)$ represents the mathematical expectation, $V(\cdot)$ is the variance of the profit, and $\lambda$ is a parameter representing the risk attitude. Positive $\lambda$ represents risk-averse, negative $\lambda$ represents risk seeking, and $\lambda = 0$ indicates risk-neutral attitude. Intuitively, a risk-averse decision maker would like to maximize the expected profit and minimize the variance of the profit at the same time. A variant of the mean–variance method is the mean–standard deviation method, which uses standard deviation instead of variance to represent the risk. The utility function under the mean–standard deviation criterion is given as follows, where $\mathrm{SD}(\cdot)$ represents the standard deviation,

$$U = E(\pi) - \lambda \cdot \mathrm{SD}(\pi). \tag{1.2}$$

The advantage of the mean–variance method is that it can be interpreted intuitively and is often analytically tractable. However, the mean–variance is a symmetric measure that treats desirable outcomes as the same as undesirable outcomes in the risk measure. As a result, it is not suitable for the cases where decision makers are more concerned with undesirable outcomes, e.g., losses (Zheng *et al.*, 2017).

### 1.3.2. VaR method

VaR can be defined as the maximum amount of money that is expected to be lost at a predefined confidence level. From the profit perspective, VaR refers to the threshold value of the profit that the probability of the profit falling below the threshold value does not exceed a prespecified level (Sarykalin *et al.*, 2008).

Suppose profit $\pi$ is a random variable. Let $v^\eta(\pi)$ be the $\eta$-quantile of the profit $\pi$, i.e., $\mathrm{Prob}\,\{\pi \le v^\eta(\pi)\} = \eta$. Namely, $v^\eta(\pi)$ represents the threshold value of the profit such that the probability of the profit falls below this threshold value would not exceed $\eta$. Let $F_\pi(\cdot)$ denote the cumulative distribution function of profit $\pi$. The VaR is then given by

$$\mathrm{VaR}^\eta(\pi) := v^\eta(\pi) = \max\{z \mid F_\pi(z) \le \eta\}. \tag{1.3}$$

Statistically, $(1-\eta)$ represents the confidence level that profit $\pi$ is greater than $v^\eta(\pi)$. In that sense, the VaR criterion allows decision makers to limit the likelihood of the resulting profits (or losses), which represents the decision makers' risk attitudes.

Specifically, the parameter $\eta$ can be interpreted as a risk-averse indicator when taking a value in the interval (0, 1]. When $\eta = 1$, the decision maker is risk neutral; otherwise it is risk-averse. As the parameter $\eta$ decreases toward 0, the decision maker becomes more risk-averse, i.e., tends to prefer a higher confidence level to generate at least a specific amount of profit.

### 1.3.3. CVaR method

Note that VaR has a limitation that the tail end of the distribution of profit (or loss) is not assessed. Therefore, when the profits (or losses) that are incurred at the tail end are substantially large or small, such volume is not properly measured. CVaR was created as an extension of VaR to overcome this shortcoming.

Mathematically, the CVaR can be defined as (Rockafellar and Uryasev, 2000, 2002; Sarykalin *et al.*, 2008):

$$\mathrm{CVaR}^{\eta}(\pi) = \int_{-\infty}^{+\infty} z dF_{\pi}^{\eta}(z), \tag{1.4}$$

where $F_{\pi}^{\eta}(z) = 1$, if $z \geq \mathrm{VaR}^{\eta}(\pi)$; $F_{\pi}^{\eta}(z) = F_{\pi}(z)/\eta$, if $z < \mathrm{VaR}^{\eta}(\pi)$. In the context of the objective function being profit, the profits less than VaR should be accounted for. Suppose the random variable $\pi$ has a continuous probability distribution function, $\mathrm{CVaR}^{\eta}(\pi)$ can be interpreted as the conditional expectation of $\pi$ subject to $\pi < \mathrm{VaR}^{\eta}(\pi)$. Therefore, CVaR is actually derived by taking a weighted average between the VaR and profits less than the value-at-risk (Zheng *et al.*, 2017).

An equivalent and more convenient definition of CVaR for a profit function $\pi$is given as follows (Rockafellar and Uryasev, 2000):

$$\mathrm{CVaR}^{\eta}(\pi) = \max_{v \in R}\left\{v + \frac{1}{\eta}E[\min(\pi - v, 0)]\right\}. \tag{1.5}$$

The crucial feature of the above definition is that the function defined within the curly bracket in (1.5) is concave and continuously differentiable. This is especially useful to analyze the maximization problem, and to calculate the $\mathrm{CVaR}^{\eta}(\pi)$, because $\mathrm{CVaR}^{\eta}(\pi)$

defined in (1.5) can be calculated without first having to calculate the $\text{VaR}^{\eta}(\pi)$, which would be more complicated.

### 1.3.4. Comparisons of the three risk measure methods

The mean–variance method is more intuitive and easier to analyze than the VaR and CVaR methods. However, the mean–variance is a symmetric measure and uses the same weight for desirable outcomes and undesirable outcomes, which may not capture the decision maker's risk attitude appropriately.

The VaR and CVaR are more suitable for the situations where decision makers are more concerned with undesirable outcomes. The VaR allows the decision makers to set a confidence level $\eta$, and the VaR can be defined as a threshold value such that the probability that the profit falls below this threshold value is $\eta$. The disadvantages of VaR include: the tail end of the distribution of objective function is not assessed, and it suffers from being unstable and difficult to work with numerically when losses are not "normally" distributed (Rockafellar and Uryasev, 2000). The CVaR is an extension of VaR that can overcome the shortcoming of VaR. It measures the average profit falling below the $\eta$-quantile level, and ignores the contribution of profit above the specified quantile (Rockafellar and Uryasev, 2000). In addition, the CVaR is analytically tractable. However, the disadvantage of CVaR is its complex form and its physical meaning is not easy to understand and interpret by practitioners.

In this book, most of the chapters will use conditional value-at-risk to measure agents' risk-averse behavior to optimize the decisions in dual-channel supply chains. Nevertheless, a couple of chapters will also apply the mean–variance or VaR method.

## 1.4. Typical Decision-Making Problems in Dual-Channel Supply Chains

Balasuburamanian (1998) was among the first to model the competition in the dual-channel or multiple-channel supply chains environment, in which direct channels (catalog and Internet marketers) and the conventional retail stores co-exist (Li, 2018). Since then, the research on dual channels has been increasing rapidly.

Existing research on dual-channel supply chains may be classified into the following categories according to the setting and scope of the decisions in the supply chain,

- *Channel conflict and channel selection*: When a supplier engages in online sales, it will affect the relationships with its reseller partners in the traditional retail channel. This leads to channel conflict and competition. The relevant issues include whether or not opt to sell online, whether or not to open an online channel by supplier itself or via retailer, which type of channel structure to select, and how to adjust the supplier–reseller relationships (Cai, 2010; Chen *et al.*, 2007; Hsiao and Chen, 2013; Tsay and Agrawal, 2004).
- *Pricing strategies*: In a dual-channel supply chain context, the manufacturer will not only make the wholesale pricing decision in the traditional retail channel but also the online selling price in the online channel. The retailer is to make the retail price in the traditional physical channel. However, it is possible that a consistent pricing strategy (or equal-pricing strategy) is adopted in which the product selling prices are kept the same in both channels in order to mitigate the channel conflict. Determine the pricing decisions in dual-channel supply chains under various scenarios has been the predominate research topic. Moreover, inconsistent pricing strategies have also attracted attention in dual-channel supply chains (Cattani *et al.*, 2006; Li *et al.*, 2014).
- *Risk-averse behavior*: When facing uncertainties, decision makers often take risk-averse behavior attempting to lower the impact of the uncertainty. This phenomenon is very common in economics and finance. It has attracted much attention in supply chain management (Li *et al.*, 2014, 2016; Liu *et al.*, 2016).
- *Coordination and contract design*: Channel coordination and contract design are an important research topic in dual-channel supply chains. The main purpose is to resolve the channel competition and channel conflict, and improve the overall supply chain performance. By appropriately designing a contract between the supplier and the retailer, it is possible that the decentralized dual-channel supply chain can achieve the same overall performance

as the centralized supply chain and both channel members could reach a win–win outcome (Cao, 2014; David and Adida, 2015; Li *et al.*, 2016).

- *Environmental impact and green investment*: With the increasing concern on sustainable development, governments are imposing more strict carbon emission regulations. Business organizations have to consider environmental impacts of their products and commit more investment on green product development in the dual-channel SCM (Carrillo *et al.*, 2014; Xu *et al.*, 2018).
- *Asymmetric information*: Asymmetric information refers to the situations where channel members have different levels of information, e.g., market size, consumer preference, production cost, and product attributes. It is possible that one channel member may deliberately hide or distort the information so that he can gain more profit in the supply chain. The existence of information asymmetry obviously affects the decision-making in dual-channel supply chains (Cao *et al.*, 2013; Huang *et al.*, 2018b; Lei *et al.*, 2014; Li *et al.*, 2017).
- *Service strategies and impact*: In the dual-channel context, additional services could be provided to add values, e.g., returns policy, trade-in policy, free shipping, and showroom services. Such services may affect the consumers' behaviors and channel members' other decisions (Chen and Bell, 2012; Feng *et al.*, 2019; Jiang *et al.*, 2017; Li *et al.*, 2019).
- *Financing strategies and impact*: Channel members may be constrained by capital to sustain the business operations. Arranging the cash flow along the supply chain or determining the optimal investment allocation among channel members would have a significant impact on channel strategies (Li *et al.*, 2018; Salmani *et al.*, 2018; Xia *et al.*, 2017).
- *Cross-selling and free-riding*: In dual-channel supply chains, when a consumer finds a product in one channel, but he may purchase it from the other channel. This can be caused by the inconsistent pricing strategy in two channels and will have an impact on channel members' decision-making (Balakrishnan *et al.*, 2014; He *et al.*, 2016; Zhou *et al.*, 2018).
- *Inventory management and demand fulfillment*: Inventory management in dual-channel supply chain is more complicated. Interesting issues include what level of initial inventories to keep before

the sales season, how to replenish inventories over multiple periods, and how to assign inventories to satisfy incoming demands from different channels (Chiang and Monahan, 2005; Fan *et al.*, 2019; Takahashi *et al.*, 2011).

It should be noted that the above topics are not exhaustive. Many new topics are emerging. They are not exclusive either, because some of the above topics are often tackled simultaneously, e.g., the decision making with risk-averse players and/or information asymmetry. This book will cover most of the above decision-making problems in dual-channel supply chain systems with explicit consideration of risk-averse behaviors of the decision makers.

## 1.5. Structure of the Book

This book consists of 10 chapters. Chapter 1 first introduces the relevant concepts in marketing channel theory and supply chain management, and explains their relevance to dual-channel supply chains. Secondly, we introduce the concepts of uncertainty, risk and risk attitude, which leads to an important phenomenon of decision makers in supply chain systems, i.e., the risk-averse behaviors. Three most commonly used types of risk assessment methods including mean–variance, VaR and CVaR are explained and contrasted in terms of their relative advantages. Thirdly, we categorize the existing literature on dual-channel supply chains into several groups according to the setting and scope of the decisions. Finally, the structure of the book is presented.

Chapter 2 examines the manufacturer's dual-channel selection problem concerning whether to open an own online channel or use a retailer's online channel. Consumers' heterogeneity in the valuation of a product is assumed to be a uniform distribution. Stackelberg games are applied to obtain the optimal equilibrium solutions to two channel structures. The manufacturer's preference of the channel structures and its channel control abilities are analyzed and characterized analytically. The models are then extended to the cases with uncertain demand and risk-averse behavior, where the risk-averse behavior is measured using the mean–variance method.

Chapter 3 considers the pricing decisions in a dual-channel supply chain with one risk-neutral supplier and one risk-averse retailer.

The supplier provides one perishable product with price-dependent stochastic demand. The CVaR criterion is used to measure the retailer's risk-averse behavior. A Nash bargaining model is presented to model the players' decisions such as the wholesale price, the retail price and the order quantity under equal bargaining power. With the assumption of a uniform distributed demand uncertainty, the Nash bargaining equilibrium is obtained analytically. The supplier's profit share among the supply chain is then analyzed. The effects of the risk-averse indicator on the performance of two agents in various situations with varying channel powers, demand uncertainty and price sensitivities are illustrated.

Chapter 4 investigates the pricing decisions and channel coordination in a dual-channel supply chain consisting of a risk-neutral supplier and a risk-averse retailer, in which the market demand is uncertain. Both members need determine an initial stock at the beginning of the sales season. The consistent pricing practice is assumed for the product selling prices in both channels. The retailer's risk-averse behavior is measured using either the VaR criterion or the CVaR criterion. Stackelberg game models are formulated, where the manufacturer is a leader in making decisions on initial inventory quantity and product selling price, and the retailer is a follower in making decisions on the order quantity. The equilibrium solutions are obtained in the decentralized and centralized situations. A new concept of channel coordination is defined. Based on that, an improved risk-sharing contract is designed to coordinate the dual-channel supply chain and ensure that both supply chain members achieve a win–win outcome.

Chapter 5 seeks optimal pricing and greening strategies in a dual-channel supply chain. The consistent pricing practice is assumed for the product selling prices in both channels. Stackelberg game models are formulated for both centralized and decentralized cases. Optimal pricing and greening level of products are obtained analytically. The channel choice problem is discussed by comparing the dual-channel supply chain with the single-channel supply chain under the green strategy. The channel conflict and coordination are resolved by designing a two-part tariff contract between two agents. Finally, the extension of the model to the situations where the retailer takes risk-averse behavior in the dual-channel green supply chain is discussed.

Chapter 6 considers a dual-channel supply chain consisting of a risk-neutral manufacturer and a risk-averse retailer, where the manufacturer offers a consumer returns policy in the online channel. The market demand is uncertain and related to the refund-amount. The CVaR criterion is used to measure the retailer's risk-averse behavior. The impacts of customer returns policy and risk-averse behavior on the equilibrium solutions and supply chain agents' performance are analyzed. A buyback revenue-sharing contract is designed to coordinate the dual-channel supply chain, which essentially resolves the channel conflict problem. In addition, whether the returns policy can help improve the competitiveness of the online channel, and how the returns policy would affect the retailer's profit share among the supply chains are also discussed.

Chapter 7 studies the financing strategies in a supply chain where the retailer is capital-constrained and the supplier is risk-averse. The supplier makes wholesale pricing decisions and the retailer makes order quantity decisions facing uncertain demand. The supplier's risk-averse behavior is measured using the CVaR method under two financing strategies: partial credit guarantee (PCG) and trade credit financing (TCF). The optimal equilibrium solutions under PCG and TCF are obtained, respectively, and the sensitivities of the solutions to some parameters are analyzed. It is shown that the preference of two financing strategies can be characterized by the switching curves in two-dimensional space of credit guarantee coefficient and risk aversion degree. There exists a region where TCF outperforms PCG for both players. In addition, the extension of the model to the dual-channel situations is discussed.

Chapter 8 examines the pricing and order quantity decisions in a dual-channel supply chain consisting of a risk-neutral manufacturer and a risk-averse retailer with asymmetric information on market size. The market demand information is uncertain, but the retailer has more information regarding the market size than the manufacturer. It is assumed that market demand size takes two types, high and low, and at each type the demand follows a truncated normal distribution. The mean–variance method is used to measure the retailer's risk-averse behavior. Stackelberg game models are developed for three scenarios: the benchmark scenario without the manufacturer's encroachment, the manufacturer's encroachment under symmetric information, and the manufacturer's encroachment under asymmetric information. It is found that whether the manufacturer and the retailer can be better off after manufacturer encroachment or information sharing depends on the manufacturer's per-unit selling cost and the retailer's risk-averse level.

Chapter 9 considers the contracting and pricing decisions in a dual-channel supply chain consisting of a risk-neutral manufacturer and a risk-averse retailer with asymmetric information on production cost. The retailer's risk-averse behavior is measured using the CVaR. To model the production cost information asymmetry, it is assumed that the manufacturer's production cost takes two types (a high type and a low type), which are privately known to the manufacturer. The retailer is assumed to be the principal and more powerful than the manufacturer. The retailer provides a menu of contracts to the manufacturer for selection. From the manufacturer's selection, the retailer can better estimate the production cost of the manufacturer and determine her retail price in the traditional channel. After that, the manufacturer sets the price for his online channel. Four situations are examined depending on the combinations of whether the manufacturer opens an online channel or not, and whether the manufacturer keeps his production cost information private or not.

Chapter 10 investigates the pricing decisions of two competing shipping companies (large and small) facing uncertain spot market demand considering risk-averse behavior and capacity constraint. This case can be regarded as two parallel channels competing for the same market. The larger shipping company is risk-neutral with sufficient capacity; while the smaller shipping company is risk-averse with limited shipping capacity. The CVaR is used to measure the risk-averse attitude of the smaller supplier. A Nash game model is formulated to model two suppliers' pricing decisions and the equilibrium solution is obtained analytically. It is shown that the pricing decisions take two forms, which can be characterized by a threshold of the smaller supplier 2's capacity. With the assumption of uniformly distributed demand, it is found that as the smaller supplier becomes more risk-averse, both suppliers' optimal prices are decreasing, and the threshold value that determines the pricing strategy is also decreasing. The impacts of price sensitivity and competition intensity parameters on the optimal prices are also analyzed. Numerical experiments are performed to illustrate the analytical results and explore their validity in more general situations.

## References

Balakrishnan, A., Sundaresan, S., & Zhang, B. (2014). Browse-and-switch: Retail-online competition under value uncertainty. *Production and Operations Management*, 23(7), pp. 1129–1145.

Balasuburamanian S. (1998). Mail versus mall: A strategy analysis of competition between direct marketers and conventional retailers. *Marketing Science*, 17(3), pp. 181–195.

Cai, G. (2010). Channel selection and coordination in dual-channel supply chains. *Journal of Retailing*, 86(1), pp. 22–36.

Cao, E. (2014). Coordination of dual-channel supply chains under demand disruptions management decisions. *International Journal of Production Research*, 52(23), pp. 7114–7131.

Cao, E., Ma, Y., Wan, C., & Lai, M. (2013). Contracting with asymmetric cost information in a dual-channel supply chain. *Operations Research Letters*, 41(4), pp. 410–414.

Carrillo, J. E., Vakharia, A. J., & Wang, R. (2014). Environmental implications for online retailing. *European Journal of Operational Research*, 239(3), pp. 744–755.

Cattani, K., Heese, H., Gilland, W., & Swaminathan, J. (2006). Boiling frogs: Pricing strategies for a manufacturer adding a direct channel that competes with the traditional channel. *Production and Operations Management*, 15, pp. 40–56.

Chen, C., Chou, S., Hsiao, L., & Chen, P. (2007). The optimal product design and Internet channel design of competitive firms. *Journal of Management*, 24(2), pp. 113–134.

Chen, J., & Bell, P. C. (2012). Implementing market segmentation using full-refund and no-refund customer returns policies in a dual-channel supply chain structure. *International Journal of Production Economics*, 136(1), pp. 56–66.

Chiang, W. K., & Monahan, G. E. (2005). Managing inventories in a two-echelon dual-channel supply chain. *European Journal of Operational Research*, 162(2), pp. 325–341.

Chiu, C. H., & Choi, T. M. (2016). Supply chain risk analysis with mean-variance models: A technical review. *Annals of Operations Research*, 240(2), pp. 489–507.

Clement, J. (2020). *E-commerce Worldwide*. Hamburg, Germany: Statista.

David, A., & Adida, E. (2015). Competition and coordination in a two-channel supply chain. *Production and Operations Management*, 24(8), pp. 1358–1370.

Fan, D., Xu, Q., Fan, T., & Cheng, F. (2019). Inventory optimization model considering consumer shift and inventory transshipment in dual-channel supply chains. *RAIRO-Operations Research*, 53(1), pp. 59–79.

Feng, L, Li, Y., Xu, F., & Deng, Q. (2019). Optimal pricing and trade-in policies in a dual-channel supply chain when considering market segmentation, *International Journal of Production Research*, 57(9), pp. 2828–2846.

He, R., Xiong, Y., & Lin, Z. (2016). Carbon emissions in a dual channel closed loop supply chain: The impact of consumer free riding behavior. *Journal of Cleaner Production*, 134, pp. 384–394.

Hsiao, L., & Chen, Y. J. (2013). The perils of selling online: Manufacturer competition, channel conflict, and consumer preferences. *Marketing Letters*. 24(3), pp. 277–292.

Huang, S., Guan, X., & Xiao, B. (2018b). Incentive provision for demand information acquisition in a dual-channel supply chain. *Transportation Research Part E: Logistics and Transportation Review*, 116, pp. 42–58.

Jiang, Y. S., Li, B., & Song, D. P. (2017). Analysing consumer RP in a dual-channel supply chain with a risk-averse retailer. *European Journal of Industrial Engineering*, 11(3), pp. 271–302.

Kotler, P., & Keller, K.L. (2015). *Marketing Management*, 15th Ed., New York: Pearson.

Lei, M., Liu, H., Deng, H., Huang, T., & Leong, G. K. (2014). Demand information sharing and channel choice in a dual-channel supply chain with multiple retailers. *International Journal of Production Research*, 52(22), pp. 6792–6818.

Li, B., An, S., & Song, D. (2018). Selection of financing strategies with a risk-averse supplier in a capital-constrained supply chain. *Transportation Research Part E: Logistics and Transportation Review*, 118, pp. 163–183.

Li, B., Chen, P., Li, Q., & Wang, W. (2014). Dual-channel supply chain pricing decisions with a risk-averse retailer. *International Journal of Production Research*. 52(23), pp. 7132–7147.

Li, B., Hou, P.-W., Chen, P., & Li, Q.-H. (2016). Pricing strategy and coordination in a dual channel supply chain with a risk-averse retailer. *International Journal of Production Economics*, 178, pp. 154–168.

Li, G., Li, L., & Sun, J. (2019). Pricing and service effort strategy in a dual-channel supply chain with showrooming effect, *Transportation Research Part E: Logistics and Transportation Review*, 126, pp. 32–48.

Li, Q., Li, B., Chen, P., & Hou, P. (2017). Dual-channel supply chain decisions under asymmetric information with a risk-averse retailer. *Annals of Operations Research*, 257(1–2), pp. 423–447.

Li, Y. Y. (2018). Overview of research on dual-channel supply chain management, *Advances in Economics, Business and Management Research*, 51, pp. 205–212.

Liu, M., Cao, E., & Salifou, C. K. (2016). Pricing strategies of a dual-channel supply chain with risk aversion. *Transportation Research Part E: Logistics and Transportation Review*, 90, pp. 108–120.

Markowitz, H. (1959). *Portfolio Selection: Efficient Diversification of Investment*. New Haven, NH:Yale University Press.

Perez, S. (2020). COVID-19 pandemic accelerated shift to e-commerce by 5 years, new report says, *Tech Crunch*, 24 August 2020 (https://techcrunch.com/2020/08/24/covid-19-pandemic-accelerated-shift-to-e-commerce-by-5-years-new-report-says/).

Redtechnology (2020). Why manufacturers should be trading direct online (D2C), *Redtechnology.com*, 22 May 2020. (www.redtechnology.com/news-and-insights/Why-manufacturers-should-be-trading-direct-online/).

Rockafellar, R. T., & Uryasev, S. (2000). Optimization of conditional value-at-risk. *Journal of Risk* 2, pp. 21–42.

Rockafellar, R. T., & Uryasev, S. (2002). Conditional value-at-risk for general loss distributions. *Journal of Bank and Finance,* 26(7), pp. 1443–1471.

Rosenbloom, B. (2004). *Marketing Channels: A Management View*, 7th Ed. Mason, OH:Thomson.

Salmani, Y., Partovi, F. Y., & Banerjee, A. (2018). Customer-driven investment decisions in existing multiple sales channels: A downstream supply chain analysis. *International Journal of Production Economics*, 204, pp. 44–58.

Sarykalin, S., Serraino, G., & Uryasev, S. (2008). Value-at-risk vs. conditional value-at-risk in risk management and optimization. In *Tutorials in Operations Research*. pp. 270–294. INFORMS.

Takahashi, K., Aoi, T., Hirotani, D., & Morikawa, K. (2011). Inventory control in a two-echelon dual-channel supply chain with setup of production and delivery. *International Journal of Production Economics*, 133(1), pp. 403–415.

Tapiero, C. S. (2005). Value at risk and inventory control. *European Journal of Operational Research,* 163(3), pp. 769–775.

Tsay, A., & Agrawal, N. (2004). Channel conflict and coordination in the e-commerce age. *Production and Operations Management*, 13(1), pp. 93–110.

Xia, Y., Xiao, T., & Zhang, G. P. (2017). The impact of product returns and retailer's service investment on manufacturer's channel strategies. *Decision Sciences*, 48(5), pp. 918–955.

Xu, L., Wang, C., & Zhao, J. (2018). Decision and coordination in the dual-channel supply chain considering cap-and-trade regulation. *Journal of Cleaner Production.* 197(Part 1), pp. 551–561.

Zheng, W., Li, B., & Song, D. P. (2017). Effects of risk-aversion on competing shipping lines' pricing strategies with uncertain demands. *Transportation Research Part B*, 104, pp. 337–356.

Zhou, Y. W., Guo, J., & Zhou, W. (2018). Pricing/service strategies for a dual-channel supply chain with free riding and service-cost sharing. *International Journal of Production Economics*, 196, pp. 198–210.

© 2022 World Scientific Publishing Europe Ltd.
https://doi.org/10.1142/9781800610408_0002

# Chapter 2

# Channel Selection in Dual-Channel Supply Chains

**Rufeng Wang**[*,‡], **Bo Li**[*,§], **and Dong-Ping Song**[†,¶]

[*] *College of Management and Economics, Tianjin University, China*
[†] *School of Management, University of Liverpool, Liverpool, UK*

[‡] *wangrus992@163.com*
[§] *libo0410@tju.edu.cn*
[¶] *Dongping.Song@liverpool.ac.uk*

## 2.1. Introduction

In a dual-channel supply chain, the basic question for the suppliers is the channel selection problem, e.g., whether or not to open a new channel and how to choose the appropriate distributing channels for their products. With the rapid development of electronic commerce, besides the traditional supplier–retailer physical channel, the suppliers may open an online channel by their own (Cattani *et al.*, 2006; Chiang *et al.*, 2003); meanwhile, the retailer may operate an online channel to distribute the suppliers' products to the market (Ofek *et al.*, 2011; Tsay and Agrawal, 2004). This gives rise to two types of dual-channel supply chains according to who opens the online channel, which are regarded as two channel strategies: the supplier (or manufacturer) dual-channel strategy, and the retailer dual-channel strategy, respectively. An interesting question is which channel strategy is more beneficial for the channel members (Wang *et al.*, 2018).

It should be noted that in a manufacturer dual-channel model, in addition to specialized manufacturing, the manufacturers must pay additional attention to market demand and the demand fluctuation associated with their online channel, which is usually not to their advantage (Li *et al.*, 2015). In the retailer dual-channel model, the manufacturers can focus on manufacturing the products. However, because all products are sold through the retailer's channels, the manufacturer may slowly lose market control (Balakrishnan *et al.*, 2014; Chiang *et al.*, 2003; Luo and Sun, 2016). This chapter will discuss the manufacturer dual-channel model and the retailer dual-channel model using the traditional single-channel supply chain as a benchmark; then, we analyze whether the manufacturer should open online channel or cooperate with retailers to distribute products through the retailers' dual-channels.

It is assumed that there is consumers' heterogeneity in the valuation of a product, also denoted as willingness to pay (WTP) (Balakrishnan *et al.*, 2014; Chiang *et al.*, 2003; Hsiao and Chen, 2014). That is, suppose that $v$ is willingness to pay from consumers, and it follows a uniform distribution in [0,1] with its density of 1. If one of the members in the supply chain makes the price of the product at $p$, then through purchasing the product, a consumer with WTP $v$ will obtain a net surplus of $v - p$. Obviously, when the consumers meet $v - p \geq 0$, they will buy the product, shown in Fig. 2.1. On the other hand, if $v < p$, the consumer will not buy the product. Therefore, when the consumer whose WTP is equal to $p$ will be indifferent to purchase from the member or not, and all consumers with WTP in $[p, 1]$ will buy the product from the member (Chiang *et al.*, 2003).

The assumption that consumers' valuations are heterogeneous for a product may be explained as follows (Balakrishnan *et al.*, 2014). For the products like cellphones, tablet computers, cars and furniture etc., because they are high-priced products, consumers often prefer to go shopping in physical stores and test the products by themselves. Several researchers have shown that consumers have a lower

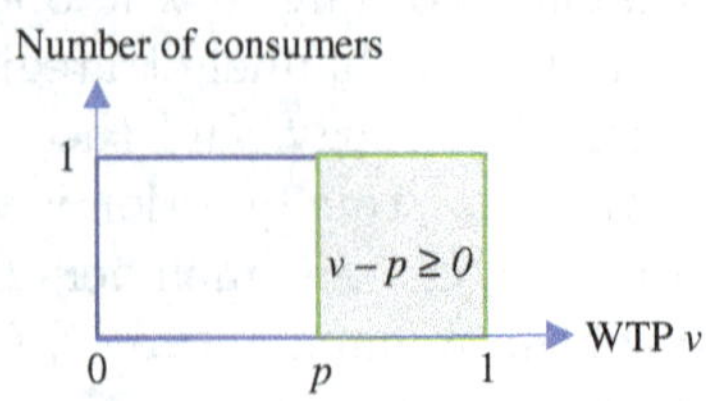


Fig. 2.1. The distribution of consumers' WTP.

valuation for the same product in online channel than that in offline (brick-and-mortar) channels (Ma *et al.*, 2013; Yan and Ghose, 2010; Yan *et al.*, 2010). Further, some empirical evidence has also demonstrated that consumers' acceptance to the products in online channels is not higher than that in offline channels (Kacen and Lee, 2002; Luo and Sun, 2016). According to the more recent survey, which compares the 30 most popular smartphones from various offline retailers and leading e-commerce portals, it is found that the online prices for smartphones are 5% lower than that in offline channels (Aulak, 2014). This indicates that price discounting on the products in online channels is a popular phenomenon, which may greatly promote the actual purchasing amount (Chellappa *et al.*, 2011).

In this chapter, a supply chain with a manufacturer and a retailer is investigated, where the manufacturer makes his decisions about the channel selection strategies, either the manufacturer dual-channel model or the retailer dual-channel model. The following problems are discussed:

(1) With regard to new distribution channel modes, how does the manufacturer decide to better capture the demand in online channels?
(2) To the manufacturer, if he decides to introduce an online channel into his distribution system, then how can he control his different channels under the different models and how will his choice influence the retailer's preferences on channel selection?
(3) How will some parameters, such as consumer acceptance of the e-channel, the price discount rate, influence the two members' decisions in the dual-channel supply chain?
(4) How can the models be extended to the cases where channel members have risk-averse behavior?

## 2.2. Channel Structures and Demands

Four channel structures are considered, including a benchmark with a manufacturer (he) and a traditional retailer (she) (Model 0), the manufacturer dual-channel model (Model 1), the retailer dual-channel model (Model 2) and the multichannel model where both the manufacturer and the retailer will insert e-channels (Model 3), shown in Figs. 2.2(a), 2.2(b), 2.2(c) and 2.2(d), respectively.

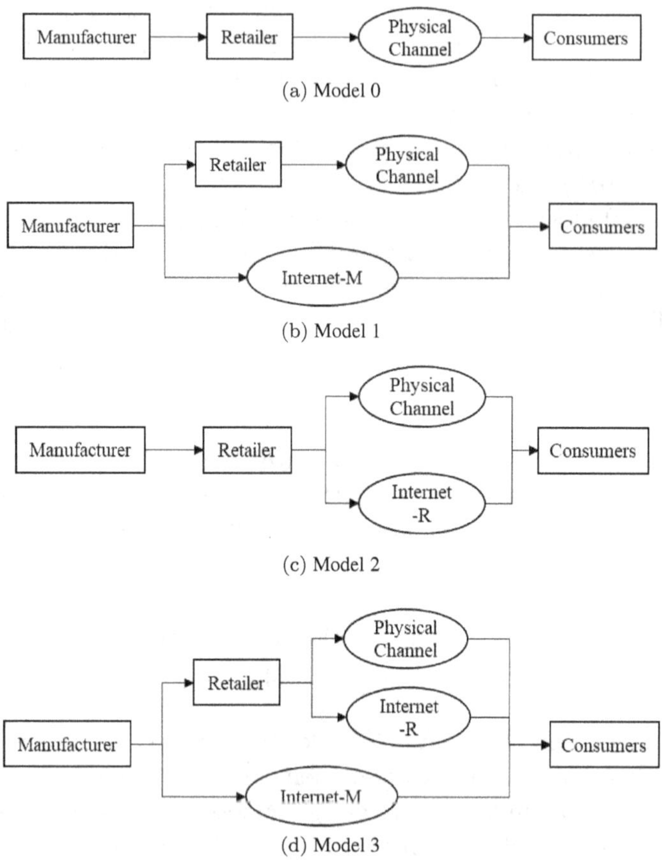


Fig. 2.2. Structures of the supply chains.

It is assumed that only one kind of product is produced by the manufacturer, and consumers are willing to buy only one unit of the product. The manufacturer will first decide his wholesale price $w$, and then the retailer will determine her retail price $p$ in Model $i$, where $i = 0, 1, 2, 3$. Thus, when the manufacturer/retailer introduces an online channel, he/she will decide the online price $\eta p$ based on the retailer's retail price in Model $i (i = 1, 2, 3)$, where $\eta$ is the discount rate, and it represents the ratio between the retail price on the e-channel and that in the physical channel.

The market demand is normalized to 1 and consumers are heterogeneous with product utility $v$. Further, $v$ follows the uniformly distribution in [0,1], and the similar assumption has been widely applied in the literature (e.g.,Chiang *et al.*, 2003; Chiang and Monahan, 2005; Luo and Sun, 2016; Ma *et al.*, 2013). We assume the lower consumer acceptance of the e-channel, and define the parameter $\delta \in [0, 1]$ as consumers' willingness to pay (WTP) for a product in the e-channel. This implies that if a consumer's utility is $v$ concerning with the product in the physical channel, then this consumer will own the utility $\delta v$ to that product in the online channel.

For simplicity, all operation costs in the supply chains are normalized to zero, such as the retailer's operating cost, the manufacturer's production cost and his e-channel operating cost (Yan and Ghose, 2010). Meanwhile, the manufacturer is supposed as a Stackelberg leader, and can utilize his channel power over the retailer. All members in the supply chains share the same information and are risk-neutral (Hsiao and Chen, 2014; Ma *et al.*, 2013). Furthermore, this chapter assumes the discount rate as an exogenous parameter. In fact, some empirical research have indicated that smartphones, digital cameras and GPS navigators are about 5%, 8% and 10% cheaper in online channel than that in physical channel, respectively (Aulak, 2014).

In Model 0 shown in Fig. 2.2(a), the consumer's utility is given by $u_0 = v - p$. If $u_0 \geq 0$, then the consumer will buy it; otherwise, he will not. Note $v$ is uniformly distributed in [0, 1]. Therefore, the demand in Model 0, $q_0$, can be determined by $q_0 = 1 - p$.

In Model $i, i = 1, 2$, a consumer who buys the product will obtain utilities $u_{i1} = v - p$ or $u_{i2} = \delta v - \eta p$ from the physical channel or the e-channel, respectively. If $u_{i1} \geq 0$ and $u_{i1} \geq u_{i2}$, then this consumer will buy the product from the physical channel. As a result, if $v \in \left[\frac{1-\eta}{1-\delta}p, 1\right]$, then the consumer will purchase the product in the physical channel. Similarly, if $u_{i2} \geq 0$ and $u_{i2} \geq u_{i1}$, that is, $v \in \left[\frac{\eta}{\delta}p, \frac{1-\eta}{1-\delta}p\right]$, then the consumer will buy in the online channel. Based on the above, we can easily obtain the demands $q_{i1} = 1 - \frac{1-\eta}{1-\delta}p$ and $q_{i2} = (\frac{1-\eta}{1-\delta} - \frac{\eta}{\delta})p$ through the physical channel and the online channel, respectively, and the total demand in the supply chain is $q_i = q_{i1} + q_{i2} = 1 - \frac{\eta}{\delta}p$.

In Model 3, an online channel is introduced by the manufacturer and the retailer simultaneously. To simplify the narrative, we assume that e-channel demand is segmented into two parts and the proportions for the manufacturer's and the retailer's online channels are divided into $s$ and $(1 - s)$, that is, $s$ is called as the market share of the retailer's online channel. Thus, when $s = 0$, Model 3 will be simplified into Model 1, and when $s = 1$, it will be reduced to Model 2. That is, Model 3 is a generalized model to Model 1 and Model 2, as shown in Fig. 2.2. Using the above similar method, we can obtain the demands in Model 3 which are similar to those in Model $i, i = 1, 2$.

It should be pointed out that $0 < \eta < \delta < 1$ need be satisfied to ensure the positive demands of the two channels in the dual-channel supply chain. In addition, in the Model $i, i = 1, 2, 3$, the constrains $0 < w < p$ and $p < \min\left\{\frac{1-\delta}{1-\eta}, \frac{\delta}{\eta}\right\}$ should be satisfied. Moreover, in Model $i, i = 1, 2, 3$, in order to ensure the positive profit from the e-channel, the condition $w < \eta p$ is needed. In summary, the constraints required in Model $i, i = 1, 2, 3$ are $0 < w < \eta p$ and $p < \frac{1-\delta}{1-\eta}$.

## 2.3. Equilibrium Solutions

The sequence of decision-making in the Stackelberg game is as follows: the manufacturer firstly decides the wholesale price, and then the retailer decides the retail sale price. Thus, the manufacturer is a leader and the retailer is a follower in the game. The profit functions of the retailer, the manufacturer, and his online channel are represented as $\pi_{iR}$, $\pi_{iM}$ and $\pi_{id}$, $i = 0, 1, 2, 3$. Through the Stackelberg games, the optimal equilibrium solutions under the different channel structures can be solved by applying the backward induction approach. We denote the optimal solutions using the superscript $*$.

**Scenario 0: Model 0—The benchmark.** In this benchmark model, the retailer acts like a monopolist and the manufacturer distributes the product through the retailer. For a given wholesale price $w$, the retailer's and the manufacturer's optimal profits are determined by

$$\max_{p} \pi_{0R} = q_0(p - w) = (1 - p)(p - w), \tag{2.1}$$

$$\max_{w} \pi_{0M} = (1 - p)w. \tag{2.2}$$

**Scenario I: Model 1—The manufacturer's dual-channel model.** In Model 1, the manufacturer opens an online channel by his own. As we discuss earlier on, the demand in the physical channel is given by $q_{11} = 1 - \frac{1-\eta}{1-\delta}p$. Given the manufacturer's wholesale price $w$, the retailer's and the manufacturer's optimal profits are as follows:

$$\max_{p} \pi_{1R} = q_{11}(p-w) = \left(1 - \frac{1-\eta}{1-\delta}p\right)(p-w), \tag{2.3}$$

$$\max_{w} \pi_{1M} = \left(1 - \frac{1-\eta}{1-\delta}p\right)w + \left(\frac{1-\eta}{1-\delta} - \frac{\eta}{\delta}\right)\eta p^2. \tag{2.4}$$

**Scenario II: Model 2—The retailer's dual-channel model.** In Model 2, the retailer introduces the online channel in addition to her physical store. Similar to Scenario II, given the manufacturer's wholesale price $w$, the retailer's and the manufacturer's optimal profits are

$$\max_{p} \pi_{2R} = \left(1 - \frac{1-\eta}{1-\delta}p\right)(p-w) + \left(\frac{1-\eta}{1-\delta} - \frac{\eta}{\delta}\right)(\eta p - w)\,p, \tag{2.5}$$

$$\max_{w} \pi_{2M} = \left(1 - \frac{\eta}{\delta}p\right)w. \tag{2.6}$$

**Scenario III: Model 3—Both members all introduce e-channels.** In Model 3, both the manufacturer and the retailer will introduce an e-channel simultaneously. In this case, given the wholesale price $w$, the optimal profits of both members are as follows:

$$\pi_{3R} = \left(1 - \frac{1-\eta}{1-\delta}p\right)(p-w) + s\left(\frac{1-\eta}{1-\delta} - \frac{\eta}{\delta}\right)p(\eta p - w), \tag{2.7}$$

$$\pi_{3M} = \left(1 - \frac{1-\eta}{1-\delta}p\right)w + s\left(\frac{1-\eta}{1-\delta} - \frac{\eta}{\delta}\right) \times pw + (1-s)\left(\frac{1-\eta}{1-\delta} - \frac{\eta}{\delta}\right)\eta p^2. \tag{2.8}$$

Then the backward induction method is applied to solve the above three scenarios and the equilibrium solutions can be obtained. The solutions are summarized in Table 2.1. Because the solutions in Model 3 are complex, here we can omit them.

Generally, $RGM$ can be interpreted as the manufacturer's ability to control the distribution channels. The higher the value of the $k_i^*$ is, the weaker the manufacturer can control his channels. In Model 3, the optimal profits are omitted here because the expressions are too complicated to reveal insight.

Table 2.1. The optimal equilibrium solutions in the four scenarios.

| | Model 0 | Model 1 | Model 2 |
|---|---|---|---|
| $w_i^*$ | $\frac{1}{2}$ | $\frac{\delta-\eta^2}{1-\eta}\cdot A$ | $\frac{1}{2}\cdot\frac{[2(\delta-\eta^2)-(1+3\delta)\eta]\delta}{(1-\delta)\eta^2}$ |
| $p_i^*$ | $\frac{3}{4}$ | $\frac{3}{2}\delta\cdot A$ | $\frac{1}{4}\cdot\frac{\delta}{\eta}\cdot B$ |
| $\pi_{iM}^*$ | $\frac{1}{8}$ | $\frac{1}{4}\cdot\frac{-4\eta^2+3\delta\eta+\delta}{1-\eta}\cdot A$ | $\frac{1}{8}\cdot\frac{\delta[2\eta^2-(3\delta+1)\eta+2\delta]^2}{(1-\delta)\eta^2(\eta^2-2\delta\eta+\delta)}$ |
| $\pi_{iR}^*$ | $\frac{1}{16}$ | $\frac{1}{4}\cdot\frac{(2\eta^2-3\delta\eta+\delta)^2}{(1-\eta)(1-\delta)}\cdot A^2$ | $\frac{1}{16}\cdot\frac{\delta[(-23\eta^2+36\eta-12)\delta^2+(36\eta^3-50\eta^2+12\eta)\delta+\eta^2+12\eta^3-12\eta^4]}{(1-\delta)\eta^2(\eta^2-\delta\eta+\delta)}$ |
| $\Pi_{id}^*$ | $\frac{3}{16}$ | $\frac{3}{4}\cdot\frac{\delta(\delta-\eta^2)}{1-\delta}\cdot A^2$ | $\frac{1}{16}\cdot\frac{\delta[-2\eta^2+(3+\delta)\eta-2\delta]}{(1-\delta)\eta^2}\cdot B$ |
| $q_i^*$ | $\frac{1}{4}$ | $1-\frac{3}{2}\eta\cdot A$ | $1-\frac{1}{4}\cdot B$ |
| $q_{i1}^*$ | / | $1-\frac{3}{2}\cdot\frac{\delta(1-\eta)}{1-\delta}\cdot A$ | $1-\frac{1}{4}\cdot\frac{\delta(1-\eta)}{(1-\delta)\eta}\cdot B$ |
| $q_{i2}^*$ | / | $\frac{3}{2}\cdot\frac{\delta-\eta}{1-\delta}\cdot A$ | $\frac{1}{4}\cdot\frac{\delta-\eta}{(1-\delta)\eta}\cdot B$ |
| $k_i^*$ | $\frac{1}{3}$ | $1-\frac{3}{2}\cdot\frac{\delta-\eta^2}{\delta(1-\eta)}$ | $1-2\cdot\frac{2\eta^2-(3\delta+1)\eta+2\delta}{(1-\delta)\eta\cdot B}$ |

*Note:* $A=\frac{1-\delta}{\eta^2-3\delta\eta+2\delta}$, $B=\frac{2\eta^2-(5\delta-1)\eta+2\delta}{\eta^2-2\delta\eta+\delta}$. $k_i^*$ means the retail gross margin (*RGM*) under the above four cases and it is defined as $k_i^*=(p-w)/p$ (Steiner, 2004).

In addition, it is interesting to evaluate the channel efficiency of supply chains in Model $i, i=0,1,2$. If we consider the optimal prices and profits under the centralized supply chains in Model $i, i=0,1,2$, then we can obtain the results in Table 2.2. The channel efficiency can be defined as $\tau_i=\pi_{iD}^*/\pi_{iC}^*, i=0,1,2$, where $\pi_{iD}^*$ represents the total optimal profit of the decentralized supply chain in Model $i$ and $\pi_{iC}^*$ represents the optimal profit of the centralized supply chain corresponding to Model $i$. That is, channel efficiency as the ratio of the optimal profit of the decentralized supply chain to that of the centralized supply chain. It is stated that the channel efficiency in a static decentralized supply chain is 75% because of the double marginalization effect (Spengler, 1950). According to Tables 2.1 and 2.2, we can see that $\tau_2<\tau_0<\tau_1$. That is to say, relative to the benchmark, if the manufacturer opens an e-channel, the double marginalization effect in the supply chain will be alleviated, but if the retailer introduces an online channel, it will be exacerbated.

Table 2.2. The optimal equilibrium of the centralized supply chain.

| Solutions | Model 0 | Model 1 | Model 2 |
|---|---|---|---|
| $p_{ci}^*$ | $\frac{1}{2}$ | $\frac{\delta(1-\delta)}{2(\eta^2-2\delta\eta+\delta)}$ | $\frac{\delta(1-\delta)}{2(\eta^2-2\delta\eta+\delta)}$ |
| $\pi_{ic}$ | $\frac{1}{4}$ | $\frac{\delta(1-\delta)}{4(\eta^2-2\delta\eta+\delta)}$ | $\frac{\delta(1-\delta)}{4(\eta^2-2\delta\eta+\delta)}$ |

## 2.4. Analysis of Channel Control Abilities and Profits

This section will compare the optimal prices, the retail gross margin, and the optimal profits under three models ($i = 0, 1, 2$) that are obtained in Sec. 2.3. Moreover, the influences of some parameters on two members' channel selection decisions will be analyzed, e.g., the discount rate and consumer acceptance of the e-channel. Management implications are discussed.

In order to ensure the positive profits under each models and compare the above models in a unified framework, we consider the joint feasibility conditions denoted by the region $R$ of $(\delta, \eta)$ in Models $i, i = 0, 1, 2, 3$. Based on $0 < w_i^* < \eta p_i^*$, and $p_i^* < \frac{1-\delta}{1-\eta}$, we can obtain the feasible region as

$$R = \{(\eta, \delta)|2/3 < \eta < 1, \eta < \delta < \min\{C_0(\eta), C_1(\eta), C_2(\eta)\}\}, \quad (2.9)$$

where

$$C_0(\eta) = \frac{(2\eta^4 - 8\eta^3 + 10\eta^2 - 2\eta) - 2\eta(\eta - 1)^2\sqrt{\eta^2 + 6\eta + 1}}{2(5\eta^3 - 14\eta^2 + 14\eta - 4)},$$

$$C_1(\eta) = \frac{2\eta^2}{3\eta^2 - 3\eta + 2},$$

$$C_2(\eta) = \frac{(2\eta^2 + 9\eta - 3) - (1 - \eta)\sqrt{4\eta^2 - 4\eta + 9}}{2(3\eta^2 + 3\eta - 2)}\eta.$$

It is noted that the following discussion will be limited in the commonly feasible region $R$. Because of the complexity of Model 3, we focus on the comparisons of Model $i, i = 0, 1, 2$.

### 2.4.1. Comparisons on pricing and channel control abilities

Firstly, the relationships of the wholesale prices, the selling prices and the demands across Models $i, i = 0, 1, 2$ can be given as follows.

**Proposition 2.1.** *In the feasible region $R$ of Models $i$,$i = 0, 1, 2$, the pricing and the sale quantities have the following relationships, shown in Fig.* 2.3.

(1) *For the manufacturer, if $(\eta, \delta) \in A$, then $w_0^* < w_1^* < w_2^*$; and if $(\eta, \delta) \in B$, then $w_0^* < w_2^* < w_1^*$; where the regions $A$ and $B$ are shown in Fig.* 2.3.
(2) *For the retailer, her pricing decisions satisfy $p_1^* < p_0^* < p_2^*$, and her retail margin satisfies: $p_1^* - w_1^* < p_0^* - w_0^*$, and $p_2^* - w_2^* < p_0^* - w_0^*$.*
(3) *For the total demands in Models $i, i = 0, 1, 2$, we have $q_0^* < q_2^* < q_1^*$. For the demands in the physical channels, we have $q_{21}^* < q_{11}^* < q_0^*$. For the demands in the online channel, we have $q_{12}^* < q_{22}^*$.*

From Proposition 2.1(1), we can find that the wholesale price in the benchmark is the lowest among three models. Further, in Region $B$ from Fig. 2.3, the wholesale price in Model 1 is the highest; however when $(\eta, \delta)$ is located in Region $A$, the wholesale price in Model 2

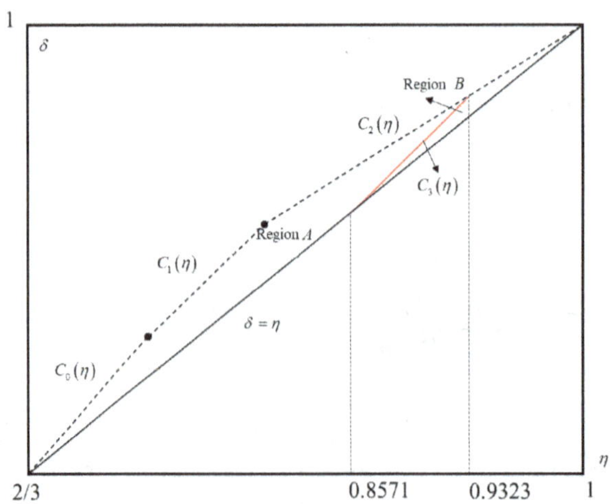


Fig. 2.3. Region divisions considering wholesale pricing in Models $i, i = 0, 1, 2$.

is the highest in three models. Obviously, compared with the benchmark, when the manufacturer inserts the e-channel (Model 1) or the retailer introduces the e-channel (Model 2), the manufacturer increases his wholesale price. Proposition 2.1(3) reveals that after introducing the online channel, the total demand of the manufacturer will be improved, thus the manufacturer will benefit from inserting the online channel. This result confirms the previous contributions in Chiang *et al.* (2003) and Cattani *et al.* (2006).

Meanwhile, from Proposition 2.1(2), it is concluded that if the manufacturer decides to open an e-channel, consumers not only purchase the product from the physical retailer, but also directly from the manufacturer's online channel. That is, the channel conflict will be intensified, and the retailer will reduce the price in the retailer's physical channel to avoid losing demand in Model 1; thus, the retail margins of the retailer in Model $i (i = 1, 2)$ decrease. It is the decline in the retail price which can alleviate the double marginalization problem in the supply chain. When the retailer decides to open an e-channel by her own, she is still a monopolist in the market and will give a higher retail price in her physical channel for more profits, thereby the double marginalization effect may be exacerbated.

Finally, Proposition 2.1(3) exhibits that no matter who introduces an e-channel, the total market demand will expand, especially by the manufacturer's dual-channels. From the viewpoint of expanding the market, when the retailer opens an e-channel, her demand also expands because $q_{12}^* < q_{22}^*$. In fact, because of the invasion of the online channel, the demand through the physical channel will decline relative to the benchmark, that is, on the one hand, the insertion of an e-channel will increase demand in the online channel; on the other hand, it will also decrease gradually appropriate part of the demand in the physical channel.

Next, we consider the retail gross margin ($RGM$) $k_i^* := (p_i^* - w_i^*)/p_i^*$ in Model $i$. As we know, the indicator $k_i^*$ represents the channel control ability of the manufacturer. The following result can be obtained.

**Proposition 2.2.** *In the feasible regions shown in Fig. 2.4, concerning with the RGMs in Model $i$ $(i = 0, 1, 2)$, the following relationships are satisfied:*

(1) *If $(\eta, \delta) \in A$, then $k_2^* < k_1^* < k_0^*$.*
(2) *If $(\eta, \delta) \in B$, then $k_1^* < k_2^* < k_0^*$.*

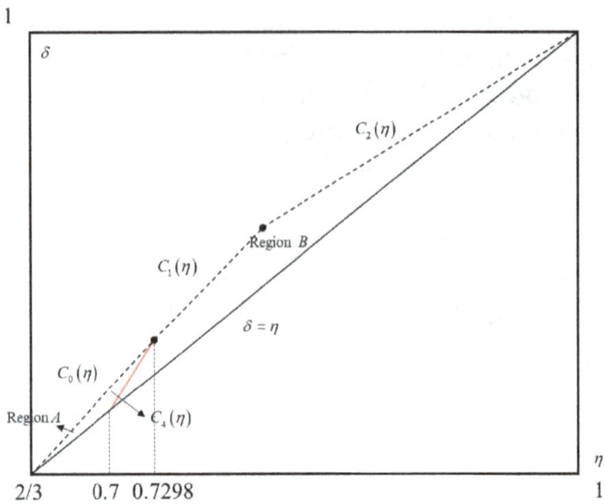


Fig. 2.4. The region divisions considering RGM in Model $i$.

Proposition 2.2 shows that once an online channel is opened by the manufacturer or the retailer, the manufacturer's channel control ability $k_i^*$ increases greatly compared with that in the benchmark. If $(\eta, \delta)$ is located at Region $A$ in Fig. 2.4, we can see that relative to the channel control ability in Model 2, the manufacturer owns less channel control ability in Model 1. On the other hand, in Region $B$ (which occupies the majority of the feasible region $R$), the manufacturer has more channel control ability. Therefore, the manufacturer can strengthen his channel control ability by opening his own online channel in most cases.

In terms of Model 3, because the calculation about comparing the pricing and the *RGMs* among Model 1, Model 2 and Model 3 is complex, the following corollary gives some results with regard to the pricing and the *RGMs* in Model 0 and Model 3.

**Corollary 2.1.** *In the feasible region $R$, concerning with the manufacturer's wholesale price and the RGMs in Model 0 and Model 3, we have the following results:*

(i) $w_3^* > w_0^*$ *and* $k_3^* < k_0^*$*;*
(ii) *there is a threshold* $\bar{s}$ *of the market share of the retailer's online channel, when* $0 \le s < \bar{s}$, $p_3^* < p_0^*$*; when* $\bar{s} \le s \le 1$, $p_3^* > p_0^*$.

From Corollary 2.1, we can find that when the manufacturer and the retailer simultaneously introduce an e-channel, the manufacturer will give a higher wholesale price relative to that in the benchmark and his channel control ability will be improved. That is, with the invasion of both members' online channels, the manufacturer will own more power about the channels and to win the higher profit, he will increase his wholesale price. Compared with the selling price in the benchmark, when the market share of the retailer's online channel is lower, i.e., within the range of $[0, \bar{s}]$, the retailer will choose a lower price. However, when the market share of the retailer's online channel becomes larger, she will choose a higher price than that in the benchmark. When $s$ takes the boundary values 0, or 1, we can easily find that the results are in accordance with that in Proposition 2.1(2).

### 2.4.2. Comparison of profits

With regards to the profits of the two parties in the supply chains, we calculate the differences among Model $i(i = 0, 1, 2)$ and then obtain Proposition 2.3.

**Proposition 2.3.** *In the feasible region $R$, the profits of two members in Models $i(i = 0, 1, 2)$ will satisfy the following relationships:*

(1) *For the manufacturer, $\pi_{1M}^* > \pi_{2M}^* > \pi_{0M}^*$.*
(2) *For the retailer, when $(\eta, \delta) \in A$, $\pi_{0R}^* > \pi_{1R}^* > \pi_{2R}^*$, and when $(\eta, \delta) \in B$, $\pi_{0R}^* > \pi_{2R}^* > \pi_{1R}^*$, where the regions $A$ and $B$ are shown in Fig. 2.4.*
(3) *For the entire supply chain, $\pi_{1D}^* > \pi_{0D}^* > \pi_{2D}^*$.*

Proposition 2.3(1) reveals that the manufacturer's profits will be the highest in Model 1, while his profit is the lowest in the benchmark Model 0. This may reflect the phenomenon that nowadays, most manufacturers tend to open their online channels. In contrast, for the retailer, Proposition 2.3(2) indicates that through introducing an e-channel, her profit will be reduced compared with that in the benchmark.

Moreover, comparing Model 1 with Model 2 in Fig. 2.5(a), when $(\eta, \delta)$ belongs to Region $A$, the retailer will prefer Model 1 and when $(\eta, \delta)$ is located in Region $B$, she would prefer Model 2. Obviously, the retailer's profit will decrease no matter who (the manufacturer or

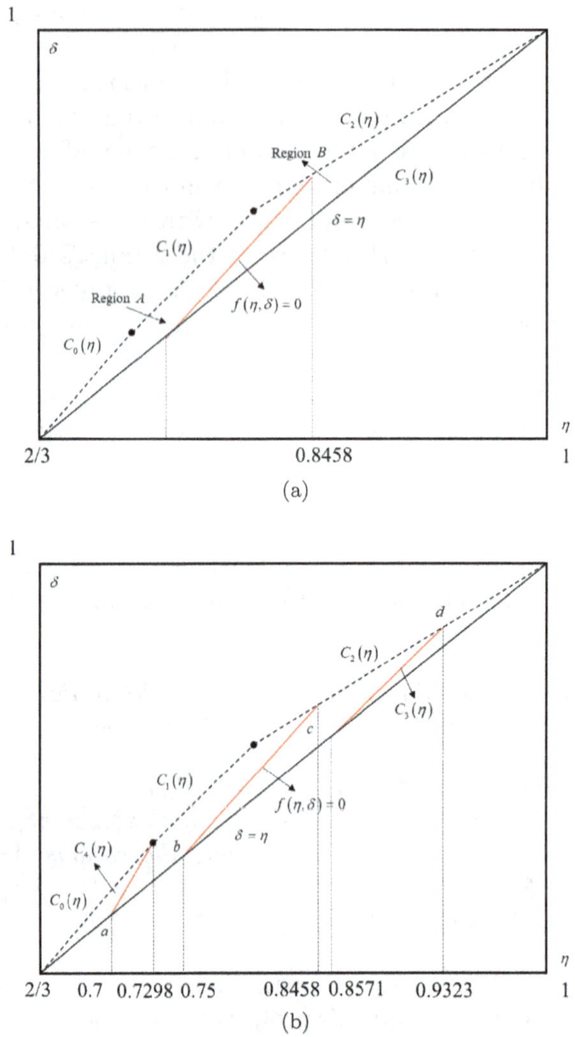


Fig. 2.5. The region divisions when comparing Model $i\,(i = 0, 1, 2)$. (a) Considering the retailer's optimal profits and (b) when comparing $w_i^*$ and $k_i^*$.

the retailer) introduces the online channel because the demand and the retail margin through the brick-and-mortar channel fall down (see Propositions 2.1(2), (3)).

Taking the supply chain's perspective, Proposition 2.3(3) demonstrates that the total profit in the supply chain will increase once

Table 2.3. The retailer's preferences for the e-channel in different regions.

| $(\eta, \delta)$ | Comparing $w_i^*$ | Comparing $k_i^*$ | The Retailer's preference |
|---|---|---|---|
| a | $w_2^* > w_1^* > w_0^*$ | $k_1^* > k_2^* > k_0^*$ | Model 1 |
| b | $w_2^* > w_1^* > w_0^*$ | $k_2^* > k_1^* > k_0^*$ | Model 1 |
| c | $w_2^* > w_1^* > w_0^*$ | $k_2^* > k_1^* > k_0^*$ | Model 2 |
| d | $w_1^* > w_2^* > w_0^*$ | $k_2^* > k_1^* > k_0^*$ | Model 2 |

the manufacturer opens an online channel. However, it will decrease when the retailer opens it. This means that in Model 1, the increased profit that the manufacturer gains by inserting an e-channel will be more than the decreased profit that the retailer loses. But, in Model 2, the manufacturer's gain from the retailer opening an e-channel is not sufficient to offset the retailer's loss.

In terms of the manufacturer's wholesale price and the channel control ability, we can further examine the channel selection issue. Figure 2.5(b) gives four sections, 'a', 'b', 'c' and 'd' in the feasible region $R$ and Table 2.3 reveals the retailer's preferences for the e-channel in different regions.

When $(\eta, \delta)$ is in Region 'a', we have $w_2^* > w_1^*$ and $k_2^* < k_1^*$. Thus, the manufacturer will give the lower wholesale price in Model 1 than that in Model 2, while his channel control ability in Model 1 is weaker than that in Model 2. From Proposition 2.3(2), the retailer is better off in Model 1 under this case. When $(\eta, \delta)$ belongs to Region 'b' or 'c', there are $w_2^* > w_1^*$ and $k_2^* > k_1^*$. We can see that the retailer is better off with Model 1 in Region 'b', or with Model 2 in Region 'c'. When facing similar conditions, why does the retailer prefer the different strategy? The reason is that the different combinations of $(\eta, \delta)$ may have different influences on the prices and profits of both agents in the supply chain. That is, when $\delta$ is fixed, the discount rate is smaller in Region 'b' relative to that in Region 'c', thus the price is lower in the retailer's e-channel and her demand in the online channel will increase. But, because the increase in the demand cannot offset the reduction in her profit, the retailer has to cede the introduction of the online channel in Region 'b'. In contrast, when $\eta$ is fixed, consumers' acceptance in Region 'c' is lower than that in Region 'b', which leads to the retailer to open an e-channel by herself in Region 'c'. When $(\eta, \delta)$ is in Region 'd', there are $w_2^* < w_1^*$ and $k_2^* > k_1^*$. Then, the retailer is better off in Model 2 from Proposition 2.3(2).

### 2.4.3. Managerial implications

Based on the above decisions about whether to introduce both members' e-channels or not, some managerial insights are revealed in our research for the manufacturer and the retailer.

In practice, the manufacturer dual-channel (Model 1) and the retailer dual-channel (Model 2) both exist. In comparison with the traditional brick-and-mortar channel (Model 0), we find that the manufacturer is always better off if he opens his own online channel, however the retailer could be better off under certain conditions that are characterized by parameter combinations of consumer acceptance of the e-channel and the online discount rate. The implication is that manufacturers will select to introduce their own e-channels. However, many traditional manufacturers in China, have paid much attention to production for many years. Therefore, they may first decide to cooperate with a retailer to open online channel. When they accumulate adequate experiences in the online market and gain consumers' acceptance, they may decide to open their own online channel.

From the retailer's perspective, her profit is not always better off after the introduction of the e-channel, and the different combinations of the consumer acceptance of the e-channel and the online discount rate $(\eta, \delta)$ may affect her preference to Model 1 or Model 2. The retailer's preferences can be determined by identifying and characterizing the regions of $(\eta, \delta)$. In addition, it is concluded that when a lower online price is provided to consumers (see Proposition 2.1(2)), the online demand of the retailer will increase. Thus, to capture the online market, the retailer has to offer an online discount periodically. For example, in China, 6.18 and Singles' Day are becoming more and more popular, attracting many consumers. Some products, such as the famous brands in the apparel industry, including Tommy Hilfiger and Ralph Lauren, have both a retailer e-channel and a manufacturer-channel in addition to the traditional retail brick-and-mortar channel. This is represented in Model 3.

## 2.5. Extension to the Case with Uncertain Demand and Risk-Averse Behavior

This section will extend the channel selection problem to the case of stochastic demand. Uncertain demand gives rise to risk-averse behavior of decision makers. In this section, we take Model 1 as an example, to analyze how the risk-averse attitude would influence on channel members' decision-making. Specifically, this section just considers a dual-channel supply chain with a monopoly manufacturer as the Stackelberg leader, an independent retailer as the follower, where the manufacturer opens his own online channel besides the retailer's physical channel and the manufacturer is risk-averse. It is noted that the definitions of most parameters in this section are the same as those in the previous sections.

### 2.5.1. Stochastic demand

To characterize consumers' preference to the online and offline channels, we assume that consumers are divided into two kinds: the grocery shoppers who obtain higher value in the retailer's physical channel and the online shoppers who gain higher value in the e-channel (Hsiao and Chen, 2014). To model their difference, the proportion $\tau{:}1-\tau$ of the grocery shoppers and the Internet shoppers are defined. Assume that each consumer's valuation of product from the retailer is $v$ and then the grocery shoppers will obtain $\alpha v (0 < \alpha < 1)$ from the e-channel and the online shoppers will obtain $\beta v$ $(1 < \beta < 2)$ from the manufacturer's online channel. Thus, when a grocery shopper decides to buy the product from the retailer's store, he will obtain the net utility $v-p$; otherwise his net utility is $\alpha v-p$ from the online channel. That is, the grocery shoppers will purchase the product only from the physical store. Similarly, the online shoppers will purchase the product only from the manufacturer's e-channel.

Furthermore, the market size is assumed to be $a = \tilde{a}+\varepsilon$, where $\tilde{a}$ is the mean of the potential demand. $\varepsilon$ denotes the demand fluctuation and is assumed to be a random variable following a normal distribution $\varepsilon \sim N(0, \sigma^2)$. Combining the consumers' utility and the market size, we characterize the demand function of the retailer's channel as $q_r = a\tau(v - p)$ and the demand function of the manufacturer's online as $q_m = a(1-\tau)(v-p/\beta)$. Similarly, the product cost and the online operating cost of the manufacturer, the operating cost of the retailer's physical channel are normalized to zero. Meanwhile, $\tilde{a}$, $v$ are also assumed to be 1 for simplicity. In this section, the subscripts $i = m, r$ denote the manufacturer and the retailer, respectively.

### 2.5.2. The models

This section will investigate the pricing decisions considering the member' risk-averse attitude. Two scenarios are designed: one is the case that two parties are all risk-neutral as a comparison benchmark (denoted as Model NN), the other is the case where the manufacturer has the risk-averse behavior but the retailer is risk-neutral (denoted as Model RN). Here, we adopt the mean–variance method to gauge the risk-averse behavior.

**Model NN—The benchmark.** Model NN provides a benchmark about the case in which the manufacturer and the reseller are all risk-neutral. For a given wholesale price $w$, the retailer's profit is $E(\pi_r^{NN}) = \tau(1-p)(p-w)$, the best response function $p_r^{NN^*}$ can be determined by

$$\max_{0<w\leq p<1} E(\pi_r^{NN}) = \tau(1-p)(p-w). \tag{2.10}$$

From the concavity of the objective functions in $p_r^{NN^*}$, we can obtain

$$p_r^{NN^*} = (1+w)/2. \tag{2.11}$$

Given the retailer's response function, the manufacturers profit is

$$\max_{0\leq w<1} E(\pi_m^{NN}) = \tau(1-p_r^{NN^*})w + (1-\tau)(1-p_r^{NN^*}/\beta)p_r^{NN^*}. \tag{2.12}$$

Simultaneously, the first-order condition on $w$ then leads to the optimal wholesale price as follows:

$$w_m^{NN^*} = \frac{\beta - 1 + \tau}{1 - \tau + 2\tau\beta}. \tag{2.13}$$

Obviously, the optimal retail price $p_r^{NN^*}$, the optimal profits $E(\pi_m^{NN})^*$, $E(\pi_r^{NN})^*$ of the manufacturer and the retailer can be obtained:

$$p_r^{NN^*} = \frac{\beta(1+2\tau)}{1-\tau+2\tau\beta},$$
$$E(\pi_m^{NN})^* = \frac{\beta+4\tau(1-\tau)(\beta-1)}{4(1-\tau+2\tau\beta)},$$
$$E(\pi_r^{NN})^* = \frac{\tau[2-\beta+2\tau(\beta-1)]^2}{4(1-\tau+2\tau\beta)^2}.$$

**Model RN—With the manufacturer's risk-averse behavior.** In Model RN, we assume that the manufacturer has the risk-averse behavior, but the retailer is risk-neutral. Similar to the above benchmark scenario, for a given $w$, the retailer's profit is given by $E(\pi_r^{RN}) = \tau(1-p)(p-w)$. Then the retailer's response function is

$$p_r^{RN^*} = (1+w)/2. \tag{2.14}$$

Hence, the mean–variance model of the manufacturer is

$$\begin{cases} \max\limits_{0\le w<1} & E(\pi_m^{RN}) = \tau(1-p)w + (1-\tau)(1-p/\beta)p \\ \text{subject to} & \sqrt{Var(\pi_m^{RN})} = [\tau(1-p)w + (1-\tau)(1-p/\beta)p] \\ & \quad \times \sigma \le K_m. \end{cases} \tag{2.15}$$

It is equivalent to the following formula:

$$\begin{cases} \max\limits_{0\le w<1} & E(\pi_m^{RN}) = \frac{(1-\tau+2\tau\beta)}{4\beta}w^2 + \frac{(\beta-1+\tau)}{2\beta}w \\ & \quad + \frac{(1-\tau)(2\beta-1)}{4\beta} \\ \text{subject to} & E(\pi_m^{RN}) \le d_m, \end{cases} \tag{2.16}$$

where $K_m$ denotes the risk-averse degree of the manufacturer measured by mean–variance method, and $K_m > 0$. $d_m = K_m/\sigma$ represents the risk tolerance of the manufacturer through combining his risk-averse behavior and the demand fluctuation. That is, given $\sigma$, the larger the manufacturer's risk-averse degree $K_m$ is, the higher risk tolerance he has. Thus, the equilibrium prices and the corresponding payoffs are shown as follows:

(1) If $d_m \ge E(\pi_m^{NN})^*$, then $w_m^{RN^*} = w_m^{NN^*}$, $p_r^{RN^*} = p_r^{NN^*}$, and $E(\pi_m^{AN})^* = E(\pi_m^{NN})^*$, $E(\pi_r^{AN})^* = E(\pi_r^{NN})^*$.

(2) If $\max\{\frac{(1-\tau)(2\beta-1)}{4\beta}, \frac{(1-\tau)(\beta-1)}{\beta}\} < d_m \leq E(\pi_m^{NN})^*$, then

(i) first solutions: $w_m^{RN^*} = w_m^{NN^*} + 2\sqrt{\Delta}$, $p_r^{RN^*} = p_r^{NN^*} + \sqrt{\Delta}$ and $E(\pi_m^{AN})^* = d_m$, $E(\pi_r^{AN})^* = E(\pi_r^{NN})^* + \tau\Delta - \tau(1 - w_m^{NN^*})\sqrt{\Delta}$;

(ii) second solutions: $w_m^{RN^*} = w_m^{NN^*} - 2\sqrt{\Delta}$, $p_r^{RN^*} = p_r^{NN^*} - \sqrt{\Delta}$, and $E(\pi_m^{AN})^* = d_m$, $E(\pi_r^{AN})^* = E(\pi_r^{NN})^* + \tau\Delta + \tau(1 - w_m^{NN^*})\sqrt{\Delta}$.

(3) If $\frac{(1-\tau)(\beta-1)}{\beta} < d_m \leq \frac{(1-\tau)(2\beta-1)}{4\beta}$ and $1 < \beta \leq 1.5$, then $w_m^{RN^*} = w_m^{NN^*} + 2\sqrt{\Delta} p_r^{RN^*} = p_r^{NN^*} + \sqrt{\Delta}$, and $E(\pi_m^{AN})^* = d_m$, $E(\pi_r^{AN})^* = E(\pi_r^{NN})^* + \tau\Delta - \tau(1 - w_m^{NN^*})\sqrt{\Delta}$.

(4) If $\frac{(1-\tau)(2\beta-1)}{4\beta} < d_m \leq \frac{(1-\tau)(\beta-1)}{\beta}$ and $\beta > 1.5$, then

$$
\begin{aligned}
w_m^{RN^*} &= w_m^{NN^*} - 2\sqrt{\Delta}, p_r^{RN^*} = p_r^{NN^*} - \sqrt{\Delta} \text{ and } E(\pi_m^{AN})^* \\
&= d_m, E(\pi_r^{AN})^* = E(\pi_r^{NN})^* + \tau\Delta + \tau(1 - w_m^{NN^*})\sqrt{\Delta},
\end{aligned}
$$

where

$$
\Delta = \frac{\beta[E(\pi_m^{NN})^* - d_m]}{1 - \tau + 2\tau\beta}.
$$

Obviously, we can see from the above optimal solutions that when the manufacturer's risk tolerance $d_m$ is large enough, the manufacturer's risk-averse behavior has no influence on the partner's decisions in the supply chain. The model will be reduced to the benchmark scenario, and the results become the same as those in Model NN.

But when the manufacturer's risk tolerance $d_m$ is mediate (i.e., $\max\{\frac{(1-\tau)(2\beta-1)}{4\beta}, \frac{(1-\tau)(\beta-1)}{\beta}\} < d_m \leq E(\pi_m^{NN})^*$), the cases become more complicated, because the manufacturer may take the higher wholesale price or the lower wholesale price. The reason may be that when the manufacturer produces the high-end product, although he has a certain degree of risk aversion, he still adopts the skimming pricing policy. That is, he will select a higher pricing and limit the demand of some consumers. However, when the manufacturer produces the low-end product, due to his risk-averse attitude, he will choose the penetration pricing policy and make a lower pricing policy to expand the demand of consumers.

Specially, when consumers' preference $\beta$ to the manufacturer's online channel is less than 1.5, it means that most consumers will buy product in the retailer's store. Because the manufacturer has much stronger risk-averse attitude, he will give a higher wholesale price to restrict the retailer's market demand. On the contrary, if $\beta > 1.5$, we can conclude that most consumers will prefer to buy the product from the manufacturer's online channel, the manufacturer undoubtedly likes to give a lower wholesale price to incent the reseller although he has more stronger risk-averse behavior.

Note that when the risk tolerance of the manufacturer is small, that is

$$d_m \in \left(0, \min\left\{\frac{(1-\tau)(\beta-1)}{\beta}, \frac{(1-\tau)(2\beta-1)}{4\beta}\right\}\right),$$

no equilibrium solutions exist under the condition $0 < w < 1$. It shows that when the manufacturer has very strong risk-averse behavior, the members in the dual supply chain cannot reach the equilibrium.

Further, we can conclude that when the manufacturer's risk-averse behavior is mediate, the manufacturer's profit will be hurt. However, the retailer's profit may increase or decrease according to the marketing strategy. Therefore, the total profit in the dual-channel supply chain may also be increased or decreased.

## 2.6. Conclusion

This chapter studies the channel selection issues through discussing whether the manufacturer or the retailer will introduce an e-channel in addition to a traditional brick-and-mortar channel. The traditional brick-and-mortar channel (Model 0), the manufacturer dual-channel model (Model 1), the retailer dual-channel model (Model 2) and the multi-channel model (Model 3) are captured in a unified framework. Two important phenomena are taken into account in these models: consumers' lower valuation of the products sold through e-channels and sellers' discount pricing behavior in e-channels to promote sales. Applying Stackelberg game, the optimal equilibrium-pricing decisions are derived. Theoretic analyzes and comparisons among these models are made with respect to the prices, demand, and the channel control ability of the manufacturer, profits for the two members and the entire supply chain.

Further, this chapter extends the pricing decision of a dual-channel supply chain to the case where the manufacturer has risk-averse behavior. Based on the consumers' channel preferences, the consumers are classified into two types: grocery shoppers and Internet shoppers. Then, using mean–variance method and Stackelberg game theoretic analysis, we examine the optimal equilibrium pricing under the dual-channel models. Taking the risk-neutral case as the benchmark, the comparative results are obtained.

Note that our models are based on the assumptions that the cost of the brick-and-mortar channel and the cost of the e-channel are both normalized to zero. However, in practice, the cost of the brick-and-mortar channel may be higher than the cost of the e-channel. In addition, the extended models could be further analyzed and compared, particularly in the cases in which both channel members are risk-averse when introducing the e-channels and deciding discount rates.

## References

Aulak, G. (2014). The average price difference between online and offline prices of smartphones is just 5%, says survey. *The Economic Times*, October 27, 2014. (https://economictimes.indiatimes.com/industry/services/retail/the-average-price-difference-between-online-and-offline-prices-of-smartphones-is-just-5-says-survey/articleshow/44943820.cms?from=mdr).

Balakrishnan, A., Sundaresan, S., & Zhang, B. (2014). Browse-and-switch: Retail-online competition under value uncertainty. *Production and Operations Management*, 23(7), pp. 1129–1145.

Cattani, K., Gilland, W., Heese, H. S., & Swaminathan, J. (2006). Boiling frogs: Pricing strategies for a manufacturer adding a direct channel that competes with the traditional channel. *Production and Operations Management*, 15(1), p. 40.

Chellappa, R. K., Sin, R. G., & Siddarth, S. (2011). Price formats as a source of price dispersion: A study of online and offline prices in the domestic US airline markets. *Information Systems Research*, 22(1), pp. 83–98.

Chiang, W. Y. K., Chhajed, D., & Hess, J. D. (2003). Direct marketing, indirect profits: A strategic analysis of dual-channel supply-chain design. *Management Science*, 49(1), pp. 1–20.

Chiang, W. Y. K., & Monahan, G. E. (2005). Managing inventories in a two-echelon dual-channel supply chain. *European Journal of Operational Research*, 162(2), pp. 325–341.

Hsiao, L., & Chen, Y. J. (2014). Strategic motive for introducing internet channels in a supply chain. *Production and Operations Management*, 23(1), pp. 36–47.

Kacen, J. J., & Lee, J. A. (2002). The influence of culture on consumer impulsive buying behavior. *Journal of Consumer Psychology*, 12(2), pp. 163–176.

Luo, L., & Sun, J. (2016). New product design under channel acceptance: Brick-and-Mortar, online-exclusive, or brick-and-click. *Production and Operations Management*, 25(12), pp. 2014–2034.

Li, T., Zhao, X., & Xie, J. (2015). Inventory management for dual sales channels with inventory-level-dependent demand. *Journal of the Operational Research Society*, 66(3), pp. 488–499.

Ma, W. M., Zhao, Z., & Ke, H. (2013). Dual-channel closed-loop supply chain with government consumption-subsidy. *European Journal of Operational Research*, 226(2), pp. 221–227.

Ofek, E., Katona, Z., & Sarvary, M. (2011). "Bricks and clicks": The impact of product returns on the strategies of multichannel retailers. *Marketing Science*, 30(1), pp. 42–60.

Spengler, J. J. (1950). Vertical integration and antitrust policy. *Journal of Political Economy*, 58(4), pp. 347–352.

Steiner, R. L. (2004). The evolution and applications of dual-stage thinking. *The Antitrust Bulletin*, 49(4), pp. 877–909.

Tsay, A. A., & Agrawal, N. (2004). Channel conflict and coordination in the e-commerce age. *Production and Operations Management*, 13(1), pp. 93–110.

Wang R. F., Li, B., Li, Z. H., & Hou P. W. (2018). Selection policy for a manufacturer's online channel: Do it oneself or cooperate with retailers. *IMA Journal of Management Mathematics*, 29, pp. 393–414.

Yan, R., & Ghose, S. (2010). Forecast information and traditional retailer performance in a dual-channel competitive market. *Journal of Business Research*, 63(1), pp. 77–83.

Yan, R., Wang, J., & Zhou, B. (2010). Channel integration and profit sharing in the dynamics of multi-channel firms. *Journal of Retailing and Consumer Services*, 17(5), pp. 430–440.

© 2022 World Scientific Publishing Europe Ltd.
https://doi.org/10.1142/9781800610408_0003

## Chapter 3

# Pricing Decisions in a Dual-Channel Supply Chain with a Risk-Averse Retailer

**Bo Li* and Ping Chen†**

*College of Management and Economics, Tianjin University, China*

**libo0410@tju.edu.cn*

†*bingling.0815@163.com*

### 3.1. Introduction

While Internet-based e-commerce has become an efficient transaction technology, many manufacturers have been motivated to introduce their online channels. On the one hand, through the online channel, the manufacturers have expanded their product distributions besides traditional retail channels to form dual-channel supply chains. On the other hand, however, channel conflict appears because of the addition of new online channels, including horizontal competition between the traditional channel and the electronic channel and vertical competition between the manufacturers and the retailers (Yao *et al.*, 2005). The uncertainties and the risks inherent in supply chain decisions are also increasing in the dual-channel context. As a result, the decision makers in supply chains may exhibit risk-averse behaviors.

In fact, the risk-averse behaviors of channel members have attracted much attention in the literature, and the existing studies have shown that such behaviors could drastically influence their decisions, such as pricing, ordering and investment (Chung *et al.*, 2010; Ma *et al.*, 2012).

This chapter considers a dual-channel supply chain system that consists of a manufacturer and a retailer. The manufacturer is risk-neutral and produces only one type of perishable product with a stochastic price-dependent demand. Meanwhile, the manufacturer opens an online channel to distribute his product to consumers besides one physical channel via the retailer. The retailer is risk-averse because of the serious channel conflict caused by the manufacturer's online channel. Under the problem setting, we investigate the following problems:

(1) Considering the retailer's risk-averse behavior, how does adding an online channel to a conventional retail channel influence the pricing strategies, the order quantity, and the profits of the entire supply chain as well as each agent?
(2) What are the effects of the risk-averse indicator on the performance of two agents in the dual-channel supply chains considering different channel power, demand uncertainty and price sensitivity?

This chapter is organized as follows. Section 3.2 describes the problem. The consistent pricing strategy (i.e., online sale price is the same as the retail sale price) is assumed to mitigate the channel conflict. We first build a Nash bargaining model in which the manufacturer and the retailer negotiate with each other on the decisions such as the wholesale price, the retail price and the order quantity. In Sec. 3.3, with the assumption of a uniform distributed demand uncertainty, a Nash bargaining equilibrium is obtained analytically. The manufacturer's profit share among the supply chain is then analyzed. In Sec. 3.4, numerical experiments are provided to illustrate interesting results concerning the effects of the risk-averse indicator on the performance of two agents in various situations with varying channel powers, demand uncertainty and price sensitivities. Section 3.5 concludes this chapter.

## 3.2. Model Description

The model comprises a manufacturer M and a retailer R in a supply chain with a single perishable product. We suppose that the manufacturer is risk-neutral and the retailer is risk-averse. The products are infinitely divisible and sold through an independent physical retail channel and the manufacturer's own online channel. The traditional channel's demand is relatively steady and predictable based on historical sales data. However, the electronic channel's demand is dynamic as well as personalized, and it is hard to predict the amount of customers ordering. Here, we concern only one sales season, and the retailer orders from the manufacturer at the beginning of the sales period, while the manufacturer applies a make-to-order policy on its own channel. It means that we assume that the manufacturer applies a mixed strategy of make-to-order on its online channel and make-to-stock on the independent retail channel (Carr *et al.*, 2000; Li *et al.*, 2014).

Furthermore, because the value of perishable products will gradually decline by time, the optimal retail price and order quantity of products are the vital decisions for the retailer, while only the wholesale price is significant for the manufacturer. Hence, to simplify the calculation in this chapter, the surplus value of the product is assumed to be 0 at the end of the sales period, and product shortage is not concerned.

The notations and parameters are defined as follows:

| Notations | Definitions |
|---|---|
| $i$ | $i = 1$ or 2 denotes the retail channel or the direct Internet channel |
| $D$ | the basic product demand, which is constant |
| $\xi$ | the market demand uncertainty that is a random number, and follows a uniform distribution on $[-U, U](0 \leq U \leq D)$, where $\varphi(\cdot)$ is the probability density function of $\xi$ and $\Phi(\cdot)$ is the cumulative distribution function of $\xi$ |
| $\bar{D}$ | the total product demand, which is stochastic, $\bar{D} = D + \xi$ |
| $\theta$ | the proportion of the traditional channel's market share, i.e., $1 - \theta$ represents the proportion of the online channel's market share, $0 \leq \theta \leq 1$ |
| $b_i$ | the marginal channel demand per respective channel price, $i = 1$ or 2 |
| $\alpha$ | the diffusion intensity, the shift between the two channels with regard to the price (Yao and Liu, 2005), where $b_i \geq \alpha$ indicates that the impact of the price on one channel is bigger than that of the other channel (Hassens *et al.*, 2001; Kurata *et al.*, 2007; Mukhopadhyay *et al.*, 2008) |
| $\gamma_i$ | the price sensitivity, which represents the marginal channel demand per respective channel price under consistent pricing |

The demands in the retail channel and in the online channel are

$$D_1 = \theta\bar{D} - b_1 p_1 + \alpha p_2, \tag{3.1}$$

$$D_2 = (1-\theta)\bar{D} - b_2 p_2 + \alpha p_1, \tag{3.2}$$

where $D_1$, and $D_2$ represent the demands in the traditional channel and in the online channel, respectively, while $p_1$, and $p_2$ denote the prices in the traditional channel and in the online channel, respectively.

According to Kevin (2002), the identical price in two channels can mitigate the channel conflict to some degree. Cattani *et al.* (2006) have also provided abundant empirical evidence for the reasonability of the consistent pricing (i.e., equal-pricing) strategy in dual-channel context. Meanwhile, a survey on popular products' prices has been conducted to demonstrate that the manufacturer's direct price and the traditional retail price are quite similar in some cases (Wen *et al.*, 2013). Hence, this chapter applies the assumption that the prices in the two channels are the same, namely $p_1 = p_2 = p$. Consequently, the demand functions can be rewritten as follows:

$$D_1 = \theta\bar{D} - \gamma_1 p, \tag{3.3}$$

$$D_2 = (1-\theta)\bar{D} - \gamma_2 p, \tag{3.4}$$

where $\gamma_1 = b_1 - \alpha, \gamma_2 = b_2 - \alpha$.

In this chapter, we adopt CVaR criterion to estimate the risk-averse behavior of the retailer. Particularly, let $\pi_r$ represent the profit function of the retailer with order quantity $q_1$ and random demand $D_1$, and $v^\eta(\pi_r)$ represent the $\eta$-quantile of $\pi_r$. A confidence indicator $\eta \in (0,1]$ (also denoted as a risk-averse indicator) is specified by the decision maker for achieving a certain level of profit which is denoted as $v$. The VaR measure can be defined as follows (Artzner *et al.*, 1997):

$$v^\eta(\pi_r) = \inf\{\Pr(\pi_r \le v) \ge \eta\}.$$

Note that the CVaR criterion which measures the average profit falling below the $\eta$-quantile level, ignores the contributions of profit beyond the specified quantile. Thus, the retailer's $\eta$-CVaR under an order quantity $q_1$ is defined as follows (Rockafellar and Uryasev, 2000):

$$\mathrm{CVaR}^{\eta}(\pi_r) = E[\pi_r \mid \pi_r \leq v^{\eta}(\pi_r)].$$

To simplify the calculation, we will adopt the following equivalent definition of CVaR (Rockafellar and Uryasev, 2000):

$$\mathrm{CVaR}^{\eta}(\pi_r) = \max_{v \in R} \left\{ v + \frac{1}{\eta} E[\min(\pi_r - v, 0)] \right\}.$$

Assuming that the manufacturer produces a single product at a unit cost $c$, $\pi_m$ represents the manufacturer's profit, while $\pi_r$ represents the traditional retailer's profit. Following the Nash bargaining framework, the manufacturer and the retailer simultaneously make decisions about the wholesale price $w$, the direct and the retail sales price $p$, and the order quantity $q_1$ to maximize the values of their objective functions. To avoid the trivial case, it is supposed that $p \geq w \geq c$.

In the marketing chain, channel members may have different bargaining power. Bargaining power can be defined as the relative power of the agents to exert impact over other parties. If two agents are on an equal footing in a debate, then they will have equal bargaining power, like in a perfectly competitive market. In a supply chain, we also refer to the channel power, which is the ability of one member to change the other members' behavior based on their relatively strong position in the demand market, when they distribute the products in the channels, including the online and offline channels.

Hence, the above problem can be formulated as follows:

$$\max_{q_1 \geq 0, c \leq w \leq p} \mathrm{CVaR}^{\eta}(\pi_r - \pi_{r0}) \cdot (\pi_m - \pi_{m0}), \tag{3.5}$$

where $\pi_{r0}$ and $\pi_{m0}$ denote the reservation payoffs of the retailer and the manufacturer, respectively. Reservation payoffs could be gained by the manufacturer and the retailer under the normal cases. We adopt the same objective function as Ma *et al.* (2012) because the solution to problem (3.5) satisfies the axioms of Pareto efficiency, symmetry, linear transformation immutability and the independence of the irrelevant choice. Thus, we select the same treatment like that in Ma *et al.* (2012) to keep the model tractable.

### 3.3. Equilibrium and Analysis

In this section, the solutions under equal bargaining power are firstly solved and then the profits of two members, the relative profitability of channel members in the dual-channel supply chain are revealed.

#### 3.3.1. The solutions under equal bargaining power

First, we assume that two agents have equal bargaining power. Then, the problem needed to be solved is as follows:

$$\max_{q_1 \geq 0, c \leq w \leq p} \mathrm{CVaR}^{\eta}(\pi_r) \cdot \pi_m. \tag{3.6}$$

To simplify the narrative, denote $\min(q_1, D_1) = q_1 - (q_1 - D_1)^+$, and $(\cdot)^+ = \max(\cdot, 0)$.

The manufacturer's profit function is

$$\begin{aligned} \pi_m &= (w-c)q_1 + (p-c)D_2 \\ &= (w-c)q_1 + (p-c)[(1-\theta)\bar{D} - \gamma_2 p]. \end{aligned} \tag{3.7}$$

The manufacturer's profit expectation function is

$$\begin{aligned} E[\pi_m] &= E[(w-c)q_1 + (p-c)D_2] \\ &= (w-c)q_1 + (p-c)(1-\theta)D - (p-c)\gamma_2 p. \end{aligned} \tag{3.8}$$

The traditional retailer's profit function is

$$\pi_r = p\min(q_1, D_1) - wq_1 = (p-w)q_1 - p\{q_1 - [\theta\bar{D} - \gamma_1 p]\}^+. \tag{3.9}$$

Then, we have

$$CVaR^{\eta}(\pi_r) = \max_{v \in R}\left\{v + \frac{1}{\eta}E[\min(\pi_r - v, 0)]\right\}.$$

Therefore, the traditional retailer's $\eta - \mathrm{CVaR}$ is

$$\begin{aligned} \mathrm{CVaR}^{\eta}(\pi_r) == \max_{v \in R}\Bigg\{v + \frac{1}{\eta}E[\min((p-w)q_1 \\ -p[q_1 - \theta\bar{D} + \gamma_1 p]^+ - v, 0)]\Bigg\}. \end{aligned}$$

The above formula could be simplified in the following two cases:

(1) If $(p-w)q_1 - v \le 0$, then

$$\mathrm{CVaR}^{\eta}(\pi_r) = (p-w)q_1 - \frac{p}{\eta}\theta \int_{-U}^{\frac{q_1+\gamma_1 p}{\theta}-D} \Phi(\xi)d\xi.$$

Thus, we have

$$\begin{aligned} v^* &= \arg\max_{v\in R} \\ &\quad \times \left\{ v + \frac{1}{\eta} E[(p-w)q_1 - p[q_1 - \theta D + \gamma_1 p]^+ - v] \right\} \\ &= (p-w)q_1. \end{aligned}$$

(2) If $(p-w)q_1 - v > 0$, then

$$\begin{aligned} \mathrm{CVaR}^{\eta}(\pi_r) = \max_{v\in R} \Bigg\{ v + \frac{1}{\eta} \int_{-U}^{\frac{wq_1+v}{\theta p}+\frac{\gamma_1 p}{\theta}-D} ((p-w)q_1 \\ - p[q_1 - \theta\bar{D} + \gamma_1 p]^+ - v)d\Phi(\xi) \Bigg\}. \end{aligned}$$

Let

$$\begin{aligned} F(v) = v + \frac{1}{\eta} \int_{-U}^{\frac{wq_1+v}{\theta p}+\frac{\gamma_1 p}{\theta}-D} \\ \times((p-w)q_1 - p[q_1 - \theta\bar{D} + \gamma_1 p]^+ - v)d\Phi(\xi). \end{aligned}$$

As $\xi$ follows a uniform distribution with support over $[-U, U]$, we have

$$\Phi(\xi) = \frac{\xi+U}{2U}, \Phi(-U) = 0.$$

Then

$$\begin{aligned} \frac{dF(v)}{dv} &= 1 + \frac{1}{\eta}\left[ \int_{-U}^{\frac{wq_1+v}{\theta p}+\frac{\gamma_1 p}{\theta}-D} (-1)d\Phi(\xi) + 0 - 0 \right] \\ &= 1 - \frac{1}{\eta}\Phi\left( \frac{wq_1+v}{\theta p} + \frac{\gamma_1 p}{\theta} - D \right). \end{aligned}$$

Obviously, $\frac{dF^2(v)}{dv^2} = -\frac{1}{\eta} \cdot \frac{1}{\theta p}\varphi(\frac{wq_1+v}{\theta p} + \frac{\gamma_1 p}{\theta} - D) < 0$, which proves that $F(v)$ is a concave function and there exists a unique optimal solution.

Let $\frac{dF(v)}{dv} = 0$, thus $v^* = -wq_1 + p\theta\Phi^{-1}(\eta) + \theta pD - \gamma_1 p^2$.

Therefore,

$$CVaR^{\eta}(\pi_r) = -wq_1 + p\theta\Phi^{-1}(\eta) + \theta pD - \gamma_1 p^2 - \frac{\theta p}{\eta}\int_{-U}^{\Phi^{-1}(\eta)} \Phi(\xi)d\xi.$$

As CVaR is a continuous risk measure, we have

$$\mathrm{CVaR}^{\eta}(\pi_r) = \begin{cases} (p-w)q_1 - \frac{\theta p}{\eta}\displaystyle\int_{-U}^{\frac{q_1+\gamma_1 p}{\theta}-D} \Phi(\xi)d\xi \\ \quad \text{if } q_1 \le \theta D - \gamma_1 p + \theta\Phi^{-1}(\eta), \\ -wq_1 + p\theta\Phi^{-1}(\eta) + \theta pD - \gamma_1 p^2 - \frac{\theta p}{\eta}\displaystyle\int_{-U}^{\Phi^{-1}(\eta)} \Phi(\xi)d\xi \\ \quad \text{if } q_1 > \theta D - \gamma_1 p + \theta\Phi^{-1}(\eta). \end{cases}$$

If we assume that the demand uncertainty $\xi$ follows a uniform distribution with support over $[-U, U]$, an equilibrium solution $\{q_1^*, w^*, p^*\}$ under the Nash bargaining model can be obtained as follows:

(1) The optimal retail price and the optimal direct price are denoted by $p^*$. Furthermore, $p^*$ satisfies the equation

$$(2\gamma_1 + 2\gamma_2)p^{*3} - (D - U\theta + \gamma_1 c + \gamma_2 c + \eta U\theta)p^{*2} + \eta U\theta c^2 = 0.$$

(2) The retailer's optimal order quantity from the manufacturer is

$$q_1^* = \frac{2\eta U\theta(p^* - c) - p^*U\theta - \gamma_1 p^{*2} + \theta Dp^*}{p^*}.$$

(3) The optimal wholesale price of the manufacturer is

$$w^* = \frac{p^* + c}{2} - \frac{p^* - c}{2q_1^*}\left[\frac{\eta U\theta(p^* - c)}{p^*} + (1-\theta)D - \gamma_2 p^*\right].$$

Based on the above equilibrium solution, we have Proposition 3.1.

**Proposition 3.1.** *Assume that the parameters $D, U, \gamma_1, \gamma_2, \theta$ and $c$ are constants, then the optimal price $p^*$ is increasing as $\eta$ increases in* (0,1].

Although the expression of $p^*$ is quite complicated, some managerial insights could still be gained from its expression analytically. From Proposition 3.1, we can clearly see that the retailer will reduce the retail price to avoid the sales risk as she becomes more risk-averse. The other interesting discovery is that the relative change of $\gamma_1$ or $\gamma_2$ has no impact on $p^*$. This is because the impacts of $\gamma_1$ and $\gamma_2$ on the pricing decisions are symmetric due to the consistent pricing strategy. In addition, it is the cooperative relationship between them that makes this possible.

### 3.3.2. Analysis of the manufacturer's profit share

It is interesting to analyze the relative profitability of channel members in the supply chain context. For this purpose, we define a ratio $\theta_m$ to evaluate the manufacturer's relative percentage of the total profit in the supply chain, which is defined as $\theta_m = \frac{E\pi_m}{E\pi_m + E\pi_r}$. Then, the following proposition will be gained.

**Proposition 3.2.** *If $\xi$ follows a uniform distribution with support over $[-U, U]$, then the proportion of the manufacturer's profit among the entire supply chain satisfies $\frac{1}{4-2\eta} \leq \theta_m \leq \frac{1}{2}$.*

According to Proposition 3.2, it could be discovered that the profit share of the manufacturer under the Nash equilibrium model is actually related to the retailer's risk indicator. If the risk-averse indicator $\eta \to 1$, then the retailer tends to be a risk-neutral agent and both of them split the profit pie evenly. However, if $\eta \to 0$, then the retailer becomes an extremely risk-averse agent that will reduce her order quantity. In this case, the profits of the retailer and the manufacturer decline as the total profit of the supply chain declines. However, extreme risk-averse is not definitely advantageous for the retailer because the manufacturer still holds nearly half of the total share. Actually, while having a moderate risk-averse attitude, the retailer would obtain the highest profit share. This chapter will further investigate the impacts of the retailer's risk aversion on the decision variables and the profit allocations under various cases in the numerical experiments.

Next, the effect of the risk-averse indicator $\eta$ on the manufacturer's profit from his online channel $\pi_d$ will be observed. From Proposition 3.2, it could be easily obtained that

$$\pi_d = (p^* - c)[(1-\theta)D - \gamma_2 p^*].$$

It seems that the manufacturer's profit increases with the direct market's efforts, though the situation is not as simple as that. Notice that the manufacturer's profit on the online channel is obviously related to the risk-averse indicator $\eta$ because the retailer's risk-averse indicator influences the retail price.

In fact, because $p^*$ satisfies the equation

$$(2\gamma_1 + 2\gamma_2)p^{*3} - (D - U\theta + \gamma_1 c + \gamma_2 c + \eta U\theta)p^{*2} + \eta U\theta c^2 = 0.$$

Then, we have

$$\eta = \frac{2(\gamma_2+\gamma_1)p^{*3} - (D - U\theta + \gamma_2 c + \gamma_1 c)p^{*2}}{U\theta(p^{*2} - c^2)}.$$

For the risk-averse indicator $\eta$,

$$\eta = \frac{2(\gamma_2+\gamma_1)p^{*3} - (D - U\theta + \gamma_2 c + \gamma_1 c)p^{*2}}{U\theta(p^{*2} - c^2)} > 0.$$

Because $p^* > c, p^{*2} - c^2 > 0$, thus

$$2(\gamma_2+\gamma_1)p^{*3} - (D - U\theta + \gamma_2 c + \gamma_1 c)p^{*2} > 0.$$

It follows

$$p^* > \frac{D - U\theta}{2(\gamma_1+\gamma_2)} + \frac{c}{2}.$$

Simultaneously,

$$\eta = \frac{2(\gamma_2+\gamma_1)p^{*3} - (D - U\theta + \gamma_2 c + \gamma_1 c)p^{*2}}{U\theta(p^{*2} - c^2)} \leq 1.$$

By simplifying the above formula, we get

$$p^* < \frac{D}{2(\gamma_1+\gamma_2)} + \frac{c}{2}.$$

Apparently, when $\frac{D-U\theta}{2(\gamma_1+\gamma_2)} + \frac{c}{2} < p^* < \frac{D}{2(\gamma_1+\gamma_2)} + \frac{c}{2}, \eta \in (0,1]$ is satisfied.

However, $\pi_d = (p^* - c)[(1-\theta)D - \gamma_2 p^*]$ is a downwards opening parabola with respect to the price $p^*$. The axis of the parabola is $\frac{(1-\theta)D}{2\gamma_2} + \frac{c}{2}$ and the intersections between the parabola and $x$-axis are at points $(c, 0)$ and $\left(\frac{(1-\theta)D}{\gamma_2}, 0\right)$. Thus, the manufacturer's profit from his online channel $\pi_d$ is increasing as $p^*$ increases in $\left(c, \frac{(1-\theta)D}{2\gamma_2} + \frac{c}{2}\right]$ and is decreasing as $p^*$ increases in $\left(\frac{(1-\theta)D}{2\gamma_2} + \frac{c}{2}, \frac{(1-\theta)D}{\gamma_2}\right]$. Meanwhile, according to Proposition 3.1, $p^*$ is increasing as $\eta$ increases in (0,1], thus we could conclude with the following proposition.

**Proposition 3.3.** *Assume that the demand uncertainty $\xi$ follows a uniform distribution with support over $[-U, U]$.*

(1) *If $\frac{1-\theta}{\gamma_2} < \frac{\theta(1-U/D)}{\gamma_1}$, then the manufacturer's profit on his online channel $\pi_d$ is decreasing as $\eta$ increases in $(0, 1]$.*
(2) *If $\frac{\theta}{\gamma_1} < \frac{1-\theta}{\gamma_2}$, then the manufacturer's profit on his online channel $\pi_d$ is increasing as $\eta$ increases in $(0, 1]$.*
(3) *If $\frac{\theta(1-U/D)}{\gamma_1} \leq \frac{1-\theta}{\gamma_2} \leq \frac{\theta}{\gamma_1}$, then the manufacturer's profit on his online channel $\pi_d$ is first increasing and then decreasing as $\eta$ increases in $(0, 1]$, which means $\pi_d$ is increasing when $p^*$ is in $\left(\frac{D-\theta U}{2(\gamma_1+\gamma_2)} + \frac{c}{2}, \frac{(1-\theta)D}{2\gamma_2} + \frac{c}{2}\right)$ and is decreasing when $p^*$ is in $\left(\frac{(1-\theta)D}{2\gamma_2} + \frac{c}{2}, \frac{D}{2(\gamma_1+\gamma_2)} + \frac{c}{2}\right)$, when $p^* = \frac{(1-\theta)D}{2\gamma_2} + \frac{c}{2}, \pi_d$ obtains the maximum value.*

According to Proposition 3.3, it could be seen that when $\eta$ increases in $(0, 1]$, the manufacturer's profit on his online channel $\pi_d$ may increase or decrease. The result depends on the values of parameters $D, U, \gamma_1, \gamma_2, \theta$ and $c$.

In particular, when the axis of the parabola $\frac{(1-\theta)D}{2\gamma_2} + \frac{c}{2}$ is compared with the domain of $p^* \in \left(\frac{D-\theta U}{2(\gamma_1+\gamma_2)} + \frac{c}{2}, \frac{D}{2(\gamma_1+\gamma_2)} + \frac{c}{2}\right)$, it is easily to find that $\gamma_2$ may considerably influence $\pi_d$ if $\gamma_1$ is fixed as a constant and $\gamma_2 \to 0$. Which means the online channel's demand can hardly be affected even though the price of the online channel is increasing, so the profit naturally increases as $p^*$ is increasing. This example shows the second case in Proposition 3.3. To the contrary, if $\gamma_2$ grows up to a certain extent, then the online channel's demand is quite sensitive to price, which could cause a sharp demand reduction with an increasing retail price. Thus, the increased price is disadvantageous for the online channel to achieve profit, which is the first case in Proposition 3.4. About the third case, if $\gamma_2$ takes a suitable value in $\left(\frac{1-\theta}{\theta}\gamma_1, \frac{1-\theta}{\theta(1-U/D)}\gamma_1\right)$, the increasing $p^*$ will bring a better profit per unit product at the beginning. However, as $p^*$ increases, the online channel's profit will decline because the demand of the online channel will reduce significantly.

## 3.4. Numerical Experiments

In this section, we demonstrate the properties obtained in Sec. 3.3 and explore further managerial insights using numerical experiments. In particular, our experiments focus on the impacts of the risk-averse indicator $\eta$ on decision-making and profit allocations in various cases.

### 3.4.1. The cases with varying channel powers

Firstly, we analyze the impacts of the risk-averse indicator $\eta$ on decision making and profit sharing for different retailer's market share $\theta$. The related parameters are set as follows: $D = 150$, $\gamma_1 = 0.8$, $\gamma_2 = 0.6$, $c = 4$, and the upper bound of the uniform demand distribution $U = 25$. In this case, we set $\theta = 0.55, 0.7$, and $0.85$, because the traditional channel sales are well established and usually perform better than the online channel sales. The results are illustrated in Figs. 3.1 and 3.2.

From Fig. 3.1(a), it could be easily seen that the retailer tends to choose a higher price as she becomes less risk-averse. This result verifies Proposition 3.1. If the retailer becomes a risk-neutral agent, the market might be optimistically evaluated, which induces her to increase the retail price. However, with $\theta$ increasing from 0.55 to 0.85, namely an increase of the traditional channel's market share, the retail price will decline. Because when the retailer's potential demand is higher, she might reduce the price to achieve better sales volume. It is interesting to discover that the retail prices under different channel powers gradually converge as the retailer's attitude for risk trends toward risk-neutral. This result manifests that no matter how large $\theta$ is, the retailer will set the same highest retail price when her attitude for risk is neutral.

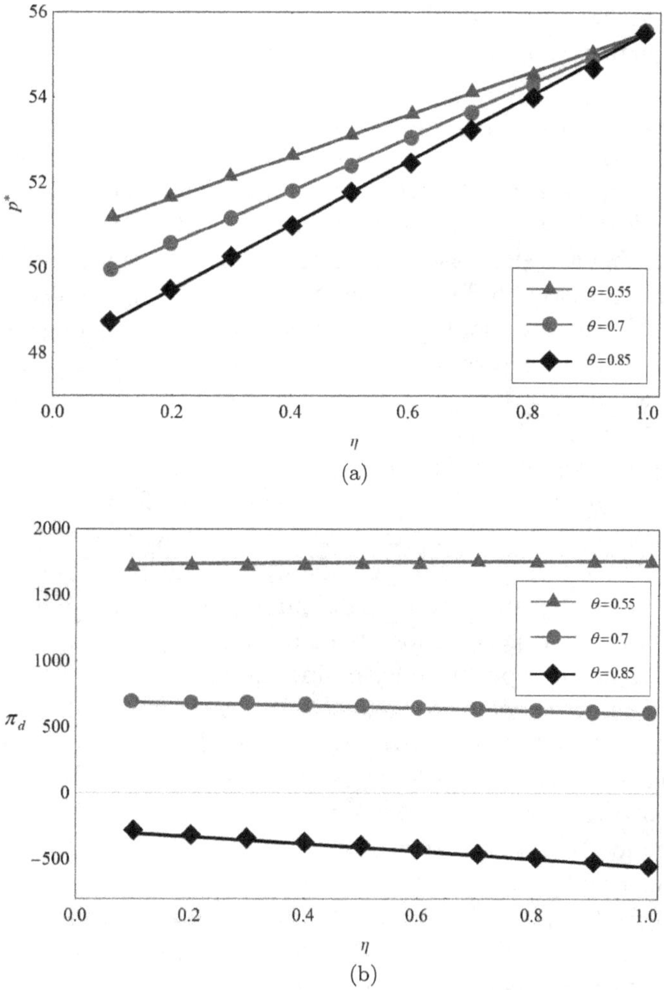


Fig. 3.1. (a) The optimal retail prices and (b) manufacturer's profits on the online channel with respect to $\eta$ under the different channel powers.

Figure 3.1(b) shows the relationship between the manufacturer's profits from his online channel and the risk-averse indicator under the different channel powers. It could be seen that when the manufacturer's market share $1 - \theta$ increases, the online channel can benefit. Nevertheless, when most of the market share ($\theta = 0.85$) has been obtained by the retailer, the manufacturer barely benefits and even bears losses on his online channel. The reason why this could happen is that the basic demand share on the online channel is far from enough to compensate the impact of the price on the channel demand. It could be explained why the manufacturer always suffers losses when he opens up an Internet online channel under this extreme case.

The profit levels of the retailer and the manufacturer are manifested in Fig. 3.2(a). It could be observed that both parties' profits are increasing as $\theta$ decreases, but the scales and the patterns are quite different. Moreover, different from Xu *et al.* (2013), we discover that the manufacturer's profit is strictly increasing as the retailer's risk-averse indicator increases, while the retailer's profit has a concave shape and reaches her peak when she has a moderate risk-averse level ($\theta \in \{0.55, 0.7, 0.85\}$).

The profit shares of the manufacturer under the different channel powers are shown in Fig. 3.2(b), by the curves of convex parabolas. For both channel members, the smaller the value of $\theta$ is ($\theta = 0.55$), the more profit they could gain. However, the profit share tells a different story, because the manufacturer could cut the market share of the retailer to obtain more benefit. It is apparently shown that the manufacturer's profit on his online channel could be substantially improved by the increased market share, which makes up for his loss on the traditional channel from the wholesale price reduction. As a special case, when the retailer is risk-neutral or extremely risk-averse, the manufacturer and the retailer obtain two same size portions of the profit, which is the highest profit share for the manufacturer proved in Proposition 3.2. For the more general case, the retailer grabs more than half of the profit pie if she has risk-averse behavior ($\eta \in (0, 1)$). In addition, the retailer will gain the highest profit share if she has a moderate risk-averse attitude.

### 3.4.2. The cases with varying demand uncertainty

In this section, the pricing and the profit allocations are analyzed with respect to the risk-averse indicator $\eta$ when the demand fluctuations are varying. The related parameters are set to be $D = 150$, $\gamma_1 = 0.8$, $\gamma_2 = 0.6$, $c = 4$, and $\theta = 0.7$. Three cases are considered in which the values of $U$ are taken as 30, 60 and 90, respectively, and $U/D$ is defined as the level of demand fluctuation. The results are illustrated in Figs. 3.3 and 3.4.

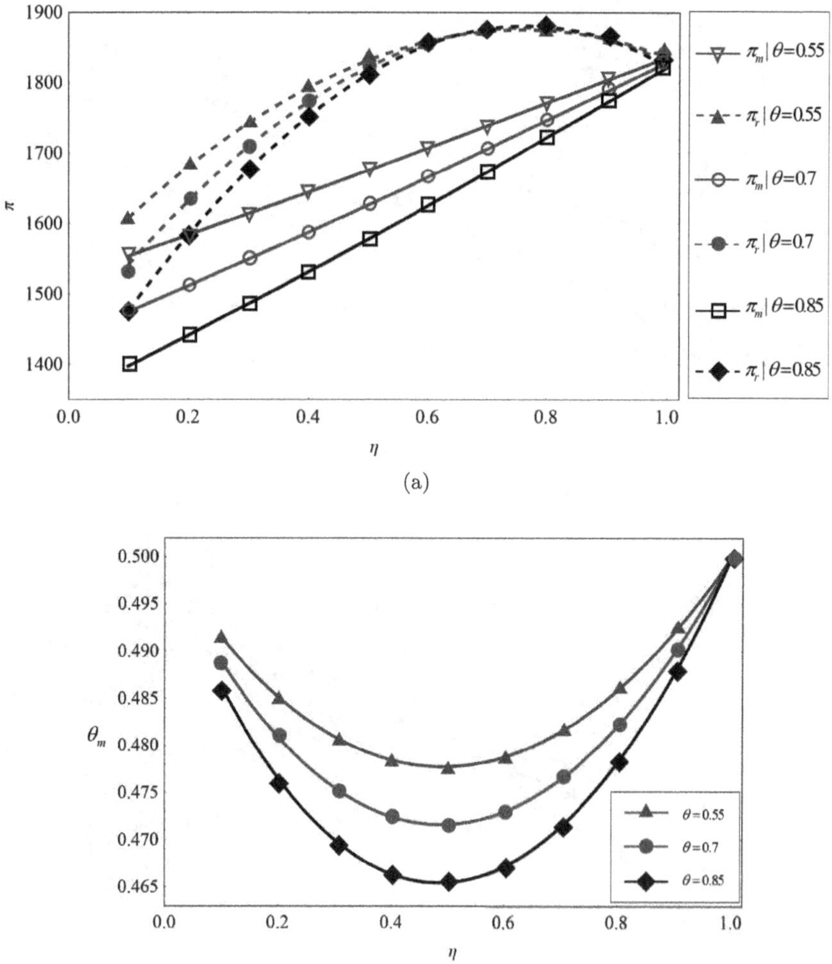


(a)



(b)

Fig. 3.2. (a) Both members' profits and (b) the manufacturer's profit shares with respect to $\eta$ under the different channel power.

Comparing Fig. 3.3(a) with Fig. 3.1(a), the same conclusion as that in Proposition 3.2 could be observed, i.e., the retail price is increasing as the retailer becomes less risk-averse. Nevertheless, under the different demand fluctuations, the growth rates are considerably different. The more violently the demand fluctuates, the higher the growth rate is. This result reveals that the risk-averse indicator has a significant impact on the retail price, especially when

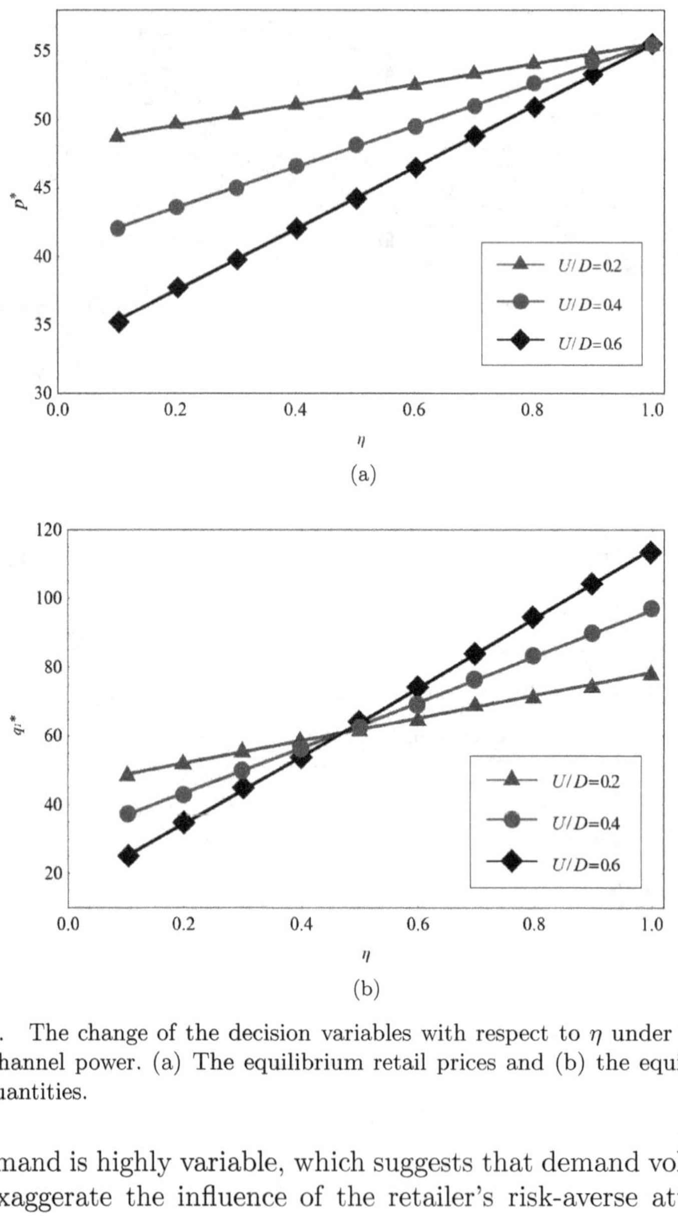


Fig. 3.3. The change of the decision variables with respect to $\eta$ under the different channel power. (a) The equilibrium retail prices and (b) the equilibrium order quantities.

the demand is highly variable, which suggests that demand volatility may exaggerate the influence of the retailer's risk-averse attitude. Thus, when the retailer is not aware of risk, the demand fluctuation is independent of the retail price.

From Fig. 3.3(b), it can be seen that the order quantities of the retailer is linearly increasing as the retailer's risk-averse indicator

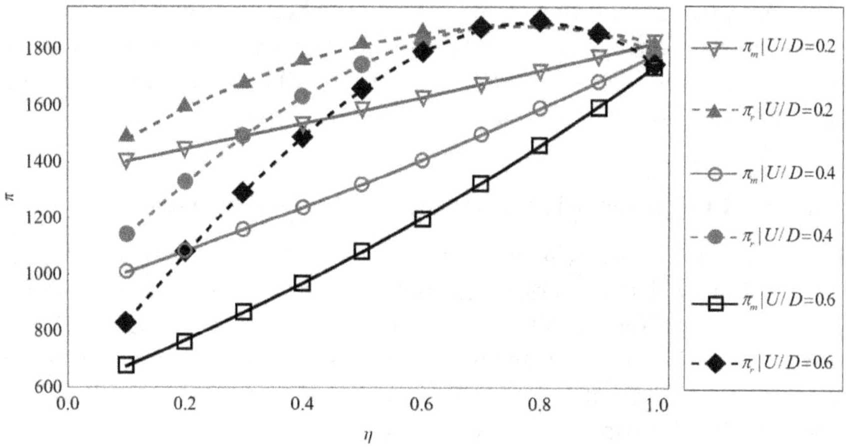


Fig. 3.4. The retailer's profits and the manufacturer's profits with respect to $\eta$ under different demand fluctuations.

increases. However, different growth gradients appear under the three different demand fluctuations. The more significant the demand fluctuation is, the more steeply the order quantity of the retailer increases. As discussed above, this consequence is mainly caused by the exaggerated impact of the demand volatility. Different from the pricing decisions (Fig. 3.3(a)), the order quantity decisions are more sensitive to demand fluctuation, thus the order quantities are totally different even though the retailer is risk-neutral. In this case, the crossing point appears in advance. This phenomenon leads to a situation where the more risk-averse retailer may reduce the order quantity, while the less risk-averse retailer may order more products, because she intends to avoid losses from being out of stock when facing a more fluctuate market. As a result, the retailer's ordering behaviors at different risk-averse levels are quite unlike under different demand volatilities.

Figure 3.4 illustrates the relationship between both members' profits and the risk-averse indicator under different demand volatilities. It indicates that high demand volatility is disadvantageous for both parties, in particular when the retailer has high risk-averse behavior. Moreover, although both parties could benefit from relatively stable demand, it happens that the manufacturer can grab more benefit from lower demand fluctuation. This observation reflects that the retailer has better adaptability when facing a highly fluctuate market environment. The reason can be fairly complicated, but the retailer may be more risk conscious than the manufacturer because she directly interacts with the market.

### 3.4.3. The cases with varying price sensitivities

Figure 3.5 manifests the impacts of the risk-averse indicator $\eta$ on the pricing decisions under different price sensitivities. The related parameters are set as follows: $D = 150$, $c = 4$, $\theta = 0.7$, $U = 60$. To test the relative price sensitivities, three sets of data are assumed to characterize three different cases, namely $\gamma_1 > \gamma_2$, $\gamma_1 = \gamma_2$, $\gamma_1 < \gamma_2$. Specifically, the three sets of data are assumed to be $\gamma_1 = 0.8$, $\gamma_2 = 0.6$, and $\gamma_1 = 0.7$, $\gamma_2 = 0.7$, and $\gamma_1 = 0.6$, $\gamma_2 = 0.8$.

Some interesting observations could be gained from Fig. 3.5(a). The retail prices are upwardly linear curves with respect to $\eta$, and the retailer would like to set the same retail price regardless of how relatively sensitive to price the two channels' demands are. This phenomenon appears to be non-intuitive at first glance. Nevertheless, some insights could be revealed from the theoretical view. Based on the objective function formulated in this chapter, it is obvious that the relationship between the manufacturer and the retailer is not just competitive but also cooperative to a certain extent. Considering the behavior of the manufacturer, if the demand from his online channel is more price-sensitive, then profit from his online channel will decline unavoidably, in which case the manufacturer would prefer to increase the wholesale price. The retailer does not decide to set a higher price to make up for the loss of the manufacturer and vice versa. This mutually beneficial relationship between them makes it possible to achieve an equitable allocation of the supply chain profit.

From Fig. 3.5(b), it could be noticed that the curves representing the relationships between the order quantities and the risk-averse indicator have the similar trend to those displayed in Fig. 3.5(a). Nevertheless, the influences of the relative price sensitivities of the demands in the two channels on the ordering decisions indicate some unlike highlights. The order quantity of the retailer declines as her relative price sensitivity increases, namely the retailer adopts a conservative strategy to avoid the disadvantage of price sensitivity. Actually, it is wise for the retailer to decrease the order quantity because

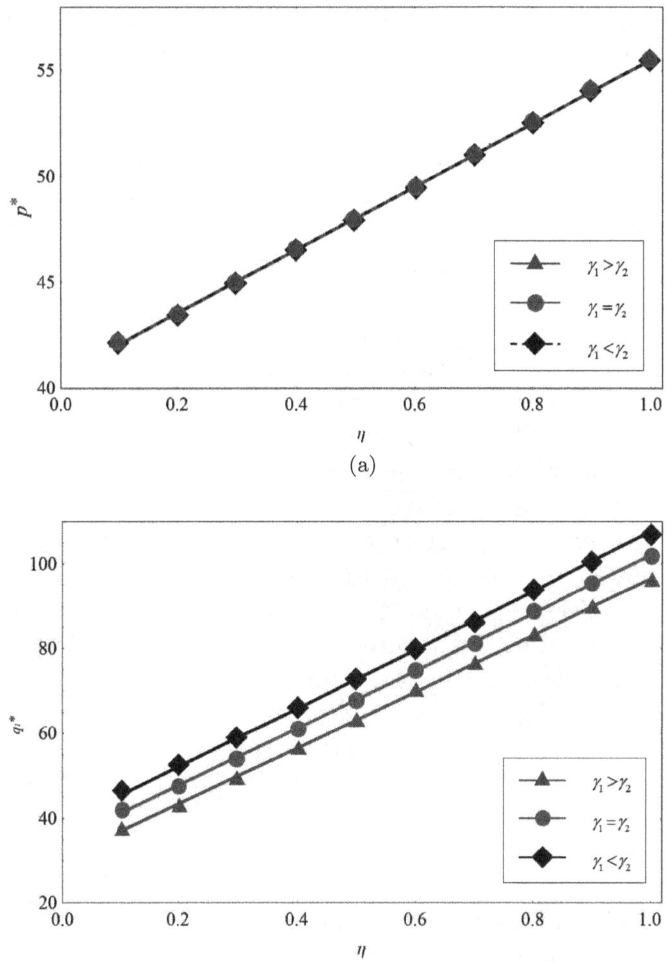


(a)

(b)

Fig. 3.5. The decision variables with varying $\eta$ and different price sensitivities. (a) The equilibrium retail prices and (b) the equilibrium order quantities.

the retail price and her price sensitivity are both considerably high, which is not beneficial.

## 3.5. Conclusion

In this chapter, we investigate a dual-channel supply chain with one type of perishable product, where the retailer has risk-averse behavior while the manufacturer is a risk-neutral agent. The manufacturer sells products through both independent traditional retail channel and his online channel. To simplify the analysis, the retail price and the online channel price are set to be the same. A Nash bargaining framework is applied to imitate the bargaining process between two agents on the decisions of the wholesale price, the retail price and the order quantity. The CVaR method is used to measure the risk-averse attitude. When the demand uncertainty follows a uniform distribution, it is proved that there exists a Nash bargaining equilibrium for the wholesale price, the retail price and the order quantity.

It is interesting to discover that the manufacturer's profit share in the entire supply chain is related to the retailer's risk-averse indicator, and his profit from the online channel may decrease, increase or decrease after increase with respect to the retailer's risk-averse indicator. Numerical experiments manifest the analytical results and provide further managerial insights. It is discovered that the wholesale price, the retail price and the order quantity are decreasing as the retailer's risk-averse indicator increases. Moreover, the impacts of the retailer's risk-averse indicator on the two members' decision making and profit allocations have unlike characteristics under different channel powers, demand volatilities and price sensitivities.

Further research could be done in several aspects. Firstly, this chapter adopts a consistent pricing strategy in two channels. What will the results be if the prices of the two channels are not the same? Secondly, if the manufacturer takes risk-averse behavior or both the manufacturer and the retailer have risk-averse attitudes, what effects will their behaviors have on decision-making? Thirdly, how to achieve supply chain coordination with risk-averse supply chain members is also a worthy further research field.

## References

Artzner, P., Delbaen, F., Eber, J. M., & Heath, D. (1997). Thinking coherently. *Risk*, 10(11), pp. 68–71.

Carr, S., & Duenyas, I. (2000). Optimal admission control and sequencing in a make-to-stock/make-to-order production system. *Operations Research*, 48(5), pp. 709–720.

Cattani, K., G. Wendell, Hans, S. H., & Jayashankar, S. (2006). Boiling frogs: Pricing strategies for a manufacturer adding a direct channel that competes with the traditional channel. *Production and Operations Management*, 15(1), pp. 1–38.

Chung, C. H., & Yu, T. L. (2010). Manufacturer's return policy in a two-stage supply chain with two risk-averse retailers and random demand. *European Journal of Operational Research*, 207(1), pp. 514–523.

Hanssens, D. M., Parsons, L. J., & Schultz, R. L. (2001). *Market Response Models: Econometric and Time Series Analysis,* 2nd Ed., Boston, MA: Kluwer Academic Publishers.

Kurata, H., Yao, D. Q., & Liu, J. J. (2007). Pricing policies under direct vs. indirect channel competition and national vs. store brand competition. *European Journal of Operational Research*, 180(1), pp. 262–281.

Li, B., Chen, P., Li Q. H., & Wang, W. G. (2014). Dual-channel supply chain pricing decision with a risk-averse retailer. *International Journal Production Research*, 52(23), pp. 7132–7147.

Ma, L. J., Liu, F. M., Li, S. J., & Yan, H. M. (2012). Channel bargaining with risk-averse retailer. *International Journal of Production Economics*, 139(1), pp. 155–167.

Mukhopadhyay, S. K., Yao, D. Q., & Yue, X. H. (2008). Information sharing of value-adding retailer in a mixed channel hi-tech supply chain. *Journal of Business Research*, 61(9), pp. 950–958.

Rockafellar, R. T., & Uryasev, S. (2000). Optimization of conditional value-at-risk. *Journal of Risk*, 2, pp. 21–41.

Wang, J. (2013). *Optimizing, Innovating, and Capitalizing on Information Systems for Operations.* Chapter 12 Equal Pricing Strategies in a Dual Channel Supply Chain. USA: Montclair State University, pp. 230–249.

Wen, U. P., Chen, Y. C., & Cheung, K. H. (2013). *Equal Pricing Strategies in a Dual Channel Supply Chain In Optimizing, Innovating, and Capitalizing on Information Systems for Operations*, Edited by J. Wang, USA: IGI Global, pp. 230–249.

Xu, G. Y., Dan B., Zhang, X. M., & Liu, C. (2013). Coordinating a dual-channel supply chain with risk-averse under a two-way revenue sharing contract. *International Journal of Production Economics*, 147, pp. 171–179.

Yao, D. Q., & Liu, J. J. (2005). Competitive pricing of mixed retail and e-tail distribution channels. *Omega*, 33(3), pp. 235–247.

© 2022 World Scientific Publishing Europe Ltd.
https://doi.org/10.1142/9781800610408_0004

# Chapter 4

# Pricing Strategy and Channel Coordination in a Dual-Channel Supply Chain with a Risk-Averse Retailer

**Bo Li*** **and Pengwen Hou**†

*College of Management and Economics, Tianjin University, China*

**libo0410@tju.edu.cn*

*†hpw0536@163.com*

## 4.1. Introduction

When a manufacturer adds an online channel to the existing traditional retail channel, it is no doubt that channel conflict will occur as the newly added channel encroaches the retailer's market share (Chiang *et al.*, 2003; Ha *et al.*, 2016). An interesting question is whether the online channel is always detrimental to supply chain performance.

Literature has demonstrated there is a variety of benefits by introducing the online channel when the agents in dual-channel supply chain are risk neutral. For example, the supplier can obtain marketing information, sales support and leave the actual sales to the retailer by establishing online channels (Cohen, 2000). Besides, through the online channel, the degree of the double marginalization problem in the supply chain can be mitigated because the supplier can influence the retailer's pricing decision even if he has no actual sales (Chiang *et al.*, 2003). Moreover, the introduction of online channels may lead to the reduction of wholesale prices, which enables the manufacturer and the retailer to achieve higher profits (Tsay *et al.*, 2004; Cattani *et al.*, 2006). Therefore, though the firms using the dual-channel strategy give rise to channel conflict, in some situations, both agents can actually benefit from the dual-channel strategy.

However, much less research has been done on the benefits of dual-channel strategy in situations where the agents are risk-averse. Nowadays, the business environment is becoming more complex with a high degree of uncertainty. As a result, the agents in the supply chain may deviate from their rational optimal decisions and pay more attention to risk aversion or loss minimization in their actual decision-making processes (Soleimani *et al.*, 2014). In addition, the introduction of an online channel will further aggravate the uncertainty and complexity of the market competition, thus prompting the retailer's risk-averse behavior. Therefore, it is necessary to analyze the dual-channel supply chain in which the retailer has risk-averse behavior. Further, with the increasing popularity of the dual-channel supply chain, marketing competition is becoming progressively fierce, and vertical competition and horizontal games coexist. How to coordinate the decisions of the channel members in the dual-channel supply chain is also an interesting question worth pondering, which is essentially related to mitigate the channel conflict (Li *et al.*, 2016).

Specifically, this chapter considers a dual-channel supply chain consisting of a risk-neutral manufacturer and risk-averse retailer producing one perishable product with stochastic price-dependent demand. Both members need construct an initial stock at the beginning of the sales season, such as the seasonal products. Thus, the manufacturer needs to predict the demand from the retailer's order, or from the historic data, and make a decision about his stock for the online channel before the sales period. A consistent pricing strategy (i.e., the same selling price in both channels) is adopted which can mitigate the channel conflict. The retailer's risk-averse behavior will be measured using the VaR and CVaR methods. We will establish a Stackelberg game where the manufacturer is a leader in making decisions on initial inventory quantity and product selling price, and the retailer is a follower in making decisions on the order quantity. In addition, a new improved risk-sharing contract will be designed to coordinate the dual-channel supply chain and enable a win–win outcome for both the manufacturer and the retailer.

The remainder of this chapter is organized as follows. In Sec. 4.2, we describe the problem and formulate the model. In Sec. 4.3, the equilibrium solutions under the VaR method and the CVaR method are derived, respectively. The comparative analysis of the results is presented. Section 4.4 proposes a new definition of coordination. An improved risk-sharing contract is developed to coordinate the dual-channel supply chain. And finally, we summarize the major findings in Sec. 4.5.

## 4.2. Model

In this section, a dual-channel supply chain facing uncertain market demand is considered in which there are a risk-neutral manufacturer and a risk-averse retailer. This is a common situation in practice that the manufacturer is risk neutral because he can diversify his risk by serving several independent retailers or channels (Gan *et al.*, 2004). Besides, the manufacturer only sells a single perishable product, and he distributes his product via the retailer's traditional store and his own online channel. At the beginning of the sales season, the manufacturer and the retailer will respectively construct their initial stocks after predicting the market demand of the online channel and the traditional retail channel. Besides, considering the properties of perishable products, we assume that at the end of sales season, the surplus value of the products is zero. To simplify the calculation, we also ignore any production shortfall.

The notations used in this chapter are summarized as follows:

| Variables | Description |
|---|---|
| $r$ or $d$ | the retail channel and the direct online channel, respectively |
| $D$ | the primary market demand (i.e., the potential demand if the goods are free of charge) |
| $D_i$ | the demand in the online channel or in the retail channel, respectively, $i = r$ or $d$ |
| $c$ | the manufacturer's production cost per unit |
| $\theta$ | the degree of customer acceptance in the traditional retail channel, correspondingly and then $(1-\theta)$ is the degree of customer acceptance in the direct online channel, where $0 \leq \theta \leq 1$ |

*(Continued)*

(*Continued*)

| Variables | Description |
|---|---|
| $a_i$ | the self-channel price sensitivity on the two channels, $i = r$ or $d$ |
| $b_i$ | the cross-channel price sensitivity, where $a_i > b_i$, $i = r$ or $d$ |
| $q_1$ | the retailer's order quantity to the manufacturer at the beginning of sales period |
| $q_2$ | the initial inventory of the direct online channel to respond to the customer's demand |
| $w$ | the manufacturer's wholesale price per unit. Note that the wholesale price may be decided as a long-term contract between members of a supply chain and here it is assumed to be an exogenous parameter |
| $p_i$ | the price in the retail channel or the direct online channel, $i = r$ or $d$ |

The demand functions in the traditional retail channel and the direct online channel are assumed as follows (Huang *et al.*, 2009):

$$D_r = \theta D - a_r p_r + b_r p_d, \tag{4.1}$$

$$D_d = (1 - \theta)D - a_d p_d + b_d p_r. \tag{4.2}$$

Moreover, under the stochastic market demand, the manufacturer adopts the make-to-stock policy to avoid the risk of demand uncertainty. Therefore, we assume that the uncertain demand $\hat{D}$ is a random variable, i.e., $\hat{D} = D + \varepsilon$, where $\varepsilon$ is a random number that reflects the degree of the demand uncertainty and follows a uniform distribution on $[-U, U]$, $0 \leq U \leq D$. $\phi(\cdot)$ and $\Phi(\cdot)$ are defined as the probability density function and cumulative distribution function for the random variable $\varepsilon$, respectively.

Further, we assume that the consistent pricing strategy is adopted in the two channels. This strategy can mitigate the channel conflict (Kevin *et al.*, 2002; (Cattani *et al.*, 2006)) and also represent practices, e.g., the prices of some high-end products are often consistent in the official online and the retail store, such as cellphones, cosmetics, famous brand clothes (Li *et al.*, 2016), especially at the beginning selling period of the new products. For that reason, we assume the prices for the two channels are the same, that is $p_r = p_d = p$. Under the consistent pricing strategy, the demand functions can be simplified as follows:

$$D_r = \theta\hat{D} - \gamma_1 p, \tag{4.3}$$

$$D_d = (1 - \theta)\hat{D} - \gamma_2 p, \tag{4.4}$$

where the price sensitivities in the retail and the online channels are denoted as $\gamma_1 = a_r - b_r$, $\gamma_2 = a_d - b_d$, respectively. Obviously, when the prices in the two channels are consistent, there is no effect of the cross-price on demand. Furthermore, we normalize the production cost $c = 0$ to simplify the calculation and assume $p \geq w$ to avoid a trivial case without losing generality.

In this chapter, three cases are designed to show how the retailer's risk-averse behavior affects the channel members' strategies: (i) the risk-neutral retailer; (ii) the risk-averse retailer under VaR criterion; (iii) the risk-averse retailer under CVaR criterion. The first case is used as a basic reference case to make comparison.

Define $\pi_r^d$, $\pi_s^d$ as the profit functions of the retailer and the manufacturer under the decentralized model with the random demands $D_r$, $D_d$ and the order quantities $q_1$, $q_2$. The timeline of a Stackelberg game in a dual-channel supply chain is as follows.

First, the manufacturer, a channel leader, decides his initial stock $q_2$ and the price $p$. Then, the retailer, a channel follower, decides his optimal order quantity $q_1$ to maximize her own profits after observing the manufacturer's decisions.

Define $(\cdot)^+ = \max\{\cdot, 0\}$, then the profit functions can be formulated as follows:

$$\pi_s^d = wq_1 + p[q_2 - (q_2 - D_d)^+], \tag{4.5}$$

$$\pi_r^d = p[q_1 - (q_1 - D_r)^+] - wq_1. \tag{4.6}$$

According to function (4.6), we can calculate the risk-neutral retailer's optimal order quantity easily:

$$\hat{q}_1 = (D - U)\theta - p\gamma_1 + \frac{2U\theta(p - w)}{p}. \tag{4.7}$$

## 4.3. Equilibrium and Analysis

In this section, the VaR and CVaR measures will be introduced to gauge the effects of the retailer's risk-averse behavior on the channel members' decisions, respectively. The equilibrium solutions will be first derived.

### 4.3.1. Under the VaR criterion

Under the VaR criterion, the retailer's decision problem is

$$\max_{q_1} E(\pi_r^d), \tag{4.8}$$

$$\text{subject to} \quad P\{\pi_r^d \leq v \leq \eta\}, \tag{4.9}$$

where the parameter $\eta \in (0, 1]$ is a risk-averse indicator that measures the risk-averse level for attaining a certain level of profit $v$ and also denoted as a confidence indicator of the decision maker.

From (4.8), we show that the retailer maximizes his expected profit $E(\pi_r^d)$ by choosing an order quantity $q_1$. Besides, the actual profit of the retailer should not fall below his target profit level of $v$ with a probability exceeding a specified $\eta$ (Artzner *et al.*, 1997). Referring to Gan *et al.* (2005), the retailer's optimal response function under VaR criterion can be obtained as follows:

$$q_{v1}^* = \begin{cases} \hat{q}_1 & \text{if } F\left(\dfrac{\gamma_1 p^2 + w\hat{q}_1 + v}{\theta p} - D\right) \leq \eta, \\ \dfrac{(D - U + 2U\eta)\theta p - \gamma_1 p^2 - v}{w} & \text{if } F\left(\dfrac{v}{p - w}\right) < \eta < F\left(\dfrac{\gamma_1 p^2 + w\hat{q}_1 + v}{\theta p} - D\right). \end{cases} \tag{4.10}$$

From Eq. (4.10), we find that when $F\left(\frac{\gamma_1 p^2 + w\hat{q}_1 + v}{\theta p} - D\right) \leq \eta$, $q_{v1}^*$ equals the optimal order quantity $\hat{q}_1$ of the risk-neutral retailer. It means that the retailer's risk-averse behavior has no effect on her ordering decision. Thus, we pay more attention to the case when $F(v/(p_v^* - w)) < \eta < F((\gamma_1 p_v^* + w\hat{q}_1 + v)/\theta p_v^* - D)$ to analyze the impact of risk aversion level on supply chain decision.

Assume that the demand uncertainty $\varepsilon$ follows a uniform distribution with support over $[-U, U]$, $0 \leq U \leq D$. Under the VaR criterion, given $F(v/(p_v^* - w)) < \eta < F((\gamma_1 p_v^* + w\hat{q}_1 + v)/\theta p_v^* - D)$, there exists a unique equilibrium solution $(q_{v1}^*, q_{v2}^*, p_v^*)$ as follows:

(1) The optimal retail price (i.e., the optimal online price) is

$$p_v^* = [D + U\theta(2\eta - 1)]/[2(\gamma_1 + \gamma_2)].$$

(2) The retailer's optimal order quantity and the manufacturer's optimal inventory for his online channel are

$$q_{v1}^* = [(D - U + 2U\eta)\theta p_v^* - \gamma_1 p_v^{*2} - v]/w,$$
$$q_{v2}^* = (D + U)(1 - \theta) - \gamma_2 p_v^*.$$

### 4.3.2. Under the CVaR criterion

Under the CVaR criterion, the $\eta$-quantile of $\pi_r^d$ is defined as $v^\eta(\pi_r^d)$ based on (Rockafellar and Uryasev, 2000), the retailer's $\eta$-CVaR under an order quantity $q_1$ is given by

$$\begin{aligned}
\mathrm{CVaR}^\eta(\pi_r^d) &= E[\pi_r^d \mid \pi_r^d \le v^\eta(\pi_r^d)] \\
&= \max_{v\in R}\left\{v + \frac{1}{\eta}E[\min(\pi_r^d - v, 0)]\right\} \\
&= \max_{v\in R}\left\{v + \frac{1}{\eta}E[\min((p - w)q_1 \right. \\
&\qquad \left. -p[q_1 - \theta\hat{D} + \gamma_1 p]^+ - v, 0)]\right\}.
\end{aligned}$$

Simplify the above equation, we can obtain the following:

$$\mathrm{CVaR}^\eta(\pi_r^d) = \begin{cases}
(p - w)q_1 - \dfrac{p}{\eta}\theta\displaystyle\int_{-U}^{\frac{q_1+\gamma_1 p}{\theta}-D}\Phi(\varepsilon)d\varepsilon & \text{if } q_1 \le \theta D - \gamma_1 p + \theta\Phi^{-1}(\eta), \\
-wq_1 + p\theta\Phi^{-1}(\eta) + \theta pD - \gamma_1 p^2 & \\
\quad -\dfrac{p}{\eta}\theta\displaystyle\int_{-U}^{\Phi^{-1}(\eta)}\Phi(\varepsilon)d\varepsilon & \text{if } q_1 > \theta D - \gamma_1 p + \theta\Phi^{-1}(\eta).
\end{cases}$$

(1) When $q_1 > \theta D - \gamma_1 p + \theta\Phi^{-1}(\eta)$, the optimal value is achieved at $q_1^*=0$ through maximizing $\mathrm{CVaR}^\eta(\pi_r^d)$. Obviously, this is also the boundary of the first case, thus we omit this situation.

(2) When $q_1 \leq \theta D - \gamma_1 p + \theta\Phi^{-1}(\eta)$, we can rewrite the profit functions of the two agents as follows:

$$\max_{q_2,p} \pi_s^d = wq_1 + p[q_2 - (q_2 - D_d)]^+, \tag{4.11}$$

$$\max_{q_1} \text{CVaR}^\eta(\pi_r^d) = (p-w)q_1 - \frac{p}{\eta}\theta \int_{-U}^{\frac{q_1+\gamma_1 p}{\theta} - U} \Phi(\varepsilon)d\varepsilon. \tag{4.12}$$

Note that the demand uncertainty $\varepsilon$ is assumed to follow a uniform distribution with support over $[-U, U]$. There exists a unique equilibrium solution $(q_{c1}^*, q_{c2}^*, p_c^*)$ as follows:

(1) The optimal retail price (and the optimal online price) satisfies the following equation:

$$2\gamma_2 p_c^{*3} - [D(1-\theta) - w\gamma_1]p_c^{*2} - 2U\eta\theta w^2 = 0.$$

(2) The retailer's optimal order quantity and the manufacturer's optimal inventory for his online channel are

$$q_{c1}^* = (D-U)\theta - p_c^*\gamma_1 + 2U\eta\theta(p_c^* - w)/p_c^*,$$
$$q_{c2}^* = (D+U)(1-\theta) - \gamma_2 p_c^*.$$

Through comparing the equilibrium solutions under VaR and CVaR measures, it is observed that the CVaR criterion has some advantages in valuing the retailer's risk-averse behavior. First, under the VaR measure, two parameters, $\eta$ and $v$, are required in order to determine the retailer's decision and these parameters represent the retailer's subjective intention. Only when the parameter $\eta$ satisfies some condition, the unique equilibrium solution exists. Even if $v$ has no influence on the sale price and the inventory of the manufacturer in his online channel, it also has a negative impact on the retailer's ordering quantity. Therefore, we can draw the conclusion that the VaR criterion is not a consistent measure. This confirms the results put forward by Soleimani *et al.* (2014), who pointed out that the VaR criterion could intuitively give the loss in monetary terms but could not measure the degree of loss and it wasn't a coherent risk measure method. On the contrary, the CVaR criterion is a consistent measure, because the equilibrium solution depends on just one risk factor $\eta$.

Second, the VaR criterion cannot completely represent the contextual uncertainty, as it just reflects a percentile of a probability distribution while the CVaR can measure the average profit falling below the $\eta$-quantile level and has been proved to be sub-additive (Artzner *et al.*, 1997). Additionally, CVaR is stable in the sense of continuity under the given confidence level proved by Rockafellar *et al.* (2002).

Therefore, in the next section, we only discuss the properties of the equilibrium results obtained by CVaR method because of its advantages.

### 4.3.3. Analysis of the equilibrium solution under CVaR

In this subsection, we will explore the analysis on the equilibrium solution under CVaR measure. As the leader of the market, the manufacturer will make his price decision and his own stock when the retailer has risk-averse behavior. The impact of the risk-averse level on the optimal decisions will first be examined in the following proposition.

**Proposition 4.1.** *Given the parameters $D$, $U$, $\gamma_1, \gamma_2$, the optimal decisions under CVaR have the following properties:*

(1) *If $\theta$ is a constant, then $p^*_{c\min} < p^*_c < p^*_{c\max}$ where $p^*_{c\min} = p^*_{c|\eta=0}, p^*_{c\max} = p^*_{c|\eta=1}$, and $p^*_c$ is increasing in the retailer's risk-averse level $\eta$ in $(0, 1]$.*

(2) *Let $f(p) = \partial q^*_{c1}/\partial p^*_c$, we assume the threshold $p_0$ is the solution of $f(p)$, the retailer's order quantity $q^*_{c1}$ satisfies the following conditions:*

   (i) *If $p_0 < p^*_{c\min}$, then $\partial q^*_{c1}/\partial \eta > 0$.*

   (ii) *If $p^*_{c\min} < p_0 < p^*_{c\max}$, then*

$$\frac{\partial q^*_{c1}}{\partial \eta} \begin{cases} > 0 & \text{if } \eta \in (0, \tilde{\eta}), \\ < 0 & \text{if } \eta \in [\tilde{\eta}, 1], \end{cases}$$

   *where $\tilde{\eta}$ satisfies the equation $p_0 = p^*_c$.*

   (iii) *If $p_0 > p^*_{c\max}$, then $\partial q^*_{c1}/\partial \eta < 0$.*

(3) $\partial q^*_{c2}/\partial \eta < 0$.

Proposition 4.1 indicates that the optimal decisions of the manufacturer depend on the retailer's risk-averse level. Proposition 4.1(1) clearly shows that although the manufacturer decides the sales price, his decision is still influenced by the retailer's risk-averse level. The retailer becomes more risk-neutral when the indicator $\eta$ tends to 1, which means that the retailer is optimistic about the marketing environment, and this attitude will naturally send signals to the manufacturer from the retailer's ordering quantity. The retailer's price will be increased and both members obtain a benefit from the retailer's attitude.

Further, we explore the managerial insight by analyzing the retailer's ordering quantity. We find that there exists a threshold $p_0$ determined by parameters $D$, $U$, $\theta$, $w$, $\gamma_1$, $\gamma_2$, then the retailer's ordering quantity $p^*_{c1}$ will increase or decrease with $p^*_c$ according to the relationship between $p_0$ and $(p^*_{c\min}, p^*_{c\max})$. Thus, according to Proposition 4.1(2), $p^*_{c1}$ may increase or decrease with respect to the retailer's risk-averse level $\eta$.

However, as the parameter $\eta$ increases, the manufacturer's initial stock is monotonically decreasing from Proposition 4.1(3), which means that the manufacturer always believes that the retailer can get closer to customers than he can, so that she can exactly grasp the market demand. Correspondingly, the retailer's optimistic attitude will send signals to the manufacturer from the retailer's ordering quantity. In this case, the manufacturer will increase the price and prefer the retailer to sell most of his products that shown from Proposition 4.1(1) and hold less initial stock for his own online channel as shown in Proposition 4.1(3).

Next, we will verify how the retailer's risk-averse level $\eta$ impacts the equilibrium solutions $p^*_c$, $q^*_{c1}$ and $q^*_{c2}$ using numerical experiments. Let $D = 205$, $\gamma_1 = 0.7$, $w = 24$. We consider three cases as follows: (i) $U = 20$, $\gamma_2 = 0.7$, $\theta = 0.7$; (ii) $U = 20$, $\gamma_2 = 1.0$, $\theta = 0.7$; (iii) $U = 5$, $\gamma_2 = 1.3$, $\theta = 0.6$. The results are shown in Figs. 4.1–4.3.

From Fig. 4.1, we can see that when the retailer's risk-averse level $\eta$ increases, $p^*_c$ is increasing under three cases and $p^*_{c\min} < p^*_c < p^*_{c\max}$, where $p^*_{c\min} = p^*_{c|\eta=0}$, $p^*_{c\max} = p^*_{c|\eta=1}$. This verifies Proposition 4.1(1). Further, by comparing Case 1 and Case 2, we find that the price decreases as the price sensitivity of the online channel increases, which means that the high price sensitivity of the customers to the online channel will force the manufacturer to reduce the price, so as to adapt to the customers' demands.

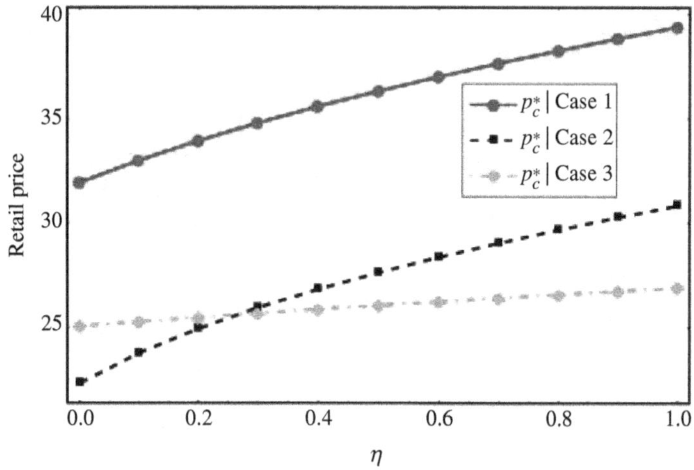


Fig. 4.1. The impacts of the retailer's risk-averse level $\eta$ on $p_c^*$.

From Fig. 4.2(a), we can see that as the retailer's risk-averse level $\eta$ increases from 0 to 1, her ordering quantity exists three different situations. The first case indicates that the ordering quantity of the retail channel $p_{c1}^*$ is increasing monotonically in $\eta$, here $p_0 = 37.2$, $p_{c\min}^* = 37.9$, $p_{c\max}^* = 44.3$, and $p_0 < p_{c\min}^*$, this verifies the first situation in Proposition 4.1(2). The retailer's ordering quantity is decreasing monotonically in $\eta$ in the third case, which is in agreement with Proposition 4.1(2), here $p_0 = 28.9$, $p_{c\min}^* = 25.5$, $p_{c\max}^* = 26.9$, where $p_0 > p_{c\min}^*$. The second case is the most complex, the optimal $p_{c1}^*$ appears to be a parabola convex. Here $p_0 = 29.6$, $p_{c\min}^* = 25.3$, $p_{c\max}^* = 33.0$ and $p_{c\min}^* < p_0 < p_{c\max}^*$. There exists a point $\tilde{\eta} = 0.46$ such that when $\eta \in (0, \tilde{\eta})$, $\partial p_{c1}^*/\partial\eta < 0$; when $\eta \in (\tilde{\eta}, 1)$, $\partial p_{c1}^*/\partial\eta > 0$. This case corresponds to Proposition 4.1(2).

From Proposition 4.1, we find that the retail price and the retailer's risk-averse behavior can significantly affect the retailer's ordering quantity. In fact, because the manufacturer decides the retail price, according to the equation $2\gamma_2 p_c^{*3} - [D(1-\theta) - w\gamma_1]p_c^{*2} - 2U\eta\theta w^2 = 0$, the retail price $p_c^*$ will be decreasing as the value of $\gamma_2$ or $U$ increases (see Fig. 4.1); as a result, it will have a positive impact on the market demand (see Fig. 4.3).

Through comparing Figs. 4.1–4.3, some interesting results can be found. The retailer's order quantity is close to the expected market

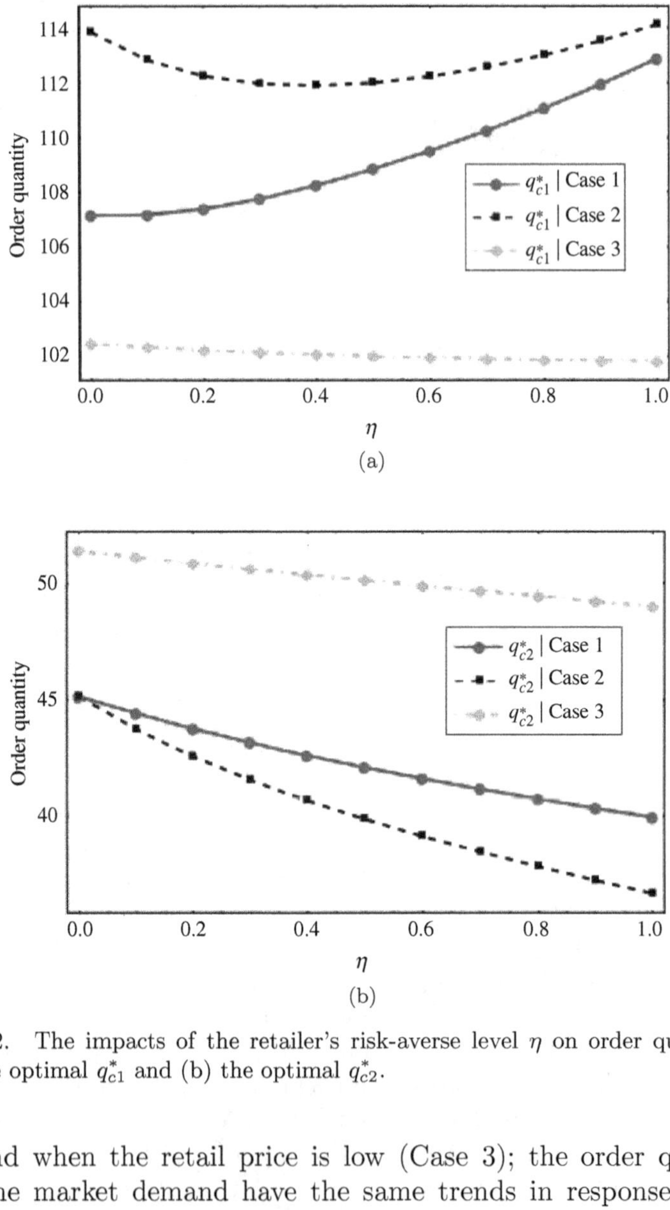


Fig. 4.2. The impacts of the retailer's risk-averse level $\eta$ on order quantities. (a) The optimal $q^*_{c1}$ and (b) the optimal $q^*_{c2}$.

demand when the retail price is low (Case 3); the order quantity and the market demand have the same trends in response to the change of the risk-averse indicator $\eta$. In contrast, there exists a big gap between the retailer's order quantity and the expected market demand when the retail price is sufficiently high (Case 1). The retailer will become more optimistic on the market demand as the risk-averse

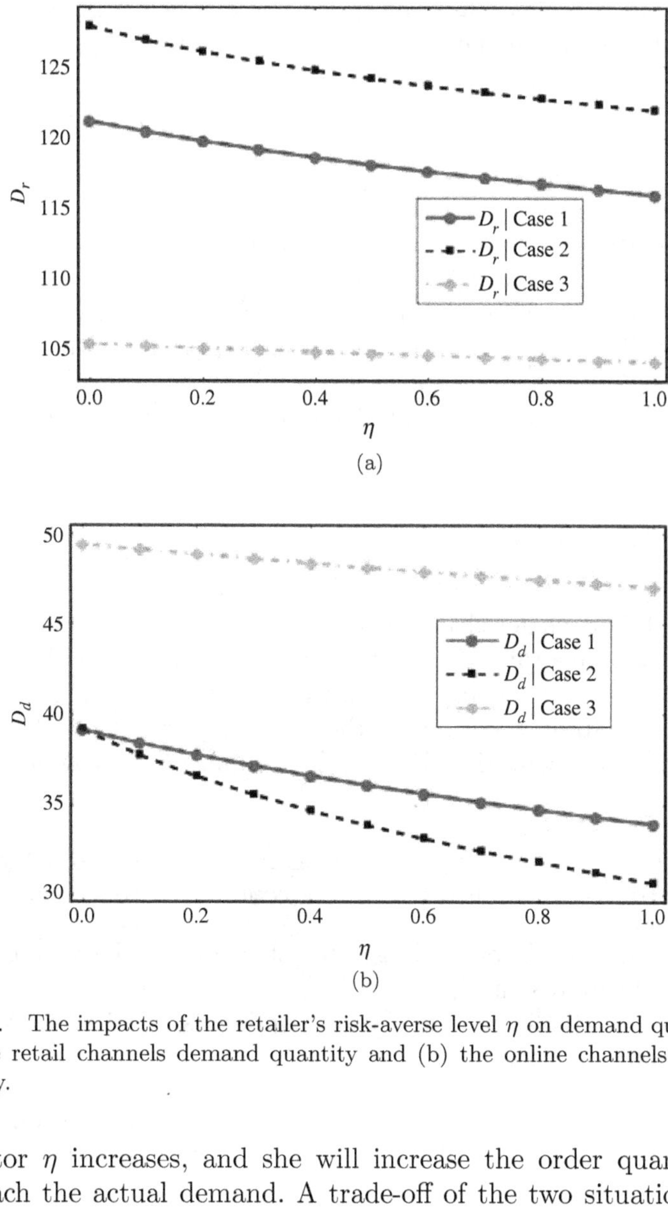


Fig. 4.3. The impacts of the retailer's risk-averse level $\eta$ on demand quantities. (a) The retail channels demand quantity and (b) the online channels demand quantity.

indicator $\eta$ increases, and she will increase the order quantity to approach the actual demand. A trade-off of the two situations discussed above is shown in Case 2.

In Fig. 4.2(b), it is clear that when the risk-averse level $\eta$ increases, the supplier's order quantity (i.e. initial inventory) will decrease in all three cases. Comparing Fig. 4.2(b) with Fig. 4.3(b), we can easily see that the supplier's initial online channel stock is larger than the expected market demand, and they have the same trends with respect to $\eta$.

## 4.4. Coordination Design

The consistent price strategy can mitigate the channel conflict to some degree, but it is often not enough to resolve the channel competition and channel conflict in dual-channel supply chains. This section will introduce the concept of coordination so that a Pareto optimal solution could be achieved for both the manufacturer and the retailer, which can essentially resolve the channel competition and conflict problems.

### 4.4.1. Benchmark

Firstly, we will adapt the definition of coordination. Gan *et al.* (2004, 2005) considered the agents' risk-averse behavior under VaR and defined a coordinating contract to obtain an acceptable Pareto-optimal solution for two agents in the supply chain.

In this chapter, according to their definition of supply chain coordination, a new definition of channel coordination is given as follows.

**Definition 4.1.** The supply chain can reach a coordinated state under a contract only if the following conditions are satisfied:

(1) Each member's profit is greater than or equal to that in the decentralized situation.
(2) The sum of the profits of two members is equal to that in the centralized situation.

In order to make a comparison between the profits under the decentralized and centralized situations, we first consider the dual-channel supply chain as a centralized system and set the entire supply chain's profit in the centralized situation as a benchmark, because the performance in the centralized situation is the best. In the centralized situation, the supplier essentially decides all the decision variables with the goal of maximizing the profit in the whole supply chain.

Thus, the total profit function in the centralized situation can be written as follows:

$$\pi^c = \pi_s^d + CVaR^\eta(\pi_r^d). \tag{4.13}$$

Note that the demand uncertainty $\varepsilon$ is assumed to follow a uniform distribution with support over $[-U, U]$. It can be proved that there exists a unique equilibrium solution $(q_1^{c*}, q_2^{c*}, p^{c*})$ as follows:

(1) The optimal retail price is

$$p^{c*} = [D - U(1-\eta)\theta]/2(\gamma_1 + \gamma_2).$$

(2) The retailer's optimal order quantity and the supplier's optimal inventory for his online channel are

$$q_1^{c*} = (D-U)\theta - p^{c*}\gamma_1 + 2U\eta\theta,$$
$$q_2^{c*} = D(1-\theta) + U(1-\theta) - p^{c*}\gamma_2.$$

Further, let $\pi^{c*}$ and $\pi^{d^*}$ denote the optimal profit of the entire supply chain in the centralized and decentralized situations, respectively. We compare their equilibrium solutions, and obtain the following results.

**Proposition 4.2.** *Given the parameters $D$, $U$, $\gamma_1, \gamma_2$, the following properties are satisfied.*

(1) $p_c^* \neq p^{c*}, q_{ci}^* \neq q_i^{c*}, i = 1, 2;$
(2) $\pi^{c*} > \pi^{d*}.$

From Proposition 4.2, it can be seen that the profit of the whole supply chain in the decentralized situation will be less than the maximum profit in the centralized situation, and the decisions in the decentralized situation deviate from that in the centralized situation. Therefore, we aim to design a contract to improve the supply chain performance in decentralized situation by achieving channel coordination in the dual-channel supply chain.

### 4.4.2. The risk-sharing contract

The wholesale price contract and the revenue sharing contract could not coordinate the supply chain in our model, although the combination of these two contracts has been proved to be able to coordinate the supply chain in the general situation (Chen *et al.*, 2012). However, due to the competition between online and offline channels and the retailer's risk-averse behavior, it is difficult to achieve coordination through the combination of the wholesale price contract and the revenue-sharing contract. Thus, Xu *et al.* (2014) proposed the coordination of the dual-channel supply chain through designing a two-way revenue contract. Next, we will design a new contract to coordinate the dual-channel supply chain considering the retailer's risk-averse behavior.

Through observing the retailer's profit function (4.12), we can easily find that the retailer's expected surplus stock

$$\frac{1}{\eta}\theta\int_{-U}^{\frac{q_1+\gamma_1 p}{\theta}-D}\Phi(\varepsilon)d\varepsilon$$

increases with $\eta$ decreasing, which means that her risk-averse behavior is mainly reflected in the expected surplus stock. By comparing with the risk-neutral retailer, the risk-averse retailer's expected surplus stock is amplified by her risk-averse behavior. Therefore, the source of the retailer's risk on the expected surplus stock need to be eliminated in order to coordinate the dual-channel supply chain.

According to the above discussion, a new contract which combines the wholesale price contract, the revenue-sharing contract and the risk-return contract is designed and described as $(w, \lambda, b)$, where $w$ is the wholesale price, $\lambda$ is the revenue share proportion and $b$ is a buyback factor considering the expected surplus stock. This contract is called an improved risk-sharing contract, because it is not a simple combination of those three traditional contracts. Thus, we can rewrite the profit functions of the supplier and the retailer as follows:

$$\begin{aligned}\pi_s{}^{sd} = wq_1 + &\left[pq_2 - p(1-\theta)\int_{-U}^{\frac{q_2+\gamma_2 p}{1-\theta}-D}\frac{\varepsilon+U}{2U}d\varepsilon\right]\\ &+(1-\lambda)\left[pq_1 - \frac{p\theta}{\eta}\int_{-U}^{\frac{q_1+\gamma_1 p}{\theta}-D}\frac{\varepsilon+U}{2U}d\varepsilon]\right.\\ &\left.\qquad -\frac{b\theta}{\eta}\int_{-U}^{\frac{q_1+\gamma_1 p}{\theta}-D}\frac{\varepsilon+U}{2U}d\varepsilon\right],\end{aligned} \tag{4.14}$$

$$\text{CVaR}^{\eta}(\pi_r^{sd}) = \lambda p \left[ q_1 - \frac{\theta}{\eta} \int_{-U}^{\frac{q_1+\gamma_1 p}{\theta} - D} \frac{\varepsilon + U}{2U} d\varepsilon \right]$$
$$+ \frac{b\theta}{\eta} \left[ \int_{-U}^{\frac{q_1+\gamma_1 p}{\theta} - D} \frac{\varepsilon + U}{2U} d\varepsilon \right] - wq_1. \quad (4.15)$$

When the agents of the supply chain adopt this contract, there exists the unique equilibrium solution $(q_1^{s*}, q_2^{s*}, p_s^*)$ as follows:

(1) The retail price $p_s^*$ satisfies the equation

$$A(1-\theta\lambda) - 2p_s^*[\gamma_2 + \gamma_1(1-\lambda)]$$
$$-w\gamma_1 - \frac{U\eta\theta(b-w)^2}{p_s^*\lambda - b}\left[\frac{2b}{(p_s^*\lambda - b)^2} + \frac{b+p_s^*}{p_s^*\lambda - b} - \frac{1}{p_s^*}\right] = 0,$$

where $A = (D - U + U\eta)\theta$.

(2) The retailer's optimal order quantity is

$$q_1^{s*} = (D-U)\theta - p_s^*\gamma_1 + \frac{2U\eta\theta(w - p_s^*\lambda)}{b - p_s^*\lambda}.$$

(3) The supplier's optimal inventory for his online channel is

$$q_2^{s*} = (D{+}U)(1-\theta) - p_s^*\gamma_2.$$

From Propositions 4.2 and 4.3, we can know that only when the conditions $p_c^* = p^{c*}$, $q_{ci}^* = q_i^{c*}$, $i = 1, 2$, are satisfied, the whole supply chain will be coordinated. Thus, firstly, we substitute $w = b, p^{s*} = p^{c*}$, into the following formula:

$$A(1-\theta\lambda) - 2p_s^*[\gamma_2 + \gamma_1(1-\lambda)] - w\gamma_1$$
$$-\frac{U\eta\theta(b-w)^2}{p_s^*\lambda - b}\left[\frac{2b}{(p_s^*\lambda - b)^2} + \frac{b+p_s^*}{p_s^*\lambda - b} - \frac{1}{p_s^*}\right] = 0.$$

Then, simplify this equation, we have

$$b = \lambda\{(D - D\theta)\gamma_1 - [D - U(1-\eta)]\theta\gamma_2\}/[\gamma_1(\gamma_1+\gamma_2)].$$

Thus, we gain Proposition 4.4 as follows.

**Proposition 4.3.** *Under an improved risk-sharing contract, when* $w = b, b = \lambda\{(D - D\theta)\gamma_1 - [D - U(1-\eta)]\theta\gamma_2\}/[\gamma_1(\gamma_1+\gamma_2)]$, *there are* $q_1^{s*} = q_1^{c*}, q_2^{s*} = q_2^{c*}, q_s^* = q^{c*}$.

The above results imply that through the contract $(w, \lambda, b)$, the total profit of the decentralized dual-channel supply chain is equal to that in the centralized situation. Note that when $\lambda \in (0,1)$, the value of $b$ is always positive, that is, $\lambda\{(D - D\theta)\gamma_1 - [D-U(1-\eta)]\theta\gamma_2\}/[\gamma_1(\gamma_1 + \gamma_2)] > 0$. By simplifying this equation, we can obtain that if $\theta < D\gamma_1/\{D\gamma_1 + [D - U(1-\eta)]\gamma_2\}$, then the values of $w$, $b$ is positive. This condition means that the retailer will be willing to accept this contract only if the degree of the retail channel's acceptance is small. In contrast, if $D\gamma_1/\{D\gamma_1 + [D - U(1-\eta)]\gamma_2\} \leq \theta < 1$ which means a large part of the market demand is occupied by the retailer, this contract may not be able to coordinate the dual-channel supply chain. However, in some special situations, for example, the supplier wants to open the market through the retailer at the beginning of the new product launch or the supplier is less powerful than the retailer, two agents may accept this contract and the dual-channel supply chain will achieve the channel coordination.

When $w = b$, the principle of the improved risk-sharing contracts appears to be no different from traditional revenue sharing contract. But in fact, these two contracts differ substantially from each other. In our model, the difficulty in coordinating the dual-channel supply chain is that the retailer's risk-averse behavior enlarges the expected surplus inventory as we discussed in Sec. 4.4.1. Under the traditional revenue-sharing contract, all the risk of the surplus stock was undertaken by the retailer, because she only shares a proportion of her sales revenue to the manufacturer, which means that the effect of the expected surplus stock cannot be eliminated by the traditional revenue sharing contract.

However, under the improved risk-sharing contract, the retailer can order $q_1$ at price $w$ from the manufacturer firstly, and the manufacturer will buy them back at price $w$ when there are surplus stocks. It means that all the risk will be undertaken by the manufacturer. Thus, the retailer will be encouraged by this contract and she will establish an optimal level of order quantity based on the real marketing demand. Furthermore, the manufacturer will receive a fraction of the retailer's revenue to guarantee the manufacturer's interest in this contract. In other words, under this improved risk-sharing contract, the make-to-order policy can be realized by the retailer in her retail channel.

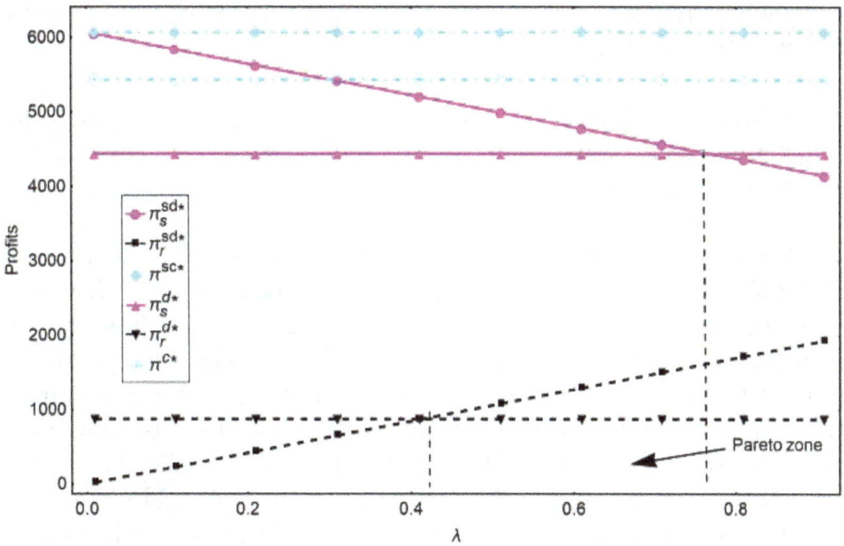


Fig. 4.4. Both agents' profits change with the share proportion $\lambda$.

**Proposition 4.4.** *There exists a menu of the improved risk-sharing contract $\{w^*, \lambda^*, b^*\}$ to make both agents in the supply chain gain a win–win outcome. That is, there exists a Pareto zone to satisfy the conditions as follows:*

$$\pi_s^{sd*}(w^*, \lambda^*, b^*) > \pi_s^{d*}$$
$$\text{CVaR}^{\eta}(\pi_r^{sd*}(w^*, \lambda^*, b^*)) > \pi_r^{d*},$$

*where $\pi_i^{sd*}$ and $\pi_i^{d*}$ represent the optimal profit of the member $i$ with and without the improved risk-sharing contract, respectively.*

We illustrate the results in Proposition 4.4 using numerical examples. Set the parameters as follows: $U = 20$, $\gamma_1 = 0.7$, $\gamma_2 = 1$, $D = 205$, $\theta = 0.4$, $\eta = 0.8$. The results are shown in Fig. 4.4. We can see from Fig. 4.4 that, under this new contract, there is a Pareto zone with the share proportion $\lambda$. In this Pareto zone, not only the profits of two channels can be reached to the coordination state, but also the two agents will be a win–win outcome. Further, the specific parameter values of $\{w^*, \lambda^*, b^*\}$ depends on the bargaining power between the two parties.

**Corollary 4.1.** *Under the improved risk-sharing contract, the total profit in the dual-channel supply chain will increase as the risk-averse indicator $\eta$ increases.*

Due to the profit function $\pi^{c*} = [D - U(1-\eta)\theta]^2/[4(\gamma_1 + \gamma_2)]$ under the centralized situation, Corollary 4.1 can be easily obtained.

Corollary 4.1 implies that when the risk-averse indicator $\eta$ increases, the profits of the agents increase. It means that the lower level of the retailer's risk aversion is beneficial to both agents under the improved risk-sharing contract. The implication is that after adopting the improved risk-sharing contract, the retailer is encouraged to be less risk-averse. Moreover, the online channel opened by the supplier will increase the profit of the total channel in the supply chain. At this time, when the parameters in the improved risk-sharing contract are fixed to allocate income properly, the retailer is unwise to boycott the supplier's online channel. Therefore, the channel competition and channel conflict can be successfully resolved.

## 4.5. Conclusion

In this chapter, we consider a distribution channel that consists of a risk-neutral supplier and a risk-averse retailer where the supplier acts as a leader of the Stackelberg game and both of them face uncertain demand. We first analyze the equilibrium solutions under VaR method and CVaR method, and then explore the contract design to coordinate the supply chain. Through the analysis, we conclude that when the retailer shows a high degree of risk aversion, the sales price will decrease and the supplier's initial stock may increase. In addition, the agents' profits and channel efficiency will always be damaged by the retailer's risk-averse behavior. Further, the supply chain could not be coordinated by only using the wholesale price contract or the traditional revenue share contract. Thus, we design an improved risk-sharing contract by combining the wholesale price contract, the revenue share contract and the risk-return contract to achieve supply chain coordination. We show that there exists a Pareto zone for the share proportion that encourages both agents to implement this risk-sharing contract.

Several aspects deserve further research. In this chapter, the demand uncertainty is assumed to follow a uniform distribution. Will the results be carried over to the demand uncertainty following general distributions? We only consider the case in which the retailer has risk-averse behavior, it will be interesting to study the case that both players have risk-averse behavior in a dual-channel supply chain.

## References


Artzner, P., Delbaen, F., Eber, J. M., & Heath, D. (1997). Thinking coherently. *Risk*, 10(11), pp. 68–71.

Cattani, K., Wendell, G., Hans, S. H., & Jayashankar, S. (2006). Boiling frogs: Pricing strategies for a manufacturer adding a direct channel that competes with the traditional channel. *Production and Operations Management*, 15(1), pp. 1–38.

Chen, J., Zhang, H., & Sun, Y. (2012). Implementing coordination contracts in a supplier Stackelberg dual-channel supply chain. *Omega*, 40(5), pp. 571–583.

Chiang, W. K., Chhajed, D., & Hess, J. D. (2003). Direct marketing, indirect profits: A strategic analysis of dual-channel supply-chain design. *Management Science*, 49(1), pp. 1–20.

Cohen, A. (2000). When channel conflict is good. *Sales and Marketing Management*, 152(4), p. 13.

Gan, X., Sethi, S. P., & Yan, H. (2004). Coordination of supply chains with risk-averse agents. *Production and Operations Management*, 13, pp. 135–149.

Gan, X., Sethi, S. P., & Yan, H. (2005). Channel coordination with a risk-neutral supplier and a downside risk-averse retailer. *Production and Operations Management*, 14(1), pp. 80–89.

Ha, A., Long, X., & Nasiry, J. (2016). Quality in supply chain encroachment. *Manufacturing & Service Operations Management*, 18(2), pp. 280–298.

Huang, W., & Swaminathan, J. M. (2009). Introduction of a second channel: implications for pricing and profits. *European Journal of Operational Research*, 194, pp. 258–279.

Li, B., Hou, P., Chen, P., & Li, Q. (2016). Pricing strategy and coordination in a dual channel supply chain with a risk-averse retailer. *International Journal of Production Economics*, 178, pp. 154–168.

Kevin, L. W. (2002). Managing channels of distribution in the age of electronic commerce. *Industrial Marketing Management*, 31, pp. 95–102.

Rockafellar, R. T., & Uryasev, S. (2000). Optimization of conditional value-at-risk. *Journal of Risk*, 2, pp. 21–41.

Rockafellar, R. T., & Uryasev, S. (2002). Conditional value-at-risk for general loss distributions. Journal of Banking & Finance, 26(7), pp. 1443–1471.

Soleimani, H., Seyyed-Esfahani, M., & Kannan, G. (2014). Incorporating risk measures in closed-loop supply chain network design. *International Journal of Production Research*, 52(6), pp. 1843–1867.

Tsay, A. A., & Agrawal, N. (2004). Channel conflict and coordination in the e-commerce age. *Production and Operations Management*, 13(1), pp. 93–110.

Xu, G., Dan, B., Zhang, X., & Liu C. (2014). Coordinating a dual-channel supply chain with risk-averse under a two-way revenue sharing contract. *International Journal of Production Economics*, 147, pp. 171–179.

© 2022 World Scientific Publishing Europe Ltd.
https://doi.org/10.1142/9781800610408_0005

# Chapter 5

# Pricing and Greening Strategies in Dual-Channel Supply Chain

**Bo Li*** **and Mengyan Zhu†**
*College of Management and Economics, Tianjin University, China*
**libo0410@tju.edu.cn*
*†18222236171@qq.com*

## 5.1. Introduction

Achieving environmental sustainability has gradually become a global consensus. An increasing number of enterprises have paid more attention to the sustainable investment such as low-carbon technology and green products, and the research on green supply chain management (GSCM) has also been developing quickly (El Saadany and Jaber, 2010; Li *et al.*, 2020). GSCM requires reconsideration of many SCM problems, e.g., green R&D, technology improvement, return management, reverse logistics design, inventory decisions, product innovation and coordination among supply chain members, etc. (Asif *et al.*, 2020; Hall and Vredenburg, 2012). It has been demonstrated that the environmental performance and economic performance of the enterprises can be improved through the adoption of GSCM, which can promote their green management (Green *et al.*, 2012; Li *et al.*, 2016).

Many factors need to be considered in the implementation of GSCM, such as the importance level of greening activities, financial and non-financial benefits, and costs/performance (Lin and Tseng, 2014; Tseng *et al.*, 2014). One of the most important green activities is the design and selection of the green levels of products. Navinchandra (1990) was among the first to put forward the idea of green product design. He pointed out that green product design should improve the compatibility of product and environment without damaging product function and quality. Pujari (2006) believed that the green level of innovative products not only had a positive impact on the environment, but also increased the competitive advantage of manufacturers. In addition, the enterprises in the supply chain nowadays feel enormous pressure from the government, non-governmental organizations and consumers, and have to increase the development and introduction of sustainable products (Seuring, 2013; Seuring and Müller, 2008). Therefore, the primary task of GSCM is innovation, which is particularly significant in green product development (Lin and Tseng, 2014).

In fact, many enterprises are concerned with green products and have put them into practice. For example, PepsiCo, an established beverage manufacturer, uses reusable plastic containers to reduce its environmental impact. From the perspective of manufacturing materials and packaging materials, Adidas, a famous sports brand manufacturer all over the world, is devoted to reducing the impact of its products on the environment (www.adidas-group.com). Patagonia, a clothing company in California, has taken green fashion as an important strategy for several years (Ghosh and Shah, 2012). In addition, some enterprises in the retail industry also focus on green products, such as home appliance retailers, Best Buy, Wal-Mart, etc.

To sum up, manufacturers and retailers are encouraged to produce or sell green products to mitigate the environmental impact and fulfill social responsibility. Particularly, with the rapid development of e-commerce, and due to the consumer consciousness of green products, many manufacturers introduce online stores to sell green products, such as green agriproducts (http://www.oabc.cc/), that is, the physical retail stores and online platforms jointly constitute a dual channel supply chain. Through online sales, the green product demand for manufacturers can be increased significantly, and their benefits will be added. However, the development of direct marketing channels leads to competition between traditional retailers and manufacturers. In addition, because manufacturers have to invest huge R&D expenses to innovate green products, this incurs higher cost compared with that of traditional products (Pujari, 2006). Accordingly, green products are likely to have higher prices in the market. However, consumers may have difficulty to evaluate the green level of the products, or because the retailers lack historical sales data and experience with green products, they also have difficulty in predicting market demands. All of these factors may bring about much trouble in identifying consumers' acceptance of green products, which leads to risk concern. Some researchers pointed out that when the market demand was uncertain, the retailers tended to behave in a risk-averse way (Ye *et al.*, 2020).

Based on the above discussion, this chapter will study the pricing and greening strategies in a dual-channel supply chain (Li *et al.*, 2016). Specifically, we aim at addressing the following questions:

(1) How will the agents make pricing and greening strategies in dual-channel context under different channel relationships (e.g., centralized relationship and decentralized relationship)?
(2) How will the degree of customer loyalty to the retail channel, the expansion effectiveness coefficients of the green level per unit, and the greening cost impact on the pricing policies, the green level choice and the profits of both agents in the dual-channel supply chain?
(3) Under the greening strategy, when should the manufacturer introduce an online channel and how could the channel conflict be resolved? What if an agent has risk-averse behavior?

The remainder of this chapter is organized as follows. In Sec. 5.2, the problem setting is introduced, including the notations, the assumptions and the model. In Sec. 5.3, both centralized dual-channel model and decentralized dual-channel model are analyzed. Optimal pricing and greening strategies are obtained analytically. In Sec. 5.4, the channel choice problem is first discussed by comparing the dual-channel supply chain with the single-channel supply chain under the green strategy; then the channel coordination is resolved by designing a two-part tariff contract between two agents. Section 5.5 presents an extension of the model to the situations where the retailer takes risk-averse behavior under the dual-channel green supply chain. Finally, conclusions and directions for future research are summarized in Sec. 5.6.

## 5.2. Problem Setting and the Model

Consider a dual-channel supply chain including a manufacturer producing green product and an independent, traditional retailer. Apart from the traditional retail channel, the manufacturer also sets up his own electronic channel to sell green products. Customers can choose online or offline channel to purchase the green product according to their own preferences.

The notations in this chapter are as follows:

| Variable Name | Variable Description |
|---|---|
| $D_r$ | the demand of the green product in the retail channel |
| $D_m$ | the demand of the green product in the online channel |
| $a$ | the basic market demand of the green product, which is a constant |
| $\rho$ | the degree of customer loyalty to the retail channel, $1-\rho$ is the degree of customer loyalty to the online channel, and $0 \leq \rho \leq 1$ |
| $p_r$ | the price in the traditional retail channel |
| $p_m$ | the price in the online channel |
| $\theta$ | the green level of the green products |
| $\beta_r$ | the expansion effectiveness coefficient of the green level per unit product to the retail demand |
| $\beta_m$ | the expansion effectiveness coefficient of the green level per unit product to the direct demand |
| $b_1$ | the marginal channel demand per respective channel price, representing the sensitivity of demand to the own channel price ($b_1 > \beta_r$ and $b_1 > \beta_m$) |
| $b_2$ | the marginal channel demand per respective channel price ($b_1 > b_2$), representing the sensitivity of demand to the other channel price. |
| $\pi_r$ | the retailer's profit |
| $\pi_m$ | the manufacturer's profit |

To establish the model, we make the following assumptions.

**Assumption 5.1.** The demands faced by the manufacturer and the retailer are linear functions of the green level and the sale price of the green products, that is, in both retail channel and online channel. We assume the demand is upward sloping in green level and downward sloping in sale price (Ghosh and Shah, 2012).

Therefore, the demand functions of the retail channel and the online channel are defined as follows:

$$D_r = \rho a - b_1 p_r + b_2 p_m + \beta_r \theta, \tag{5.1}$$

$$D_m = (1-\rho)a - b_1 p_m + b_2 p_r + \beta_m \theta. \tag{5.2}$$

**Assumption 5.2.** Consistent pricing strategy is adopted in both channels to reduce channel conflict, i.e., the price in the online channel is the same as that in the retail channel (Cattani *et al.*, 2006). That is, $p_r = p_m = p$.

To avoid the trivial situations, let $p \geq w \geq c$, here $c$ is the per-unit manufacturing cost of the traditional product, $p$ is the selling price of the green, which is determined by the retailer, $w$ refers to the unit wholesale price of green products determined by the manufacturer. Therefore, we can rewrite the demand functions as follows:

$$D_r = \rho a - bp + \beta_r \theta, \tag{5.3}$$

$$D_m = (1-\rho)a - bp + \beta_m \theta, \tag{5.4}$$

where $b = b_1 - b_2$.

**Assumption 5.3.** It is assumed that the manufacturer's traditional marginal cost is not affected by producing green products. However, the manufacturer has to invest some extra money to achieve the green innovation based on the original production process to produce green products, and the green cost is supposed as a quadratic function of green level (Ghosh and Shah, 2012; Swami and Shah, 2012). Therefore, the extra cost for the manufacturer to produce the green products can be expressed as $C(\theta) = \eta\theta^2/2$, where $\eta$ is the cost coefficient of the green level per unit.

**Assumption 5.4.** Both the direct and the retail channels have their own potential customers. For the same green level of the product, the effect on customers in the online channel is smaller than that in the retail channel. This reflects the fact that when consumers observe the actual product, they can evaluate the green level of the product by themselves and more positively influenced. Thus, here we assume $\beta_m < \beta_r$.

**Assumption 5.5.** The basic market demand is large enough to be significantly greater than the impact of other parameters of the model.

Two conditions need to be satisfied before analyzing the model. First, the demand at each channel is non-negative. Second, the manufacturer and the retailer must gain non-negative profits to sustain the supply chain. These two conditions can be transformed into the following constraints:

$$c \leq w \leq p \leq \min\left(\frac{\rho a + \beta_r \theta}{b}, \frac{(1-\rho)a + \beta_m \theta}{b}\right). \tag{5.5}$$

In the framework of Stackelberg game, to maximize the profit, the wholesale price and the green level of green products are determined by the manufacturer who is the leader, and the sale price is decided by the retailer, who is the follower. Then, the profit functions of the manufacturer and the retailer are given as follows:

$$\begin{aligned}\pi_m &= (w-c)(\rho a - bp + \beta_r \theta) + (p-c) \\ &\quad \times [(1-\rho)a - bp + \beta_m \theta] - \frac{1}{2}\eta\theta^2, \end{aligned} \tag{5.6}$$

$$\pi_r = (p-w)(\rho a - bp + \beta_r \theta). \tag{5.7}$$

## 5.3. Solutions and Analysis

In this section, we derive the optimal decisions of manufacturer and retailer in a centralized and decentralized dual-channel supply chain. The optimal decisions of the two supply chain structures are compared in order to find out which one is beneficial to the green supply chain and the environment. Further, some management insights are obtained through the sensitivity analysis of parameters and decision variables. Finally, a contract is designed to coordinate the decentralized dual channel green supply chain.

### 5.3.1. Centralized and decentralized dual-channel green supply chain models

Under the centralized model, manufacturer and retailer are vertically integrated as a whole system, and the green level and sales price are determined simultaneously to maximize the whole system performance. Let $\pi^c$ denote the total profit in the centralized dual-channel supply chain, which can be written as follows:

$$\begin{aligned}\pi^c &= (p-c)D - \frac{1}{2}\eta\theta^2 \\ &= (p-c)[a - 2bp + (\beta_r + \beta_m)\theta] - \frac{1}{2}\eta\theta^2, \end{aligned} \tag{5.8}$$

where $D = D_r + D_m$ represents the total demand in the centralized model.

It can be verified that the above function is jointly concave on the decision variables when $\eta > \frac{(\beta_r+\beta_m)^2}{4b}$. Therefore, the optimal solutions can be calculated as follows:

$$\theta_c^* = \frac{(\beta_r + \beta_m)(a - 2bc)}{A}, \tag{5.9}$$

$$p_c^* = \frac{\eta(a - 2bc)}{A} + c, \tag{5.10}$$

where $A = 4\eta b - (\beta_r + \beta_m)^2$.

By substituting the optimal solution into equation (5.8), the optimal profit of the centralized dual-channel supply chain is given as follows:

$$\pi^C = \frac{\eta(a - 2bc)^2}{2A}. \tag{5.11}$$

Next, we consider the decentralized model, i.e., manufacturer and retailer are independent, and they make decisions separately to maximize their own profits. We use Stackelberg game with the manufacturer as a leader and the retailer as a follower, that is, the wholesale price of the retail channel and the green level are determined by manufacturer first. Then, the retailer makes decision on the sale price. To obtain the optimal solution, we first determine the best response function of the retailer, in which $p$ is expressed by $\theta$ and $w$. Substituting the expression of $p$ into equation (5.6), we can derive an expression for $\pi_m$ in terms of $\theta$ and $w$ as follows:

$$\begin{aligned}\pi_m = (w-c)\cdot\frac{\rho a + \beta_r\theta - bw}{2} + \frac{\rho a + \beta_r\theta + bw - 2bc}{2b} \\ \cdot\frac{(2-3\rho)a + 2(2\beta_m - \beta_r)\theta - bw}{2} - \frac{1}{2}\eta\theta^2. \end{aligned} \tag{5.12}$$

It is easy to see that $\pi_m$ is jointly concave on $\theta$ and $w$ when $\eta > \frac{(\beta_r+\beta_m)^2}{4b}$, we have the optimal solutions as follows:

$$\theta_d^* = \frac{-2\rho a(3\beta_r - \beta_m) + a(3\beta_r + \beta_m) - 4bc\beta_m}{B}, \tag{5.13}$$

$$w_d^* = \frac{-\rho aE + aG - bc(2\eta b + \beta_r^2 - 2\beta_r\beta_m + \beta_m^2)}{bB} + c, \tag{5.14}$$

where $B = 6\eta b + 3\beta_r^2 - \beta_m^2 - 6\beta_r\beta_m$, $E = 2\eta b + \beta_r^2 - \beta_m^2$, $G = 2\eta b + \beta_r^2 - \beta_r\beta_m$.

Furthermore, the optimal sale price can be obtained as follows:

$$p_d^* = \frac{2\rho aH + a(\eta b + 2\beta_r^2) - 2bcG}{bB} + c, \tag{5.15}$$

where $H = \eta b - \beta_r^2 - \beta_r\beta_m$.

The manufacturer's, the retailer's and the total supply chain's optimal profits can be obtained by substituting the above optimal decisions into equations (5.6) and (5.7). Moreover, $\pi_m^*$, $\pi_r^*$ and $\pi^D$ are utilized to denote the manufacturer's, the retailer's and the decentralized dual-channel supply chain's optimal profits, where $\pi^D = \pi_m^* + \pi_r^*$.

Note that the decision variables $p$, $\theta$ and $w$ need to meet the condition (5.5) in order to ensure the feasible solutions to both centralized and decentralized dual-channel green supply chain models. The condition (5.5) can be represented by a constraint to the input parameters as follows.

**Proposition 5.1.** *When the customer's loyalty to the retail channel is within a certain range* $\max(0, \rho_1) \leq \rho \leq \rho_2$, *the optimal game solutions exist, where*

$$\rho_1 = \frac{aH + bcE}{aA},$$

$$\rho_2 = \frac{a(5\eta b + \beta_r^2 - 3\beta_r\beta_m) - bc(2\eta b + \beta_r^2 + 3\beta_m^2 - 4\beta_r\beta_m)}{a(8\eta b + \beta_r^2 - 3\beta_m^2 - 2\beta_r\beta_m)}.$$

The left-hand side of the inequality indicates that when $\rho$ is greater than a certain threshold, the retailer is willing to cooperate with the manufacturer, even though the manufacturer has his own online channel. When $\rho$ is too small, the demand faced by retailer is negative, or the retail price is lower than the wholesale price, which means that the retailer will not benefit from the cooperation. The right-hand side of the inequality indicates that when $\rho$ is less than a certain threshold, the manufacturer is willing to open the online channel and accept the consistent pricing strategy. When $\rho$ is too large, the manufacturer faces negative demand in the online channel. In this situation, the manufacturer will not choose to open the online channel or accept the consistent pricing strategy.

**Proposition 5.2.** *Comparing the centralized model with the decentralized model, the corresponding optimal solutions have the following relationships*:

(1) *The green levels of the products in the centralized model and the decentralized model satisfy* $\theta_c^* \geq \theta_d^*$.
(2) *The relationships of the sales prices in the centralized model and the decentralized model can be characterized into the following types*:
   (i) *if* $\frac{(\beta_r+\beta_m)^2}{4b} < \eta < \frac{\beta_r^2+\beta_m\beta_r}{b}$, *then* $p_c^* > p_d^*$;
   (ii) *if* $\eta = \frac{\beta_r^2+\beta_m\beta_r}{b}$, *then* $p_c^* = p_d^*$;
   (iii) *if* $\eta > \frac{\beta_r^2+\beta_m\beta_r}{b}$, *then* $p_c^* < p_d^*$.
(3) *The total profits in the centralized model and the decentralized model satisfy* $\pi^C \geq \pi^D$.

Proposition 5.2(1) shows that the green level under the decentralization case is lower than that in the case of centralization. We know that green level means the degree of environmental protection of green products. If the manufacturer and the retailer are vertically integrated into a whole system to make decisions, then the product can get a higher green level, that is, the product produced by the manufacturer is more environmentally friendly. On the other hand, the decentralized decision-making will result in the lower green level, which is unfavorable to the effective environment protection.

Proposition 5.2(2) indicates that when $\eta$ is located within some thresholds, the sale price in the decentralized case is lower than that in the centralized case. This conclusion seems to be different from the intuition, but it is reasonable because in the case of centralization, the unit product will have higher cost. When $\eta$ is equal to the threshold value, the sale prices in two cases are equal. When $\eta$ exceeds the threshold, the sale price in the decentralized case is higher than that in the centralized case. The result is consistent with previous studies on channel coordination, which is called "double marginalization". We have proved that in the case of centralization, the green level of the supply chain will be increased in Proposition 5.2(1).

Proposition 5.2(3) shows that under the centralized case, the supply chain can obtain more profits than that under the decentralized supply chain. This result is reasonable and consistent with the early channel coordination research.

In summary, Proposition 5.2 reveals that when the degree of customer loyalty to the retail channel $\rho$ satisfies the condition $\max(0, \rho_1) \leq \rho \leq \rho_2$, the centralized dual-channel green supply chain is better than the decentralized dual-channel green supply chain in terms of green level and total profit, but the sale price will be determined according to the threshold values. However, it should be pointed out that in the case of centralization, higher green level leads to higher sale price, which is beneficial to green supply chain management. Therefore, it is necessary to coordinate the decentralized channels for the members in the green supply chain.

### 5.3.2. Sensitivity analysis

In this subsection, we perform sensitivity analysis to analyze how the customer loyalty to the retail channel and the green level of green products will impact the optimal decisions in the decentralized model.

**Proposition 5.3.** *In the decentralized model, the sensitivity of the optimal prices and the optimal green level to the parameter of the customer loyalty is given by*

(1) $\frac{d\theta_d^*}{d\rho} < 0$, $\frac{dw_d^*}{d\rho} < 0$;

(2) *if* $\frac{(\beta_r+\beta_m)^2}{4b} < \eta < \frac{\beta_r^2+\beta_m\beta_r}{b}$, *then* $\frac{dp_d^*}{d\rho} < 0$, $\left|\frac{dp_d^*}{d\rho}\right| < \left|\frac{dw_d^*}{d\rho}\right|$;

*if* $\eta > \frac{\beta_r^2+\beta_m\beta_r}{b}$, *then* $\frac{dp_d^*}{d\rho} > 0$;

*if* $\eta = \frac{\beta_r^2+\beta_m\beta_r}{b}$, *then* $\frac{dp_d^*}{d\rho} = 0$.

Proposition 5.3(1) shows that when the customer loyalty to the retail channel $\rho$ increases, the green level and the wholesale price decrease, that is, when $\rho$ is small, the basic demand in the online channel is large. Therefore, the considerable profit can be obtained by the manufacturer in the dual-channel green supply chain. Motivated by the above, in order to increase demand and further increase profits, more investment will be committed by the manufacturer in production innovation. Obviously, the relatively high unit cost of green products will lead to the increase of the wholesale price. Naturally, with the increase of $\rho$, the wholesale price decreases.

Proposition 5.3(2) indicates that when $\eta$ is within a certain interval, the sale price is decreasing as $\rho$ increases. This is reasonable, because the wholesale price is also falling. In addition, the rate of the wholesale price change is greater than that of sale price. When $\eta$ is greater than a threshold, the sale price is increasing as $\rho$ increases. In this situation, a higher retail price should be set by the retailer when facing an increasing basic market share.

**Proposition 5.4.** *In the decentralized model, the sensitivity of the optimal price decisions to the green level is given by*

(1) $\frac{dp_d^*}{d\theta} > 0$, $\frac{d\pi_r^*}{d\theta} > 0$;

(2) *if* $\theta < \frac{\beta_r}{2\eta b}$, *then* $\frac{dp_d^*}{d\theta} > \frac{dc(\theta)}{d\theta}$; *if* $\theta \geq \frac{\beta_r}{2\eta b}$, *then* $\frac{dp_d^*}{d\theta} \leq \frac{dc(\theta)}{d\theta}$, *where* $C(\theta) = \eta\theta^2/2$.

Proposition 5.4(1) shows that $p_d$ and $\pi_r$ are increasing as $\theta$ increases. Such an effect is intuitive; note that the cost of green products will increase with the increase of green level of the green products $\theta$; this further makes the wholesale price higher than before. As a result, the retailer will raise the retail price to protect its own profit. Another explanation is that a larger demand caused by the increase of $\theta$ allows the retailer to raise the retail price. When $p_d$ increases, the demand in the retail channel decreases more slowly when $\theta$ is increasing. These factors lead to an increase in $\pi_r$.

Proposition 5.4(2) shows that when $\theta$ is less than the threshold, if the manufacturer increases $\theta$ per unit, then the impact of $\theta$ on the price increase is greater than that on the cost increase. Therefore, the manufacturer can gain more profits by improving the green level of products. When $\theta$ is more than a threshold, if the manufacturer increases $\theta$ per unit, the impact of $\theta$ on the price increase is smaller than that on the cost increase. The results reveal that excessive effort to the improvement of green level of green products will reduce the profit of the manufacturer. Therefore, there exists an optimal green level in the manufacturer's decision.

## 5.4. Channel Choice and Channel Coordination

In this section, we investigate the channel choice problem and identify the conditions when the manufacturer should introduce an online channel. This is done by comparing the dual-channel green supply chain with the single-channel green supply chain. Secondly, we design a two-part tariff contract to coordinate the decentralized dual-channel green supply chain, which can resolve the channel conflict between the manufacturer and the retailer.

### 5.4.1. Channel choice

Similar to the analysis in Sec. 5.3, the equilibrium solutions to the decentralized single-channel green supply chain can be obtained (Ghosh and Shah, 2012). The main results from the decentralized single- and dual-channel green supply chains are given in Table 5.1.

Table 5.1. Comparisons of equilibrium solutions under single- and dual-channel green supply chain.

| Optimal decisions or profits | Single-channel | Dual-channel |
|---|---|---|
| Green level | $\frac{\beta_r(a-bc)}{4\eta b-\beta_r^2}$ | $\frac{-2\rho a(3\beta_r-\beta_m)+a(3\beta_r+\beta_m)-4bc\beta_m}{B}$ |
| Wholesale price | $\frac{2\eta(a-bc)}{4\eta b-\beta_r^2}+c$ | $\frac{-\rho aE+aF-bc(2\eta b+\beta_r^2-2\beta_r\beta_m+\beta_m^2)}{bB}+c$ |
| Price | $\frac{2\rho aG+a(\eta b+2\beta_r^2)-2bcF}{bB}+c$ | $\frac{3\eta(a-bc)}{4\eta b-\beta_r^2}+c$ |
| Manufacturer's profit | $\frac{\eta(a-bc)^2}{2(4\eta b-\beta_r^2)}$ | $\pi_m^*$ |
| Retailer's profit | $\frac{b\eta^2(a-bc)^2}{(4\eta b-\beta_r^2)^2}$ | $\frac{1}{b}\cdot(\frac{\rho aA-aG-bcE}{B})^2$ |
| Total profit | $\frac{\eta(a-bc)^2(12\eta b-2\beta_r^2)}{(8\eta b-2\beta_r^2)^2}$ | $\pi_m^*+\frac{1}{b}\cdot(\frac{\rho aA-aG-bcE}{B})^2$ |

From the results in Table 5.1, we are able to analyze whether the manufacturer opens the online channel is beneficial to both agents of the supply chain from the perspective of their respective profit (see Proposition 5.5). Let $\pi_m^s$ represent the manufacturer's profit, and $\pi_r^s$ denote the retailer's profit, in the decentralized single channel green supply chain.

**Proposition 5.5.**

(1) *For the manufacturer, there exists a threshold* $\underline{\rho}$ *and* $\underline{\rho} \in [\max(0, \rho_1), \rho_2]$. *Moreover, the following results are satisfied:*
   (i) *if* $\max(0, \rho_1) \leq \rho \leq \underline{\rho}$, *then* $\pi_m^* \geq \pi_m^s$;
   (ii) *if* $\underline{\rho} < \rho \leq \rho_2$, *then* $\pi_m^* < \pi_m^s$. *The existence of* $\underline{\rho}$ *makes the equation* $\pi_m^* = \pi_m^s$ *holds;*
   (iii) *if the threshold* $\underline{\rho}$ *is out of range of* $[\max(0, \rho_1), \rho_2]$, *then* $\pi_m^* < \pi_m^s$ *always holds when* $\rho$ *falls in the range of* $\max(0, \rho_1) \leq \rho \leq \rho_2$.

(2) *For the retailer,* $\pi_r^* < \pi_r^s$ *always holds when* $\rho$ *falls in the range of* $\max(0, \rho_1) \leq \rho \leq \rho_2$.

From Proposition 5.5, it can be seen that when $\rho$ is relatively small ($\max(0, \rho_1) \leq \rho \leq \underline{\rho}$), it means that in the online channel, the basic market demand is larger than that in the traditional channel, and more profits can be obtained by the manufacturer in the dual-channel supply chain. Compared with the profit in a single retail channel, some profits of the manufacturer are lost in the dual-channel green supply chain, when $\rho$ is increasing and falling in the range of $\underline{\rho} < \rho \leq \rho_2$. However, for the retailer, under the dual-channel green supply chain, she is always less profitable. Note that the extra profit that the manufacturer earns by opening the online channel comes from the profit the retailer could obtain in a single retail channel green supply chain. That is the reason that channel conflict occurs and the retailer is opposed to the online channel introduced by the manufacturer. Furthermore, when $\rho$ falls in the range of $\underline{\rho} < \rho \leq \rho_2$, both members will earn less profits in the dual-channel green supply chain than they would in the single retail channel green supply chain. The effect of double marginalization may be the reason of this outcome. If $\underline{\rho}$ does not exist, then this phenomenon always occurs when $\max(0, \rho_1) \leq \rho \leq \rho_2$.

From the above analyzes, we have the following corollary.

**Corollary 5.1.** *The manufacturer's channel choice can be determined by the following conditions*:

(1) *When* $\eta > \eta^*$, *the manufacturer should choose the single retail channel.*
(2) *When* $\eta_1 < \eta \leq \eta^*$,
   (i) *if* $\max(0, \rho_1) \leq \rho \leq \underline{\rho}$, *then the manufacturer should open his wholly owned online channel*;
   (ii) *if* $\underline{\rho} < \rho \leq \rho_2$, *then the manufacturer just distributes his product via the offline channel; where* $\eta_1 = \frac{(\beta_r + \beta_m)^2}{4b}$, *and the threshold* $\eta^*$ *satisfies the equation:* $\rho_1 = \underline{\rho}$.

From Corollary 5.1, we can identify the conditions under which the manufacturer will introduce his wholly owned online channel in order to earn more profit. This corollary reveals that when $\eta$ is greater than the threshold $\eta^*$, the manufacturer does not introduce the online channel. The reason is that the high cost of the green products leads to the high price, thus more consumers would select the retail channel to buy green products due to the high price. In the physical retail store, consumers can go there and check the actual green product. Therefore, the offline retail channel is profitable. When $\eta_1 < \eta \leq \eta^*$, whether to introduce the online channel depends on the value of $\rho$. If $\max(0, \rho_1) \leq \rho \leq \underline{\rho}$ is satisfied, the manufacturer will open his online channel, otherwise not, that is, the relatively low cost of the green products will result in a relatively low price, then, consumers will select to buy in the online channel for saving time and costs. But, if a considerable number of consumers are loyal to the retail channel, then they will influence the manufacturer's decision. In summary, both $\eta$ and $\rho$ can influence the choice of the channel structure.

### 5.4.2. Coordinating supply chain

As dual-channel structure will cause channel conflict, it is interesting to examine how to resolve channel conflict by coordinating the dual-channel green supply chain. In Sec. 5.3, we have found that the centralized model can achieve higher total profit than the decentralized model, and the total profit is increasing in the green level. In this section, a simple two-part tariff contract is designed to coordinate the decentralized dual-channel green supply chain so that two agents can achieve win–win outcome.

Firstly, the manufacturer makes the decisions about the wholesale price for the green products, and then charges a lump sum fee $F$ from the retailer for the payment. Then, the profit functions of the manufacturer and the retailer are as follows

$$\pi_r = (p - w)(\rho a - bp + \beta_r \theta) - F, \tag{5.16}$$

$$\pi_m = (w - c)(\rho a - bp + \beta_r \theta) + (p - c)[(1 - \rho)a - bp + \beta_m \theta] - \frac{1}{2}\eta\theta^2 + F. \tag{5.17}$$

To achieve the dual-channel coordination, we use the values of $\theta_c^*$ and $p_c^*$ in the centralized model to derive the expression of the parameters $w^c$ and $F$ in the two-part tariff contract. The results are provided as follows:

$$w^c = \frac{a(2\eta b - \beta_r^2 - \beta_r\beta_m) + bc(\beta_r^2 - \beta_m^2)}{b(4\eta b - \beta_r^2 - \beta_m^2 - 2\beta_r\beta_m)} - \frac{\rho a}{b} + c, \tag{5.18}$$

$$\pi_r(w^c) = (p_c^* - w^c)(\rho a - bp_c^* + \beta_r\theta_c^*) - F, \tag{5.19}$$

$$\pi_m(w^c) = (w^c - c)(\rho a - bp_c^* + \beta_r\theta_c^*) + (p_c^* - c) \times [(1 - \rho)a - bp_c^* + \beta_m\theta_c^*] - \frac{1}{2}\eta\theta_c^{*2} + F. \tag{5.20}$$

It is noted that if $\rho \geq \max(0, \rho_1)$, then $w^c \leq w_d^* \leq p_c^*$, that is, if there is not a lump sum fee $F$, then the manufacturer loses some profit and the retailer earns more profits under this contract. Thus, the fee $F$ greatly impacts the successful implementation of the contract. If $\pi_m^*$ and $\pi_r^*$ are assumed as the reservation profits of the manufacturer and the retailer which are the lowest bounds for them, then when $F$ satisfies $\pi_m(w^c) + F > \pi_m^*$, the manufacturer is willing to offer the contract, i.e.,

$$F > F_1 = \pi_m^* - \left\{(w^c - c)(\rho a - bp_c^* + \beta_r\theta_c^*) + (p_c^* - c) \times [(1 - \rho)a - bp_c^* + \beta_m\theta_c^*] - \frac{1}{2}\eta\theta_c^{*2}\right\}. \tag{5.21}$$

Further, when $F$ satisfies $\pi_r(w^c) - F > \pi_r^*$, the retailer is willing to accept the contract, and then we have

$$F < F_2 = (p_c^* - w^c)(\rho a - bp_c^* + \beta_r\theta_c^*) - \pi_r^*. \tag{5.22}$$

Thus, the above results are summarized in the following proposition.

**Proposition 5.6.** *When the lump sum fee $F$ that the retailer pays to the manufacturer is within the interval $[F_1, F_2]$, the two-part tariff contract between the manufacturer and the retailer can coordinate the decentralized dual-channel green supply chain and obtain a win–win result.*

From the contract structure, we can find that a wholesale price charged by the manufacturer is smaller than that in the decentralized model without a contract. But, the low wholesale price can provide extra incentives to the retailer to decide a lower retail price, which can increase the demand in the manufacturer's online channel. Meanwhile, the retailer is requested to pay a lump sum fee $F$ to the manufacturer for boosting his profit. Formulas (5.19) and (5.20) suggest that a larger $F$ will benefit the manufacturer, and a smaller $F$ will benefit the retailer. Thus, the size of $F$ depends on both members' bargaining power in the negotiation, and this two-part tariff contract can coordinate the dual-channel green supply chain to realize the win–win situation.

## 5.5. Extension to the Case with the Risk-Averse Retailer

In this section, we discuss the extension of the model to the case where the retailer is risk-averse, that is, here a green supply chain built in which there is a manufacturer and a retailer, and assumes that the manufacturer is risk neutral, while the retailer is risk-averse. We assume that the risk is caused by uncertain demand. Specifically, assume the total basic demand for green products $a$ is a random demand with mean $E(a)$ and standard deviation $\mathrm{SD}(a)$. From (5.6) and (5.7), the profits of two agents are given by:

$$\pi_m = (w-c)(\rho a - bp + \beta_r\theta) + (p-c)[(1-\rho)a - bp + \beta_m\theta] - \frac{1}{2}\eta\theta^2, \tag{5.23}$$

$$\pi_r = (p-w)(\rho a - bp + \beta_r\theta). \tag{5.24}$$

If we use the mean–variance criterion to measure the retailer's risk-averse attitude (see Chapter 1 for the definition of mean-variance method), then the utility functions of two agents can be defined as follows:

$$\begin{aligned} U_m &= E(\pi_m) = (w-c)(\rho E(a) - bp + \beta_r\theta) + (p-c) \\ &\quad \times [(1-\rho)E(a) - bp + \beta_m\theta] - \frac{\eta\theta^2}{2}, \qquad (5.25) \\ U_r &= E(\pi_r) - \lambda \cdot SD(\pi_r) = (p-w)(\rho E(a) - bp + \beta_r\theta) \\ &\quad - \lambda(p-w)\rho \cdot SD(a). \qquad (5.26) \end{aligned}$$

The parameter $\lambda$ represents the degree of the retailer's risk-averse attitude. From (5.25) and (5.26), we can analyze the equilibrium solutions and the sensitivity of the solutions to key parameters similar to that in previous sections.

## 5.6. Conclusion

In this chapter, a dual-channel supply chain with green investment is discussed under the consistent pricing assumption (i.e., both channels have the same selling price to consumers). The pricing and greening strategies for the manufacturer and the retailer are explored in both centralized and decentralized cases. Furthermore, the influences of the green level, the greening cost and greening sensitivity on both agents' pricing decisions are analyzed. Through the comparison of the dual-channel green supply chain with the single-channel green supply chain, the channel choice problem is examined and the conditions to open an online channel are identified. To overcome the channel conflict and promote green innovation, a coordination mechanism in the decentralized dual-channel green supply chain is designed to ensure both members' win–win profits. In addition, the extension of the model to the case with the risk-averse retailer under random market demand is discussed based on the mean–variance criterion.

The work could be generalized in several directions. First, this chapter assumes that there is only one kind of green products in the supply chain. An interesting extension is that when there are multiple green products, how do the chain members make their decisions? Moreover, all information here is known and symmetric to both members in the dual-channel supply chain, whether the results can carry over to the cases with asymmetric information requires further research.

## References

Asif, M. S., Lau, H., & Nakandala, D. (2020). Adoption of green supply chain management practices through collaboration approach in developing countries-from literature review to conceptual framework. *Journal of Cleaner Production*, 276, pp. 124–191.

Cattani, K., Wendell, G., Hans S. H., & Jayashankar, S. (2006). Boiling frogs: Pricing strategies for a manufacturer adding a direct channel that competes with the traditional channel. *Production and Operations Management*, 15(1), pp. 1–38.

El Saadany, A., & Jaber, M. Y. (2010). A production/remanufacturing inventory model with price and quality dependent return rate. *Computers & Industrial Engineering*, 58(3), pp. 352–362.

Ghosh, D., & Shah, J. (2012). A comparative analysis of greening policies across supply chain structures. *International Journal of Production Economics*, 135(2), pp. 568–583.

Green Jr, K. W., Zelbst, P. J., Meacham, J., & Bhadauria, V. S. (2012). Green supply chain management practices: Impact on performance. *Supply Chain Management: An International Journal*, 17(3), pp. 290–305.

Hall, J., & Vredenburg, H. (2012). The challenges of innovating for sustainable development. *MIT Sloan Management Review*, 45(1), pp. 61–68.

Li B, Zhu, M., Jiang Y., & Li Z. (2016). Pricing policies of a competitive dual-channel green supply chain. *Journal of Cleaner Production*, 112, pp. 2029–2042.

Li, G., Li, L., Choi, T. M., & Sethi, S. P.(2020). Green supply chain management in Chinese firms: Innovative measures and the moderating role of quick response technology. *Journal of Operations Management*, 66(7–8), pp. 958–988.

Lin, Y. H., & Tseng, M. L. (2014). Assessing the competitive priorities within sustainable supply chain management under uncertainty. *Journal of Cleaner Production*, 24(1), pp. 1–12.

Navinchandra, D. (1990). *Steps Toward Environmentally Compatible Product and Process Design: A Case for Green Engineering*, Carnegie Mellon University, Robotics Institute, Pittsburgh, PA.

Pujari, D. (2006). Eco-innovation and new product development: Understanding the influences on market performance. *Technovation*, 26(1), pp. 76–85.

Rockafellar R. T., & Uryasev S. (2000). Optimization of conditional value-at-risk. *Journal of Risk*, 2, pp. 21–42.

Seuring, S. (2013). A review of modeling approaches for sustainable supply chain management. *Decision Support Systems*, 54(4), pp. 1513–1520.

Seuring, S., & Müller, M. (2008). Core issues in sustainable supply chain management–a Delphi study. *Business Strategy and the Environment*, 17(8), pp. 455–466.

Swami, S., & Shah, J. (2012). Channel coordination in green supply chain management. *Journal of the Operational Research Society*, 64(3), pp. 336–351.

Tseng, M. L., Lin, Y. H., Tan, K., Chen, R. H., & Chen, Y. H. (2014). Using TODIM to evaluate green supply chain practices under uncertainty. *Applied Mathematical Modelling*, 38(11), pp. 2983–2995.

Ye, F., Lin, Q., & Li, Y. (2020). Coordination for contract farming supply chain with stochastic yield and demand under CVaR criterion. *Operational Research*, 20(1), pp. 369–397.

© 2022 World Scientific Publishing Europe Ltd.
https://doi.org/10.1142/9781800610408_0006

# Chapter 6

# Consumer Return Policy and Channel Conflict Management in a Dual-Channel Supply Chain with a Risk-Averse Retailer

**Yushan Jiang**[*,‡], **Bo Li**[*,§], **and Dong-Ping Song**[†,¶]

[*] *College of Management and Economics, Tianjin University, China*
[†] *School of Management, University of Liverpool, Liverpool, UK*
[‡] *13803050699@163.com*
[§] *libo0410@tju.edu.cn*
[¶] *Dongping.Song@liverpool.ac.uk*

## 6.1. Introduction

New commercial patterns and opportunities are being created in the ear of e-commerce. Manufacturers may introduce online channels such as online sales in addition to the traditional offline channels. This leads to fierce competition among the members in supply chains, a phenomenon called "manufacturer encroachment" (Arya *et al.*, 2007; Li *et al.*, 2014). It has been evidenced that introducing an online channel can help firms increase market size, obtain more direct feedback from consumers, boost the total supply chain profit and mitigate double marginalization (Li *et al.*, 2015). Meanwhile, e-commerce is changing consumers' purchasing behavior. Under online transactions, consumers can easily shop through various websites, and transactions are no longer constrained by time and distance. But some psychological factors may raise consumers' concerns with online shopping because consumers are unable to see and inspect the products by themselves before making their purchases (Hsiao and Chen, 2012). Through images or videos, online descriptions may help consumers learn about the products, however, online shopping is lacking in emotional experiences and directing instructions, or the goods may be lost or damaged during the distribution. Therefore, on the one hand, by introducing an online channel, the competitiveness of manufacturers may be strengthened; on the other hand, it also brings about additional challenges in customer services. One of the most important concerns of online shopping is the difficulty in returning unsatisfactory purchases (Lee, 2002; Rao *et al.*, 2014).

In response to the purchasing uncertainty of online products, online suppliers often offer a variety of returns policies to alleviate consumers' psychological burden. In practice, many major electronic products manufacturers, such as Samsung Electronics (www.samsung.com/cn/home) and Apple Inc. (http://store.apple.com/cn) all promise returns policies for their online sales. Particularly, in the cosmetics industry such as Dabao, a sub-brand of Johnson & Johnson Company (http://dabao.tmall.com), promises a generous "no questions asked" money-back guarantee for consumers. It has been demonstrated that more than 70 percent of consumers would consider returns policies before their online purchasing (Trager, 2000). Therefore, returns services not only can enhance firm's competitiveness, but also can increase consumers' confidence in the product quality (Sullivan, 2009). Obviously, providing a consumer returns policy is a useful mechanism for the sellers (Wood, 2001). Further, according to Suwelack *et al.* (2011), returns policies can stimulate market demand and positively impact consumers' willingness to pay. However, the negative implications of the returns policy cannot be ignored. Too generous returns policies often give rise to an excessive amount of consumer returns and inventory. In addition, dealing with returned products consumes manufacturers' time and increases reverse logistics cost. Therefore, how to design an optimal returns policy is very important for manufacturers.

Manufacturer encroachment has a significant impact on the retailers (resellers) in the traditional channel (Arya *et al.*, 2007; Li and Gilbert *et al.*, 2014, 2015). Retailers believe that cannibalization effect is bound to happen in the dual-channel supply chain. The manufacturers not only carve up the market by establishing their online channels, but also offer the returns policy to offset the weakness of the online shopping. These factors may lead to channel conflict, higher degree of uncertainty and greater competitive pressure to retailers. Particularly, when the market demand is uncertain, the retailers tend to behave in a risk-averse way (Choi *et al.*, 2008). Thus, it is of great importance to incorporate the retailers' risk aversion into the decision framework in the manufacturer encroachment situation. Meanwhile, how to manage the channel conflict between the manufacturer and the retailer is another important issue.

This chapter considers a dual-channel supply chain with a risk-neutral manufacturer and a risk-averse retailer, in which the manufacturer produces a single type of products and sells them via his own online channel and the traditional retail channel, and offers consumers a returns policy for his online channel. We will examine the following issues (Jiang *et al.*, 2017):

(1) How would a risk-averse retailer make her optimal order decisions in response to the manufacturer's different returns policies for its online channel?
(2) How will the combinational factors of the manufacturer's different return policies and the retailer's risk-averse attitude influence their decisions and performance? What is the manufacturer's optimal returns policy?
(3) How to coordinate the dual-channel supply chain in the presence of consumer returns and a risk-averse retailer so that channel conflict could be mitigated?
(4) Does the returns policy play an important role in improving the competitiveness of the online channel?
(5) Does providing the returns policy always hurt the retailer's utility?

The rest of this chapter is organized as follows. Section 6.2 formulates the model for the problem. We assume that the market demand is uncertain and related to the refund-amount (Liu *et al.*, 2014; Xiao *et al.*, 2010). The objective of the risk-averse retailer is to maximize her expected utility and the objective of the manufacturer is to maximize his expected profit. Section 6.3 performs analytical analysis in terms of the equilibrium solution, and the impact of the returns policy and the risk-averse indicator on two players. Section 6.4 discusses the buyback revenue-sharing contract to coordinate the dual-channel supply chain, which essentially mitigates the channel conflict. Section 6.5 explores whether the returns policy helps improve the competitiveness of the online channel, and how the returns policy affects the retailer's profit share among the supply chains. Finally, a summary is provided in Sec. 6.6.

## 6.2. Model Formulation

Consider a dual-channel supply chain with a risk-neutral manufacturer (he) and a risk-averse retailer (she). The manufacturer produces a single type of products at unit cost $c$ at the beginning of the sales season, and operates his own online channel with a consumer returns policy. The mixed strategy of make-to-order and make-to-stock is adopted here, that is, a make-to-order policy is adopted in the online channel, while the retailer places an order to the manufacturer before the sales. This is because the demand in the retail channel is relatively stable and predictable. In addition, the manufacturer is a Stackelberg leader, and the manufacturer decides his wholesale price in the first move. Then after observing the manufacturer's choice, the retailer as a follower makes her order decision.

Several market surveys have found that online prices are usually lower than offline prices within a certain range of 4–16% for the reasons such as lower barriers to entry the market and lower operational costs of online channel (Bhatnagar and Syam, 2014). Taking into account the above observations, we assume that the online price is not greater than the retail price, but not less than the average of the production cost and the retail price, that is, assuming that the selling prices in the retail channel and the online channel are respectively $p_r$ and $p_m$, then $(p_r + c)/2 < p_m \leq p_r$ need be satisfied.

Furthermore, we assume that the manufacturer offers a consumer returns policy to the consumers in online channel, but the retailer does not offer a return policy to the offline consumers. The former can be understood as the manufacturer's customer service to overcome the disadvantage that consumers in the online channel are difficult to judge the fitness of the product without physically observing and trying it. The latter may be justified as follows. For the brick-and-mortar stores, the retailer has displayed proper samples of various product models on the shelves, and/or hired highly qualified sales agents, so the consumers can ensure they find the right product before committing the purchase. In addition, consumers are able to inspect and try-out the product in the retail store, which can further decrease the likelihood of a mismatch. Therefore, we assume that only the online channel provides the consumer returns service in this paper.

The returns policy is parameterized by a policy parameter $f$ where $f$ represents the refund amount. If $f = 0$, it means no return is allowed. If $f = p_m$, it represents full refunds (or full returns). Besides, $f \in (0, p_m)$ implies that the manufacturer offers partial refunds to consumers. For simplicity, this chapter assumes the refund amount as an exogenous factor. In fact, many researchers have shown that the quantities of returned products have a strong positive relation to the refund amount (Liu *et al.*, 2014). In our model, consumers face valuation uncertainty in the manufacturer's online channel. Thus, in the online channel, we assume that consumer valuation $v$ is an independent and identically distributed random variable with distribution $G(\cdot)$. These realizations are not known until the consumer receives the product (Su, 2009). A consumer's surplus of keeping the product bought online is $v - p_m$, and the surplus of returning this product is $f - p_m$. A consumer with post-purchase valuation $v$ will return the product if and only if $v - p_m \leq f - p_m$. And the probability of consumer returns is $G(f) = \text{prob}(v \leq f)$.

In addition, we assume that the returned products from consumers cannot be resold within this selling period due to the requirement for inspection, repackaging, and re-shelving (Chen and Bell, 2012). All leftover products are salvaged at prices $s$. Meanwhile, the manufacturer incurs a cost $l$ related to handling the returned products including verifying purchase, repackaging, re-shelving and carrying cost during the return processes.

The notations and parameters are defined as follows:

| Notations | Description |
|---|---|
| $i$ | $i = m, r$, where $m$ denotes the manufacturer's online channel and $r$ represents the retail channel |
| $w$ | the wholesale price, which is a decision variable of the manufacturer subject to $w \leq p_m$ |
| $q_r$ | the order quantity in the retail channel, which is a decision variable of the retailer |
| $\theta$ | the degree of consumer loyalty to the retail channel with $0 < \theta < 1$ and then $1 - \theta$ represents the degree of consumer loyalty to the online channel |
| $c$ | the production cost per unit with $c < w$ |
| $s$ | the salvage value per unit for the returned and leftover product, here assuming that $s < c$ |
| $v$ | a random variable which denotes the consumer's post-purchase valuation with an increasing distribution $G(\cdot)$ |
| $f$ | the refund amount in the online channel with $0 \leq f \leq p_m$ |
| $l$ | the unit cost of handling consumer returns undertaken by the manufacturer, to make the return meaningful, $l \leq s$, otherwise the manufacturer won't recycling returned products |
| $D$ | the basic demand for the product in the marketplace |
| $\xi$ | the uncertain part of demand, which is a random variable |
| $\rho_i$ | the demand's sensitivity parameter to the returns policy in each channel, here assume the returns policy's effect on the online channel is greater than it on the retail channel by $0 < \rho_r < \rho_m$ (Li *et al.*, 2013) |

The total market demand is stochastic, and is described as $\bar{D} = D + \xi$, in which $D$ is the basic demand and $\xi$ is a random variable, which follows a uniform distribution on $[-U, U]$ and $D \geq U \geq 0$, $\phi(\cdot)$, $\Phi(\cdot)$ are the density and the cumulative function of $\xi$, respectively. Besides, this chapter also assumes that the demand functions are linear in the prices and the refund amount, and the prices are assumed exogenous in the basic model (Lu and Liu, 2013).

The demand functions for the retail channel and the manufacturer's online channel are given as follows:

$$D_r = \theta\bar{D} - p_r + \alpha p_m - \rho_r f, \tag{6.1}$$

$$D_m = (1 - \theta)\bar{D} - p_m + \alpha p_r + \rho_m f, \tag{6.2}$$

where the parameter $\alpha$ is the cross-price sensitivity and $0 < \alpha < 1$. $\rho_i$ represents the intensity of competition between the two channels with regards to $f$. Note that return compensation can stimulate consumer demand and correspondingly increase sales (Li *et al.*, 2013), if the refund amount increases by one unit, $\rho_m$ units of the demand will increase in the online channel, meanwhile $\rho_r$ units of the demand will be lost in the retail channel.

The manufacturer's profit is

$$\begin{aligned}\pi_m = (w-c)\cdot q_r + (p_m - c)\cdot \bar{G}(f)D_m \\ + (p_m - c - f + s - l)\cdot G(f)D_m.\end{aligned} \tag{6.3}$$

In Eq. (6.3), the first term corresponds to the revenue generated from the retailer, the second term comes from the products sold at his online channel and not returned by consumers, and the third term represents the salvaging revenue from products that are bought but returned by the consumer in the online direct channel. It should be noted that the third term could be negative.

Then, the retailer's profit is given as follows:

$$\pi_r = p_r \cdot \min(q_r, D_r) - w\cdot q_r + s(q_r - D_r)^+, \tag{6.4}$$

where $(\cdot)^+ = \max(\cdot, 0)$. In Eq. (6.4), the first term corresponds to the retailer's sales revenue, the second term represents the money paid to the manufacturer and the third term represents the salvage value of the leftover products if there are any.

The CVaR criterion is applied to evaluate the risk-averse behavior of the retailer. From the definition of CVaR, we can obtain the following equivalent functions to denote the retailer's utility under $\eta$-CVaR criterion:

$$\mathrm{CVaR}^{\eta}(\pi_r) = \begin{cases} (p_r - w)q_r \\ \quad -\dfrac{(p_r - s)\theta}{\eta}\displaystyle\int_{-U}^{\frac{q_r - \alpha p_m + p_r + \rho_r f}{\theta} - D} \Phi(\xi)d\xi, & q_r \le \theta D - \rho_r f + \alpha p_m \\ & \quad - p_r + \theta\Phi^{-1}(\eta), \\ (p_r - s)\theta\Phi^{-1}(\eta) - (w - s)q_r \\ \quad +(p_r - s)[\theta D - \rho_r f + \alpha p_m - p_r] \\ \quad -\dfrac{(p_r - s)\theta}{\eta}\displaystyle\int_{-U}^{\Phi^{-1}(\eta)} \Phi(\xi)d\xi, & q_r > \theta D - \rho_r f + \alpha p_m \\ & \quad - p_r + \theta\Phi^{-1}(\eta). \end{cases} \tag{6.5}$$

The retailer's utility function as well as the above inference process can be done similar to that in Chapter 3 and we omit them here.

## 6.3. Equilibrium Solution and Analysis

In this section, we first derive the equilibrium solution to the model and then provide the sensitivity analyzes based on the equilibrium results.

### 6.3.1. Equilibrium solution and its properties

In Stackelberg game, the manufacturer first as a leader decides the wholesale price, then the retailer as a follower decides the order quantity. According to Eq. (6.5), we discuss two cases as follows:

Case 1: When $q_r > \theta D + \alpha p_m - p_r - \rho_r f + \theta \Phi^{-1}(\eta)$, we have

$$\frac{\partial CVaR^{\eta}(\pi_r)}{\partial q_r} = -(w - s) < 0.$$

It follows $q_r^* = \theta D + \alpha p_m - p_r - \rho_r f + \theta \Phi^{-1}(\eta)$. We can find that this situation is at the boundary of the feasible regions, and the optimal solution is included in the other case, so we can omit this situation.

Case 2: When $q_r \leq \theta D + \alpha p_m - p_r - \rho_r f + \theta \Phi^{-1}(\eta)$, we have

$$\begin{aligned} \mathrm{CVaR}^{\eta}(\pi_r) &= (p_r - w) q_r \\ &\quad - \frac{(p_r - s)[q_r - \alpha p_m + p_r + \rho_r f - \theta D + U\theta]^2}{4U\eta\theta}. \end{aligned} \tag{6.6}$$

The manufacturer's expected profit is as follows:

$$\begin{aligned} E(\pi_m) = (w - c) \cdot q_r + [p_m - c - G(f) \cdot (f - s + l)] \\ \cdot [(1 - \theta) D + \alpha p_r - p_m + \rho_m f]. \end{aligned} \tag{6.7}$$

Using the standard backward induction approach, we can obtain the equilibrium solution $(q_r^*, w^*)$ as follows:

$$q_r^* = \frac{1}{2}[(D - U)\theta - \rho_r f + \alpha p_m - p_r] + \frac{U\eta\theta(p_r - c)}{p_r - s},$$

$$w^* = \frac{p_r - s}{4U\eta\theta}[(D - U)\theta - \rho_r f + \alpha p_m - p_r] + \frac{p_r + c}{2}.$$

Some conditions are required in order to ensure that the system is physically meaningful. First, to keep the dual-channel supply chain structure feasible, both channels' demands must be non-negative. Second, $w^* \leq p_m$. Accordingly, we obtain the following constraints:

$$p_m \leq p_r < \min[(D-U)\theta + (\alpha - \rho_r)p_m, (2p_m - c)] \quad \text{and} \quad \eta \in [\underline{\eta}, 1],$$

where

$$\underline{\eta} = \frac{(D-U)\theta + \alpha p_m - p_r}{2U\theta} \cdot \frac{p_r - s}{2p_m - p_r - c}.$$

With respect to the impacts of the refund amount and the risk-averse indicator on the decision variables, we have the following results.

**Proposition 6.1.** *Under the conditions $\eta \in [\underline{\eta}, 1]$, the equilibrium solutions have the following properties*:

$$(1) \ \frac{\partial q_r^*}{\partial f} < 0, \quad \frac{\partial w^*}{\partial f} < 0;$$

$$(2) \ \frac{\partial q_r^*}{\partial \eta} > 0, \quad \frac{\partial w^*}{\partial \eta} < 0;$$

$$(3) \ \frac{\partial w^*}{\partial \theta} > 0, \quad \frac{\partial q_r^*}{\partial \theta} > 0.$$

In Proposition 6.1, the first group indicates that the retailer's order quantity is decreasing in $f$. This is intuitive because the demand in the e-channel becomes larger as $f$ increases; and this brings about more intense competition between two channels. Facing a shrinking market, the retailer reduces her order quantity to avoid too many leftovers. As for the manufacturer, a larger refund amount $f$ will decrease its profit from the e-channel and break the equilibrium between two channels. This would lead to his willingness to charge a lower wholesale price to stimulate a higher order quantity from the retailer. In other words, as $f$ increases, the manufacturer tends to shift more order quantity toward the retailer channel by lowering the wholesale price. For the impacts of the risk-averse indicator $\eta$, the retailer is decreasing her order quantity when she becomes more risk-averse. On the contrary, the manufacturer will decrease his wholesale price and transfer his cooperative willingness to the retailer when the retailer becomes less risk-averse. Further, the third group reveals that the wholesale price and the order quantity increase in $\theta$, which represents the degree of consumer loyalty to the retail channel. When $\theta$ is small, the basic demand in the retail channel is low. So too many order quantities may give rise to excessive leftovers. However, as $\theta$ increases, the basic demand in the retail channel becomes larger. The retailer bears less risk in overstocking. Her order quantity is responsive to the increase in $\theta$. With regards to the effect of $\theta$ on the wholesale price, when $\theta$ is small, the manufacturer can earn considerable profit in his online channel. Then, he is willing to set a lower wholesale price to encourage the retailer to order more. As $\theta$ increases, the manufacturer knows that the retailer is bound to increase her order quantity. Motivated by this, the manufacturer increases the wholesale price to make more money.

### 6.3.2. Impact of the returns policy and the risk-averse indicator on performance

In this section, we analyze the impact of the refund amount $f$ and the retailer's risk-averse indicator $\eta$ on two members' performance. We first examine how the refund amount influences the retailer's expected utility.

**Proposition 6.2.** *The following properties can be established.*

(1) *For the fixed refund amount $f$, the retailer's expected utility is monotonically increasing as her risk-averse indicator $\eta$ increases. The risk-neutral retailer will gain the most expected utility.*
(2) *For the fixed risk-averse indicator $\eta$, there exists a threshold*

$$f_r = \frac{(D-U)\theta + \alpha p_m - p_r}{\rho_r} - \frac{2U\eta\theta}{3\rho_r} \cdot \frac{p_r - s}{p_r - c}$$

*such that:*

(i) *when $f_r < 0$, the retailer's expected utility is monotonically decreasing in $f$;*
(ii) *when $0 \leq f_r < p_m$, the retailer will achieve the maximum expected utility when $f = f_r$;*
(iii) *when $f_r \geq p_m$, the retailer's expected utility is monotonically increasing in $f$.*

In Proposition 6.2(1), we can see that as the retailer's risk-averse indicator $\eta$ increases, the retailer's expected utility is increasing.

This result highlights an important conclusion that the retailer can achieve the highest expected utility when she is risk-neutral.

Proposition 6.2(2) reveals that at a given risk-averse level of the retailer, the relationship between the retailer's expected utility and the manufacturer's refund amount can be characterized by a single threshold value $f_r$. Here $f_r$ can be interpreted as a parameter that is associated with the market environment such as the basic demand, the degree of consumer loyalty, etc. Specially, when $f_r > p_m$, the retailer's expected utility will monotonically increase in $f$ for any $f \leq f_r$. This appears to be a counter-intuitive phenomenon because firstly manufacturer encroachment arouses channel competition between the retailer and the manufacturer; secondly, the manufacturer is enhancing the return service in his online channel to attract more consumers, which should intensify the competition between two channels. We explain this surprising phenomenon from two aspects. On the one hand, larger degree of consumer loyalty to the retail channel and higher basic market demand ensure higher market demand sharing for the retailer. This will decrease the retailer's risk of ordering. On the other hand, because the wholesale price will decrease as the increase of $f$. The manufacturer would like to compensate the retailer by reducing the wholesale price when he raises the refund amount in his online channel. When the basic market demand is relatively low, i.e., $f_r < 0$, the retailer will face higher risk of ordering. Meanwhile, the higher refund amount will also bring greater damage to retailer's basic market sharing. Thus, the retailer's expected utility is decreasing in $f$. When the market demand is moderate, i.e., $0 \leq f_r < p_m$, the retailer's expected utility is first increasing then decreasing in $f$. There is enough market demand when the refund amount keeps in a low level, thus the retailer's expected utility is first increasing in $f$. When $f$ gradually increases further, retailer's market demand share shrinks, thus retailer's expected utility starts decreasing.

Furthermore, we will examine the impact of $f$ on the manufacturer's expected profit from another perspective. The relative expected profit is used to measure the manufacturer's performance, that is, assume that consumer's post-purchase valuation $v$ follows a uniform distribution on $[0, \bar{v}]$ where $\bar{v} > p_m$ (Li and Xu *et al.*, 2014). Thus, the manufacturer's relative profit can be defined as the difference between the expected profits under the returns policy (RP) and no returns policy (NRP), i.e., $\Delta\pi_m = E(\pi_m)|_{RP} - E(\pi_m)|_{NRP}$. It is clear that,

- when $\Delta\pi_m > 0$, providing the returns option to consumers is better for the manufacturer;
- when $\Delta\pi_m \leq 0$, the manufacturer prefers not to offer returns service.

The next proposition characterizes the manufacturer's preferences under different combinations of the highest pre-purchase valuation $\bar{v}$ and the risk-averse indicator $\eta$.

**Proposition 6.3.** *Given the retailer's risk-averse indicator $\eta$, there exists thresholds $v_1$, $v_2$ and $\bar{\eta}$ such that:*

(1) *if $\bar{v} \leq v_1$, then it is optimal for the manufacturer to offer a partial returns policy;*
(2) *if $v_1 < \bar{v} \leq v_2$ and $0 < \underline{\eta} \leq \eta < \bar{\eta} \leq 1$, then it is optimal for the manufacturer to offer a partial returns policy;*
(3) *if $v_1 < \bar{v} \leq v_2$ and $0 < \bar{\eta} < \eta \leq 1$, then it is optimal for the manufacturer to offer a full returns policy;*
(4) *if $\bar{v} > v_2$, then it is optimal for the manufacturer to offer the full returns policy.*

Proposition 6.3 states that the manufacturer's optimal returns policy can be characterized by the highest consumer's valuation of the product. Prior to purchase, consumers are uncertain about the product's fit with their tastes. A consumer faces a distribution of potential values which she might obtain after product trial. Consumers know the distribution of $v$, but no individual knows the exact value until she buys the product and tries it. Note that if $v > p_m$ means a consumer is satisfied with the product. Therefore, a higher $\bar{v}$ means the proportion of satisfied consumers is larger, or equivalently the proportion of returns is smaller.

A simple but useful construct to capture the effect of $\bar{v}$ on the selection on returns policy is to assume that the market consists of three types of consumers. One group has high valuation of the product, another group has low valuation and the rest consumers have moderate valuation of the product. Specifically, the high-valuation type is marked as $v_H = v$, the low-valuation type is $v_L = \psi_L v$ and the moderate valuation type is $v_M = \psi_M v$ $(0 < \psi_L < \psi_M < 1)$

(Li *et al.*, 2014). As a result, the distributions of the high-valuation type and the low-valuation type are $v_H \sim U[0, \bar{v}]$, $v_L \sim U[0, \psi_L \bar{v}]$ and $v_M \sim U[0, \psi_M \bar{v}]$, respectively. Obviously, the high-valuation type has higher upper bound of $v$ than the other types.

When the upper bound of $v$ is relatively low ($\bar{v} \leq v_1$), it can be interpreted as the consumers belonging to the low-valuation type. Due to the consumers' low valuation of the product, the manufacturer may experience a relatively high proportion of returns, and therefore tends to offer partial returns policy to mitigate the risk instead of offering the full returns policy. Further, when the upper bound of $v$ is moderate, the manufacturer's optimal returns policy also counts on the retailer's risk-averse level. When the retailer's risk-averse level is relatively high ($\eta < \bar{\eta}$), for the manufacturer, even if consumers have higher valuation compared to the low-valuation type, he will also provide the partial return policy to alleviate channel competition. However, if the retailer's risk-averse level is low (i.e., $\eta > \bar{\eta}$), the manufacturer could provide the full returns policy to pursue higher profit. Moreover, when the upper bound of $v$ is relatively high (e.g., $\bar{v} > v_2$), our results show that a full returns policy is optimal for the manufacturer. Under this situation, consumers belong to the high-valuation type. In practice, consumers with higher valuation are willing to pay more and they also value service more than the low-valuation type. Besides, the proportion of the returns of high-valuation type is smaller than the low-valuation type. Therefore, the manufacturer is motivated to offer a generous full returns policy to attract more high type consumers.

**Proposition 6.4.** *Given the refund amount $f$, when $\eta$ increases in the interval $[\underline{\eta}, 1]$, the manufacturer's expected profit is increasing.*

Proposition 6.4 implies that the manufacturer's expected profit is always increasing in $\eta$. Through the analysis of the manufacturer's expected profit function, we can see that the change of $\eta$ only influences the manufacturer's profit on his traditional channel. This effect is exerted by the impact of $\eta$ on the wholesale price and the order quantity. When $\eta$ increases, the order quantity will increase with it. However, the wholesale price of the manufacturer will decrease. Even though the wholesale price and the order quantity have two different trends, we reveal that manufacturer's expected profit is monotonically increasing in $\eta$. From the proof of Proposition 6.1, each unit increase in $\eta$ is associated with unit increase in order quantity. However, as $\eta$ becomes larger, each unit increase in $\eta$ is associated with less decrease in the wholesale price. Putting together, the manufacturer's expected profit is always increasing as $\eta$ increases.

## 6.4. The Buyback Revenue-Sharing Contract to Manage Channel Conflict

Dual-channel coordination is an important issue that is closely related to channel conflict management. Here, we consider when the refund amount is endogenous, how we can design a contract to coordinate the decentralized dual-channel supply chain. Before designing the contract mechanism, the centralized dual-channel supply chain will be analyzed as a benchmark. Gan *et al.* (2005) defined the concept of supply chain coordination when involving risk-averse agents under VaR. Building upon their definition, a new definition of supply chain coordination under the CVaR criterion is given here.

**Definition 6.1.** Supply chain coordination under the CVaR criterion is described as follows:

A supply chain is coordinated if the following two conditions are satisfied:

(i) each agent's profit cannot be less than that in the decentralized situation;
(ii) the expected profit of the whole supply chain is equal to that in the centralized situation.

Under the centralized case, the decisions in the supply chain are the retailer's order quantity and refund amount in the e-channel, thus the profit of the centralized supply chain is as follows:

$$\begin{aligned}\pi_{SC}^{C} &= \pi_r + \pi_m \\ &= (p_r - c)\cdot q - (p_r - s)[q - D_r]^+ + (p_m - c)\cdot \bar{G}(f)D_m \\ &\quad +(p_m - c - f + s - l)\cdot G(f)D_m. \qquad (6.8)\end{aligned}$$

Then the problem in the centralized supply chain is

$$\max_{q,f} E[\pi_{SC}^{C}], \tag{6.9}$$

$$\text{subject to} \quad f - p_2 \leq 0. \tag{6.10}$$

According to the KKT (Karush–Kuhn–Tucker) condition, the first-best solutions exist. The proof of the concavity of $E[\pi_{SC}^{C}]$ with respect to $(q, f)$ and the first-best solutions $\{q_c^*, f_c^*\}$ can be established.

Through analysis, we can find when a contract coordinates the dual-channel supply chain with risk-averse agents, it firstly makes sure that the risk-averse retailer sets an order $q_c^*$ under this contract. Meanwhile, the manufacturer may have an incentive to select the optimal refund $f_c^*$. Further, both members' performance need be Pareto improvements. As mentioned earlier, a risk-averse retailer bears double pressure from online channel's returns service and uncertainty demand in her retail channel. As a result, if the manufacturer likes to cooperate with the retailer, the retailer may have an incentive to increase her order quantity. According to the retailer's utility function, it is revealed that the retailer's risk-averse behavior is mainly reflected in the expected surplus stock and the deprived demand from the online channel.

Thus, on one hand, the manufacturer should buy back the retailer's unsold products. On the other hand, the manufacturer should share a proportion of online channel's revenue with the retailer. That is, a buyback revenue-sharing contract is proposed here to coordinate the decentralized dual-channel supply chain. The manufacturer buys back the retailer's unsold inventory at a buyback price $b(<w)$ per unit and meanwhile shares a portion $\lambda$ of the online channel's revenue with the retailer as the following proposition.

**Proposition 6.5.** *Comparing the profit in the decentralized situation with that under the benchmark, when the contract parameters $(w_b^*, b, \lambda)$ satisfy the following conditions:*

$$w_b^* = p_r - \frac{(p_r - b)(p_r - c)}{\eta(p_r - s)} \quad \text{and} \quad \lambda = 1 - \frac{\rho_r(p_r - b)(p_r - c)}{\eta\rho_2(p_r - s)p_r},$$

*the buyback revenue-sharing contract can coordinate the dual-channel supply chain with the risk-averse retailer.*

## 6.5. Competitiveness Analysis

This subsection aims to develop implications regarding the following questions: How to measure the competitiveness of the manufacturer in his online channel? By offering the consumer returns in the online channel, what effect will it have on the competitiveness of the online channel?

In fact, it is interesting to investigate the impact of the refund amount on the retailer's viability in the supply chain. First, we define a ratio $\vartheta_d = E(\pi_d)/\pi_{\mathrm{SC}}$ to evaluate the competitiveness of the online channel in the supply chain. $E(\pi_d)$ is the expected profit of the online channel and $\pi_{\mathrm{SC}}$ is the total expected profit of the supply chain. The profit of the entire supply chain $\pi_{\mathrm{SC}}$ is regarded as a profit "pie". $\vartheta_d$ is interpreted as the competitiveness of the online channel from the angle of profit share. If $\vartheta_d$ is larger, then the competitiveness of the online channel becomes greater.

Figure 6.1 illustrates the impacts of consumer returns policy on $\vartheta_d$. The input parameters are set as follows: $s = 38$, $c = 58$, $l = 10$, $D = 500$, $U = 200$, $p_r = 330$, $p_m = 300$, $\rho_r = 0.2$, $\rho_m = 0.3$, $\alpha = 0.5$. Furthermore, we set $\bar{v} = 2000$ and $\bar{v} = 2400$, respectively, in this experiment to reveal the impacts of consumer valuation uncertainty.

From Fig. 6.1, we can see that $\vartheta_d$ is monotonically increasing in $f$. This means larger refund amount leads to greater competitiveness of the online channel. This phenomenon is intuitive. Note that online consumers are unable to actually see and inspect the products before purchasing. Providing the consumer returns policy can enhance consumers' purchasing confidence and the competitiveness of the online channel. For the online consumer, the more generous the returns policy is, the more purchase intention they have. Therefore, a higher refund amount leads to greater competitiveness. When $\theta$ is lower, the share of basic demand going to the online channel $(1-\theta)$ is relatively larger. Therefore, the competitiveness of the online channel is decreasing as $\theta$ increases. Besides, according to Proposition 6.3, the manufacturer's optimal returns policies are partial returns and full returns under the data set in Figs. 6.1(a) and 6.1(b), respectively. By comparing them, we find that the competitiveness of the online channel is always increasing in the refund amount.

Further, Chow *et al.* (2015) defined minimum profit share ratio (MPSR) as the retailer's profit over the whole supply chain profit.

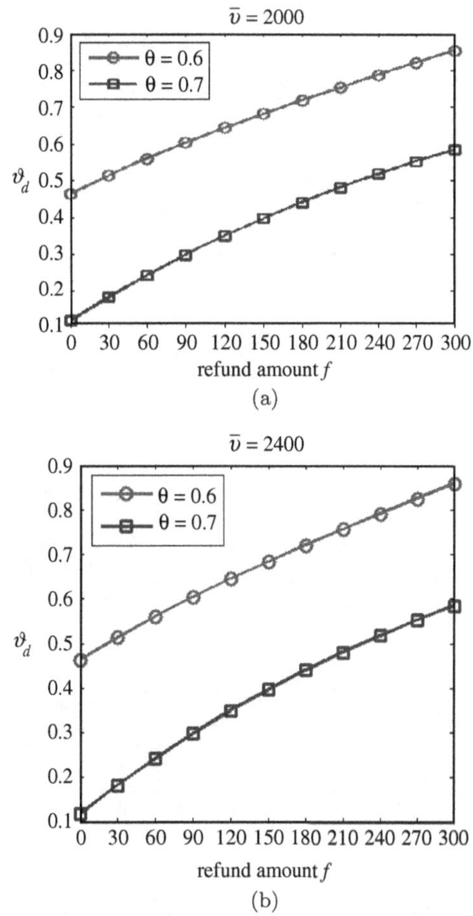


Fig. 6.1. The impact of refund amount on the competitiveness of online channels. (a) Under consumer valuation uncertainty $\bar{\upsilon} = 2000$ and (b) under consumer valuation uncertainty $\bar{\upsilon} = 2400$.

They mentioned that MPSR is related to the retailer's fairness concern. Here we define $\psi_r = \text{CVaR}(\pi_r)/\pi_{\text{SC}}$ as the retailer's profit share in the supply chain, which is an indicator on behalf of a firm's profitability. The larger $\psi_r$ means the retailer's survival ability is greater.

Through Fig. 6.2, we can see that when the market demand is low ($D = 500$), the retailer's profit share is decreasing in the refund amount $f$. When the market demand is moderate ($D = 600$), the

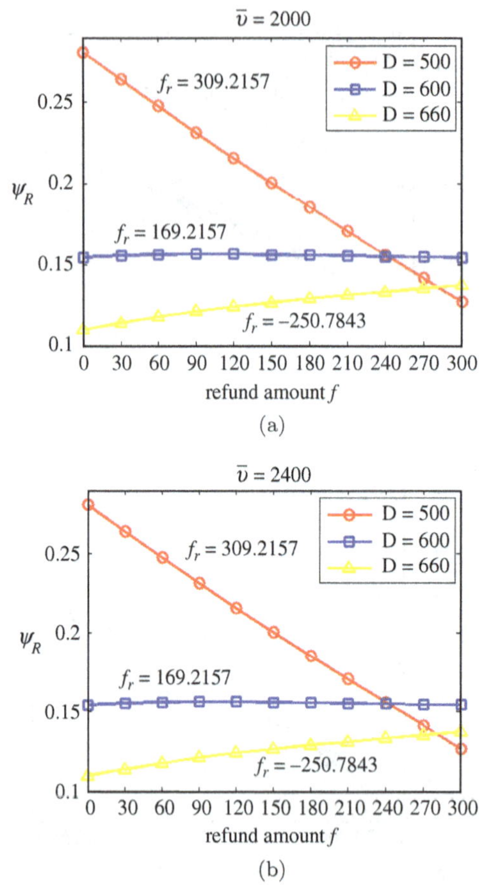


Fig. 6.2. The impact of refund amount on retailer's profit share. (a) Under consumer valuation uncertainty $\bar{v} = 2000$ and (b) under consumer valuation uncertainty $\bar{v} = 2400$.

retailer's expected utility is concave in $f$. Recall that in Proposition 6.2, we defined a threshold $f_r$ to judge the trend of the retailer's expected utility in $f$ and the thresholds are also showed in Fig. 6.2. When $D = 660$, $f_r = 309.2157$, thus the retailer's expected utility is monotonically increasing in $f$. Consequently, the growing speed of $\psi_r$ is larger when $f$ increases. Surprisingly, when the retailer's basic market demand is relatively high ($D = 660$), we find that providing the consumer returns policy in the online channel may benefit the retailer from both perspectives of her expected utility and market profit share.

Based on the numerical results, we can find that when the manufacturer offers the consumer a returns policy in the supply chain, with the refund amount increasing, then

(1) the competitiveness of the online channel is monotonically increasing;
(2) the retailer's profit share in the supply chain is increasing or firstly increasing then decreasing.

## 6.6. Conclusion

This chapter examines a dual-channel supply chain with a risk-neutral manufacturer and a risk-averse retailer, where the manufacturer provides a consumer returns policy, and consumers face valuation uncertainty of the product in the online channel. CVaR criterion is applied to evaluate the risk-averse behavior of the retailer. We focus on how customers' returns policy and the agent's risk-averse behavior influence the equilibrium solutions and performance of the supply chain.

One of our main conclusions is that the manufacturer's optimal returns policy is related to the consumer types. Facing the low-valuation type, the manufacturer should offer a partial returns policy; because under this situation, a full returns policy is so generous that the manufacturer has to bear too much costs of returns. Otherwise, the manufacturer is motivated to offer a generous full returns policy to attract high type consumers. When the consumer has moderate valuation of the product, the optimal returns policy depends on the retailer's risk-averse level. It is surprising that the retailer's expected utility may monotonically increase in the refund amount under the double pressure of manufacturer encroachment and returns service. A set of threshold values have been obtained to characterize the relationship between the retailer's expected utility and the manufacturer's refund amount, which can be determined when the retailer will achieve the maximum expected utility under a given risk-averse level. Furthermore, a buyback revenue-sharing contract is developed to coordinate the decentralized dual-channel supply chain compared with the centralized benchmark model. A number of numerical examples have been provided to verify our analytical results.

## References


Arya, A., Mittendorf, B., & Sappington, D. E. (2007). The bright side of supplier encroachment. *Marketing Science*, 26(5), pp. 651–659.

Bhatnagar, A., & Syam, S. S. (2014). Allocating a hybrid retailer's assortment across retail stores: Bricks-and-mortar vs online. *Journal of Business Research*, 67(6), pp. 1293–1302.

Chen, J., & Bell, P. C. (2012). Implementing market segmentation using full-refund and no-refund customer returns policies in a dual-channel supply chain structure. *International Journal of Production Economics*, 136(1), pp. 56–66.

Choi, T. M., Li, D., & Yan, H. (2008). Mean–variance analysis of a single supplier and retailer supply chain under a returns policy. *European Journal of Operational Research*, 184(1), pp. 356–376.

Chow, P. S., Wang, Y., Choi, T. M., & Shen, B. (2015). An experimental study on the effects of minimum profit share on supply chains with markdown contract: Risk and profit analysis. *Omega*, 57, pp. 85–97.

Gan, X., Sethi, S. P., & Yan, H. (2005). Channel coordination with a risk-neutral supplier and a downside-risk-averse retailer. *Production and Operations Management*, 14(1), pp. 80–89.

Hsiao, L., & Chen, Y. J. (2012). Returns policy and quality risk in e-business. *Production and Operations Management*, 21(3), pp. 489–503.

Jiang, Y. S., Li, B., and Song, D. P. (2017). Analysing consumer RP in a dual-channel supply chain with a risk-averse retailer. *European Journal of Industrial Engineering*, 11(3), pp. 271–302.

Lee, P. M. (2002). Behavioral model of online purchasers in e-commerce environment. *Electronic Commerce Research*, 2(1–2), pp. 75–85.

Li, Y., Xu, L., & Li, D. (2013). Examining relationships between the return policy, product quality, and pricing strategy in online direct selling. *International Journal of Production Economics*, 144(2), pp. 451–460.

Li, Y., Xu, L., Choi, T. M., & Govindan, K. (2014). Optimal advance-selling strategy for fashionable products with opportunistic consumers returns. *IEEE Transactions on Systems, Man, and Cybernetics: Systems*, 44(7), pp. 938–952.

Li, Z., Gilbert, S. M., & Lai, G. (2014). Supplier encroachment under asymmetric information. *Management Science*, 60(2), pp. 449–462.

Li, Z., Gilbert, S. M., & Lai, G. (2015). Supplier encroachment as an enhancement or a hindrance to nonlinear pricing. *Production and Operations Management*, 15(1), pp. 89–109.

Liu, J., Mantin, B., & Wang, H. (2014). Supply chain coordination with customer returns and refund-dependent demand. *International Journal of Production Economics*, 148, pp. 81–89.

Lu, Q., & Liu, N. (2013). Pricing games of mixed conventional and e-commerce distribution channels. *Computers & Industrial Engineering*, 64(1), pp. 122–132.

Rao, S., Rabinovich, E., & Raju, D. (2014). The role of physical distribution services as determinants of product returns in Internet retailing. *Journal of Operations Management*, 32(6), pp. 295–312.

Su, X. (2009). Consumer returns policies and supply chain performance. *Manufacturing & Service Operations Management*, 11(4), pp. 595–612.

Sullivan, E. A. (2009). Guaranteeing success. *Marketing News*, 43(8), p. 20.

Suwelack, T., Hogreve, J., & Hoyer, W. D. (2011). Understanding money-back guarantees: Cognitive, affective, and behavioral outcomes. *Journal of Retailing*, 87(4), pp. 462–478.

Trager, I. (2000). Not so many happy returns. *Interactive Week*, 7(11), pp. 44–45.

Wood, S. L. (2001). Remote purchase environments: The influence of return policy leniency on two-stage decision processes. *Journal of Marketing Research*, 38(2), pp. 157–169.

Xiao, T. J., Shi, K. R., & Yang, D. Q. (2010). Coordination of a supply chain with consumer return under demand uncertainty. *International Journal of Production Economics*, 124(1), pp. 171–180.

© 2022 World Scientific Publishing Europe Ltd.
https://doi.org/10.1142/9781800610408_0007

# Chapter 7

# Financing Strategies in a Capital-Constrained Supply Chain with a Risk-Averse Supplier

**Bo Li**[*,‡], **Simin An**[*,§], **and Dong-Ping Song**[†,¶]

[*] *College of Management and Economics, Tianjin University, China*
[†] *School of Management, University of Liverpool, Liverpool, UK*
[‡] *libo0410@tju.edu.cn*
[§] *ansm@tju.edu.cn*
[¶] *Dongping.Song@liverpool.ac.uk*

## 7.1. Introduction

In the past 30 years, small and medium-sized enterprises (SMEs) have played an important role in economic development. According to Business Registration Statistics, as of the end of 2016, there were more than 40 million SMEs in China, accounting for 60% of GDP (sme.gov.cn). However, with the outbreak of the global economic crisis, SMEs are facing financing difficulties or expensive financing problems. In particular, due to their low credit rate and high default risk, it is difficult for them to borrow money from banks to perform or expand their normal business, that is, the financing gap of SMEs (Hussain *et al.*, 2006; Jaffee and Russell, 1976). In recent years, supply chain financing (SCF) has received more and more attention as a means to solve the financing difficulties of SMEs and has been widely used in practice. SCF's innovative approach not only helps SMEs obtain loans, but also protects the entire supply chain from bankruptcy risks (Cai *et al.*, 2014; Fisher and Raman, 1996; Kouvelis and Zhao, 2012). SCF has two typical financing methods: bank credit financing (BCF) and TCF. The former adopts an external perspective of the supply chain, while the latter adopts an internal perspective (Kouvelis and Zhao, 2012).

In terms of BCF, due to immature market mechanisms, highly imperfect information, and default risks, it is often difficult for SMEs to directly obtain bank loans (Hussain *et al.*, 2006; Kouvelis and Zhao, 2012). Therefore, capital-constrained SMEs may have to resort to informal financial institutions for loans and be forced to pay higher loan costs (Chen *et al.*, 2016). In order to make full use of bank loans, a PCG can be designed to allow SMEs to obtain bank loans (Yan *et al.*, 2016). The core enterprise in the supply chain is the core enterprise in the supply chain that has more credit information of the SMEs than the bank. With the help of the core enterprise credit guarantee, even if the SME defaults, the guarantee enterprise will fill any part of the SME loan gap, so that the SME is more likely to obtain bank credit. In addition, PCG can be regarded as a form of insurance, which can protect banks from the possibility of SMEs' refusal to pay. If the credit of SMEs is insured, banks are willing to provide SMEs with extensive credit facilities. In fact, there have been many applications for credit guarantee programs all over the world. For example, in 2012, of nearly 90,000 guarantees in Europe, about 2.8 billion euros were provided by the credit guarantee scheme (eib.org). In addition, according to a report by the Vienna Initiative Working Group, more than 75% in Central, Eastern and Southeastern Europe of banks have PCG loans (eib.org). Similarly, China's commercial banks, such as Industrial and Commercial Bank of China (ICBC), Everbright Bank Ningbo Branch (China Everbright Bank), provide credit for many core companies in the tight supply chain guarantee contract. If the core enterprise is an upstream supplier, then downstream retailers can obtain bank loans through a credit guarantee contract. Under this contract, downstream SMEs can obtain loans without mortgage assets. With credit support from upstream suppliers, downstream SMEs can fill the financial gap and reduce financing costs. At the same time, upstream companies can speed up the return of funds and organize production as soon as possible.

On the other hand, TCF is a short-term method of debt financing between upstream suppliers and downstream retailers in a capital-constrained supply chain (Cai *et al.*, 2014). In other words, in addition to the traditional production role, upstream suppliers also play the role of investors. The lender will recover the delayed interest payment from the borrower at the end of the sale period. For example, in most American companies, TCF is the largest source of working capital, especially for small and medium enterprises. More specifically, in the United States in 1991, TCF accounted for 17.8% of the company's total assets, while in European countries such as France, Germany and Italy, TCF accounted for more than 15% of the company's assets (Rajan and Zingales, 1995). According to a survey of 674 companies on the Shenzhen and Shanghai stock exchanges from 2001 to 2007, TCF accounted for 9.1% of the total assets of Chinese companies (Cai *et al.*, 2014).

When a supplier provides credit/financing support to SMEs through PCG or TCF, there may be moral hazard issues because the retailer may go bankrupt or transfer cash to other projects. Therefore, the supplier must bear significant risks. In addition, the PCG or TCF strategy can be regarded as a risk transfer mechanism (Beck *et al.*, 2010), which increases the supplier's risk by providing credit guarantees or directly assuming bankruptcy risks. Specifically, there is evidence that the tail risk of core companies is greater than that of SMEs. It is reasonable that the supplier may take the risk-averse attitude when making decisions. Therefore, we will focus on situations where the supplier is a risk-averse and the retailer is risk-neutral in a single-channel supply chain considering demand uncertainty and bankruptcy risks. We will also discuss the extension of the model to the situation of dual-channel supply chain later on.

This chapter attempts to introduce the supplier's risk aversion behavior into the capital-constrained supply chain model, and study the interactive influence of credit guarantee parameters and risk aversion attitudes on the decision-making and profit of supply chain members. We aim to address the following research questions (Li *et al.*, 2018):

(1) Under the PCG and TCF strategies, how does the supplier's risk aversion behavior affect the decision-making and performance of supply chain members?

(2) How does the combination of key parameters such as credit guarantee coefficient and risk aversion indicators affect the decision-making and performance of the two participants under the PCG and TCF strategies?
(3) Which financing strategy do supplier and the retailer prefer? How do key parameters affect the choice of financing strategies of the two participants? In the choice of financing strategy, is there a win–win situation for the two participants?

More specifically, we consider a supply chain consisting of a core supplier (he) and a small and medium retailer (she). Before the sales season, the supplier makes wholesale pricing decisions and the retailer makes order quantity decisions. The retailer faces uncertain demand. We use CVaR to measure the supplier's risk aversion attitude, and merge it into a risk aversion newsboy problem.

The chapter is organized as follows. Section 7.2 defines the notations and presents the mathematical model under CVaR criterion. Section 7.3 derives the equilibrium solutions under PCG and TCF strategy, including the optimal order quantity and wholesale prices. Section 7.4 compares the performance of the supply chain under the two financing strategies. Section 7.5 extends the model to the case in a dual-channel setting. Section 7.6 draws the conclusions.

## 7.2. Model Description

This section studies a newsboy model of a single-cycle supply chain system consisting of a supplier and a retailer, in which the supplier has sufficient funds to support their production activities, but the retailer must rely on external funding sources to maintain their business activities. The retailer has no capital endowments and needs to borrow from banks or through trade credit contracts (Jing *et al.*, 2012). We consider two financing strategies: one where the retailer obtains a loan from the bank under the supplier's guarantee (PCG case), and the other where the supplier provides funds to the retailer and allows them to delay payment until the end of the period (TCF case). Obviously, in both cases, there may be moral hazard issues, because the retailer may go bankrupt or transfer cash to other items. Therefore, it is reasonable to consider the supplier's risk aversion behavior in SCM. We use CVaR standards to measure supplier risk aversion.

We assume that the uncertain demand $y$ is an absolutely continuous random variable with a cumulative distribution function that will not be realized until the end of the season. The probability density function is $f(y)$ ($f(y) > 0$ on $[0, +\infty]$), $\bar{F}(y) = 1 - F(y) \cdot h(y) = f(y)/\bar{F}(y)$ is the hazard rate that is assumed to increase in $y$. $c$ per unit is the production cost of the supplier, the supplier decides his wholesale price and the retail price $p$ is exogenous, where $p \geq w > c$. There are no other costs for both the retailer and supplier. Prior to the sale season, the retailer decides the order quantity $q$. For convenience, we assume that any excess inventory has no salvage value. In particular, we assume that the supplier and the retailer have symmetric information. In the PCG case, the upstream supplier provides a partial guarantee for the retailer. Here we assume that the credit guarantee coefficient is $\lambda$. For ease of description, we define the relevant notations in the following table.

| Parameters | Definition |
|---|---|
| $y$ | the random demand, where the probability density function is $f(y)$ and the distribution function is $F(y)$ |
| $p$ | the retail price which is exogenous |
| $q^j$ | the order quantity of the retailer, which is the decision variable of the retailer, where $j = P, T$ represents the two cases under PCG and TCF |
| $w^j$ | the wholesale price, which is the decision variable of the supplier, where $j = P, T$ represents the two cases under PCG and TCF |
| $c$ | the production cost per unit of the supplier |
| $R^P$ | the commercial bank's interest rate under PCG |
| $R^T$ | the interest rate of the supplier to the retailer under TCF |
| $\lambda$ | the credit guarantee coefficient of the supplier |
| $\eta$ | the supplier's degree of risk aversion |
| $\pi_i^j$ | the decision-maker's profit function, where $j = P, T$ represents the two cases under PCG and TCF, and $i = r, s$ represents the retailer and the supplier respectively |

This problem is described as a Stackelberg game of a single sales season, in which the supplier is the leader and the retailer is the follower. The timeliness of the game is shown as follows: First, given the commercial bank interest rate, the supplier provides the retailer with a credit guarantee or commercial credit contract, and announces the wholesale price: a wholesale price $w^P$ under PCG at the beginning of sale season, or a postponed wholesale price $w^T$ at the end of the sale season under TCF. We define the postponed wholesale price as $w^T = w(1 + R^T)$, in which $w$ is the wholesale price and $R^T$ is an interest rate prior to the sale season. This setting could reduce the supplier's decision variables in the TCF case (Jing *et al.*, 2012). Secondly, after observing the wholesale price $w^P$ or $w^T$ of the supplier under PCG or TCF, the retailer will decide the order quantity $q^P$ or $q^T$.

In both PCG and TCF cases, once the retailer cannot repay the loan, the supplier must repay part of the loan to the bank and bear the loss that the retailer cannot pay. Therefore, the supplier will naturally show risk aversion behavior. Here, in order to measure the impact of supplier risk aversion, the CVaR standard is selected to calculate the average profit below $\eta$-quantile level, where $\eta$ ($\eta \in (0, 1]$) is the degree of risk aversion, which is also called the supplier's confidence in reaching a certain profit level $v$ (Rockafellar and Uryasev, 2002). In fact, the smaller $\eta$, the higher the supplier's risk aversion. When $\eta = 0$, it means the supplier is extremely risk-averse; on the contrary, when $\eta = 1$, it means that the supplier is risk-neutral.

According to the definition of CVaR by Rockafellar and Uryasev (2000), the supplier's utility is defined as

$$CVaR_\eta(\pi(w, q)) = \max_{v \in R} \left\{ v - \frac{1}{\eta} E[v - \pi(w, q)]^+ \right\}, \quad \eta \in (0, 1], \tag{7.1}$$

where $\pi(w, q)$ is the supplier's profit function and $R$ represents the set of real numbers.

## 7.3. The Equilibrium Solutions with a Risk-Averse Supplier

This section will derive the equilibrium solutions to the models under PCG and TCF strategy, respectively. The impacts of the risk-averse indicator and other parameters on the optimal decisions will be analyzed.

### 7.3.1. Equilibrium under PCG strategy

Under PCG, we consider a Stackelberg game model in which the supplier acts as a leader and the retailer acts as a follower. Firstly, the supplier announces the wholesale price $w^P$, and then the retailer decides the order quantity $q^P$ after observing the wholesale price. The retailer has no capital endowment, but she can obtain loan $w^P q^P$ from the commercial bank with the credit guarantee from the upstream supplier.

At the end of the sales season, the retailer generates revenue $p\min\{y, q^P\}$, and needs to repay the bank loan and interest, that is $w^P q^P(1 + R^P)$ when $p\min\{y, q^P\} \geq w^P q^P(1 + R^P)$. If the retailer obtains revenue $p\min\{y, q^P\} < w^P q^P(1 + R^P)$, then the retailer has to repay all his revenue to the bank. As the creditor, the supplier has the responsibility to repay the partial loan to the bank, that is $\lambda[w^P q^P(1 + R^P) - p\min\{y, q^P\}]$. We assume that $p \geq w^P(1 + R^P)$ to avoid the trivial scenes (in which the retailer would not be able to stay in the game).

Let $E\pi_r^p$ be the retailer's expected profit under PCG, and then $E\pi_r^p$ can be given by

$$E\pi_r^p = E[p\min\{y, q^P\} - \min\{p\min\{y, q^P\}, w^P q^P(1 + R^P)\}]. \quad (7.2)$$

Solving Eq. (7.2) with the backward induction method, we have the following result. Given the wholesale price $w^P$ of the supplier in a capital-constrained supply chain under PCG, the retailer's optimal order quantity response function $q^{P^*}$ satisfies the following equation if $q^{P^*}$ is a stationary point:

$$p - w^P(1 + R^P) - pF(q^{P^*}) + w^P(1 + R^P)F\left(\frac{w^P q^{P^*}(1 + R^P)}{p}\right) = 0.$$

The similar results can be seen in Chen (2015).

In addition, the supplier's profit function under PCG can be expressed as

$$\pi_s^P = (w^P - c)q^P - \lambda[w^P q^P(1 + R^P) - p\min\{y, q^P\}]^+. \quad (7.3)$$

For the supplier's risk aversion attitude, we adopt the CVaR metric. Then, the supplier's objective function is as follows:

$$\mathrm{CVaR}_\eta(\pi_s^P(w^P)) = \max_{w^P \geq c, v \in R}\left\{v - \frac{1}{\eta}E[v - \pi_s^P(w^P)]^+\right\}. \quad (7.4)$$

Let

$$\begin{aligned}k(v,w^P) &= v - \frac{1}{\eta}E[v - \pi_s^P(w^P)]^+ \\ &= v - \frac{1}{\eta}\int_0^{\frac{w^P q^P(1+R^P)}{p}} [v - (w^P - c)q^P \\ &\quad + \lambda[w^P q^P(1+R^P) - py]]^+ dF(y) \\ &\quad - \frac{1}{\eta}\int_{\frac{w^P q^P(1+R^P)}{p}}^{+\infty} [v - (w^P - c)q^P]^+ dF(y). \qquad (7.5)\end{aligned}$$

Here $[y]^+ = \max\{y, 0\}$, when $y > 0$, $[y]^+ = y$; otherwise $[y]^+ = 0$. Obviously, $k(v, w^P)$ is a concave function in terms of $v$, and the optimal $v$ can be obtained by maximizing Eq. (7.5).

In order to facilitate the comparison between PCG and TCF, we assume that the demand uncertainty obeys a uniform distribution $U[0, u]$. We have the following proposition.

**Proposition 7.1.** *In a capital-constrained supply chain under PCG, if the demand uncertainty $y$ follows a uniform distribution $[0, u]$, then the optimal wholesale price of the credit guaranteed supplier and the optimal ordering quantity of the retailer are as follows:*

$$w^{P^*} = \begin{cases} \dfrac{\eta p(c + p + R^P c)}{(1+R^P)[(1+R^P)(\lambda p - c\eta) - \eta p]}, & \underline{\eta} < \eta \le \eta_1, \\ \dfrac{p}{1+R^P}, & \eta > \eta_1, \end{cases}$$

$$q^{P^*} = \begin{cases} \dfrac{u[(1+R^P)(\lambda p - c\eta) - \eta p]}{\lambda p(1+R^P)}, & \underline{\eta} < \eta \le \eta_1, \\ \dfrac{u}{2}, & \eta > \eta_1, \end{cases}$$

*where*

$$\underline{\eta} = \frac{c\lambda p(1+R^P)^2}{(c+p+cR^P)^2}, \quad \eta_1 = \frac{\lambda p(1+R^P)}{2(c+p+cR^P)}.$$

Note that $w^P$ is constrained by $c \le w^P \le p/(1+R^P)$. When $\eta \le \underline{\eta}$, we have $w^{P^*} = c$. This means that when the supplier is highly risk-averse (that is, the risk aversion index is less than $\underline{\eta}$), the supplier will not get any profit and has no intention of signing a PCG contract. It can be seen from Proposition 7.1 that the supply chain is only feasible when the supplier's risk aversion index $\eta > \eta_1$, which means that if the supplier avoids risks enough, the game does not exist.

On the other hand, when $\eta > \eta_1$ we have $w^{P^*} = p/(1 + R^P)$ and $E\pi_r^P = 0$. This means that when the supplier's risk aversion is low or relatively optimistic (that is, the risk aversion index is greater than $\eta_1$), the optimistic supplier will set the wholesale price at the upper threshold to capture the retailer's total revenue. In fact, credit guarantee schemes are like selling put options on financial projects (Honohan, 2010). When upstream supplier provides the retailer with loan guarantees, they have an incentive to set higher wholesale prices to increase their profitability.

The above discussion shows that if the supplier is too risk-averse, he will get negative profits; if the supplier tends to be risk-neutral, the retailer will not get profits. This provides theoretical support for the supplier's risk aversion behavior in the supply chain. Otherwise, the supply chain cannot be sustained.

We will focus on the risk-averse indicator being in the interval $(\underline{\eta}, \eta_1)$ to avoid trivial cases in the following analysis under PCG. The impact of the supplier's risk-averse indicator $\eta$, operational cost $c$, and credit guarantee coefficient $\lambda$ on the optimal decision variables is given in the following corollary.

**Corollary 7.1.** *Under PCG, when* $\underline{\eta} < \eta < \eta_1$, *the following properties exist*:

(1) $dw^{P^*}/d\eta > 0$, $dq^{P^*}/d\eta < 0$;
(2) $dw^{P^*}/dc > 0$, $dq^{P^*}/dc < 0$;
(3) $dw^{P^*}/d\lambda < 0$, $dq^{P^*}/d\lambda > 0$.

Corollary 7.1(1) means that the optimal wholesale price of risk aversion supplier increases with the increase of the risk aversion factor $\eta$, while the retailer's optimal order quantity decreases with the increase of the risk aversion factor $\eta$. The smaller $\eta$, the stronger the supplier's ability to avoid risks, the lower the supplier's optimal wholesale price, and the higher the retailer's optimal order quantity. This phenomenon can be explained as a risk-averse supplier will set a lower wholesale price to attract the retailer; if the supplier's wholesale price drops, the retailer's order volume will increase. Corollary 7.1(2) is intuitively correct. From Corollary 7.1(3), it can be seen that the credit guarantee coefficient $\lambda$ has a negative impact on the optimal wholesale price, while the opposite is true for the optimal order quantity. Obviously, when the credit guarantee coefficient is small, the retailer will reduce the optimal order quantity in order to avoid bankruptcy risk, and the supplier will increase the wholesale price to make up for the marginal profit. However, in order to ensure that the wholesale price is relatively large, the retailer will lower its order quantity when the guaranteed price is relatively large. Corollary 7.1(3) can be explained from the perspective of risk aversion, and can also be explained from Corollary 7.1(1), because larger $\lambda$ means the supplier's risk is higher, which is equivalent to having a smaller $\eta$.

### 7.3.2. Equilibrium under TCF strategy

In this section, we study the case of the risk-averse supplier providing TCF to the retailer under the $\eta$-CVaR standard. At the beginning of the sales season, the supplier announces the wholesale price $w$ and interest rate $R^T$ in the trade credit scenario. The delayed wholesale price at the end of the sales period can be defined as $w^T = w(1+R^T)$. By introducing delayed wholesale price $w^T$, it is possible to simplify the supplier's decision variables, and then design delayed payment contracts for the retailer. The retailer determines the order quantity $q^T$ by observing the wholesale price and obtains a loan $w^T q^T$ from the supplier. At the end of this period, if the retailer's income can cover her loan, she should repay her deferred payment and interest. Otherwise, the retailer will repay all income and declare bankruptcy.

Given $w^T$, the retailer's expected profit function under TCF is similar to the expected profit function under PCG, so the retailer's optimal order quantity $q^{T*}$ at a fixed point satisfies the following equation:

$$p - w^T - pF(q^{T*}) + w^T F\left(\frac{w^T q^{T*}}{p}\right) = 0. \tag{7.6}$$

Under TCF, the supplier 's profit function is given by

$$\pi_s^T = \min\{py, w^T q^T\} - cq^T. \tag{7.7}$$

Similarly, using CVaR measurement, the supplier's CVaR profit maximization problem is

$$\mathrm{CVaR}_\eta(\pi_s^T(w^T)) = \max_{w^T \geq c, v \in R} \left\{ v - \frac{1}{\eta} E[v - \pi_s^T(w^T)]^+ \right\}.$$

Assuming that the uncertain demand $y$ follows a uniform distribution $[0, u]$, we can obtain the following proposition.

**Proposition 7.2.** *Assuming that the random demand $y$ follows a uniform distribution $[0, u]$, then under TCF, the optimal wholesale price of the risk-averse supplier and the optimal ordering quantity of the retailer are*

$$w^{T*} = \begin{cases} \dfrac{\eta p(c+p)}{(1-\eta)p - c\eta}, & \underline{\eta}' < \eta \leq \eta_2, \\ p, & \eta > \eta_2, \end{cases}$$

$$q^{T*} = \begin{cases} \dfrac{u[p - \eta(c+p)]}{p}, & \underline{\eta}' < \eta \leq \eta_2, \\ \dfrac{u}{2}, & \eta > \eta_2, \end{cases}$$

*where*

$$\underline{\eta}' = \frac{cp}{(c+p)^2}, \quad \eta_2 = \frac{p}{2(c+p)}.$$

Similar to the case of PCG, when $\eta \leq \underline{\eta}'$, we have $w^{T*} = c$, and this implies that the supplier will have no intention of continuing this contract and earn negative profit. When $\eta > \eta_2$, the optimistic supplier will seize the retailer's total revenue, which results in the retailer with no profit.

Under TCF, because $\frac{dw^{T*}}{d\eta} = \frac{p^2(c+p)}{(c\eta - p + \eta p)^2} > 0$ (when $\underline{\eta}' < \eta \leq \eta_2$), supplier's optimal wholesale price increases in the risk-averse factor. However, due to $\frac{dq^{T*}}{d\eta} = -\frac{u(c+p)}{p} < 0$ (when $\underline{\eta}' < \eta \leq \eta_2$), the capital-constrained retailer's optimal order quantity decreases in the risk-averse factor. Thus, we can see that under TCF, the relationships between optimal wholesale price, order quantity, and risk-averse factor are the same as those under PCG scenario.

Moreover, it should be noted that the feasible intervals of the risk-averse factor $\eta$ under PCG and TCF are different. We compare the feasible intervals $(\underline{\eta}, \eta_1)$ in Proposition 7.1 with $(\underline{\eta}', \eta_2)$ in Proposition 7.2 in terms of their lower and upper bounds, respectively. As for the upper bounds, we find that there exists a threshold level of the guarantee coefficient $\lambda_0 = \frac{c(1+R^P)+p}{(1+R^P)(c+p)}$ such that $\eta_1 < \eta_2$ when $\lambda < \lambda_0$; and $\eta_1 > \eta_2$ when $\lambda > \lambda_0$. This implies that when the credit guarantee coefficient of the supplier is limited by $\lambda_0$, the upper bound of the feasible interval under PCG is smaller than that under TCF and vice versa. As for the lower bounds, there also exists a threshold level of the guarantee coefficient $\lambda_0^2$, such that $\underline{\eta} < \underline{\eta}'$ when $\lambda < \lambda_0^2$; and $\underline{\eta} > \underline{\eta}'$ when $\lambda > \lambda_0^2$. This shows that when the supplier tends to extreme risk aversion, the supplier under TCF will have a negative effect, so he has no intention of participating in the game. However, in the PCG mode, when the guarantee coefficient is lower than the threshold level $\lambda_0^2$, the supplier who are extremely risk-averse will still remain in the game and profit.

In order to clarify the difference between the feasible intervals under PCG and TCF, we numerically display the feasible intervals in the $(\eta, \lambda)$ two-dimensional space shown in Fig. 7.1. In light of Buzacott and Zhang (2004), we suppose $p = 2.5$, $R^P = 0.1$, $c = 0.4$, and that the demand follows a uniform distribution with a mean value of 5. When the supplier tends to be extremely risk-averse ($\eta < \max\{\underline{\eta}, \underline{\eta}'\}$), we can see $\underline{\eta} < \underline{\eta}'$ when $\lambda < \lambda_0^2$; and $\underline{\eta} > \underline{\eta}'$ when $\lambda > \lambda_0^2$. This shows that when the guarantee ratio is less than the threshold level $\lambda_0^2$, the extreme risk-averse supplier will stay in the game under PCG, which is represented by the area AOB in Fig. 7.1(a). In the TCF model, since he is simultaneously responsible for operation and financial functions, the extreme risk-averse supplier ($\eta < \underline{\eta}'$) will face negative utility, so he will withdraw from the game. When the guarantee ratio exceeds the threshold level $\lambda_0^2$, the supplier who is extremely risk-averse will face huge guarantee risks and thus withdraw from the game under PCG. Under TCF, the supplier with a high degree of risk aversion will continue to participate in the game, which is represented by the region AHJ in Fig. 7.1(b).

Secondly, consider that the supplier is not very risk-averse, i.e., $\eta > \max\{\underline{\eta}, \underline{\eta}'\}$. Under the guarantee coefficient $\lambda < \lambda_0$, the feasible region under PCG is represented by the ABCD region in Fig. 7.1(a), and the feasible region under TCF is given by AEFCD in Fig. 7.1(b).

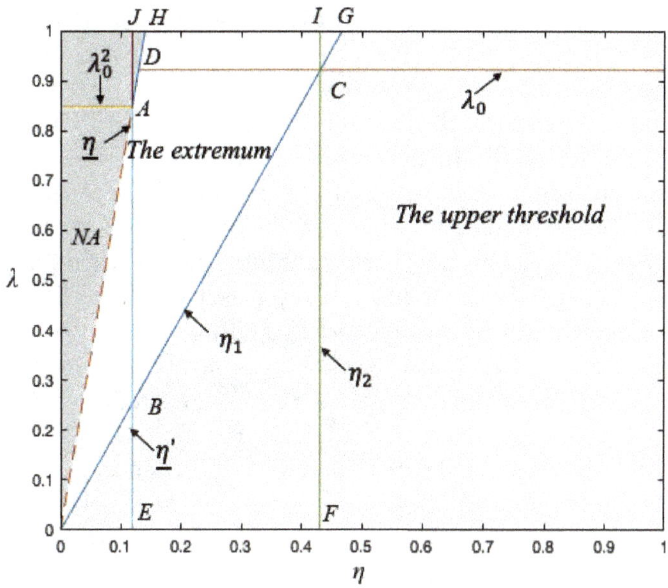


(a)

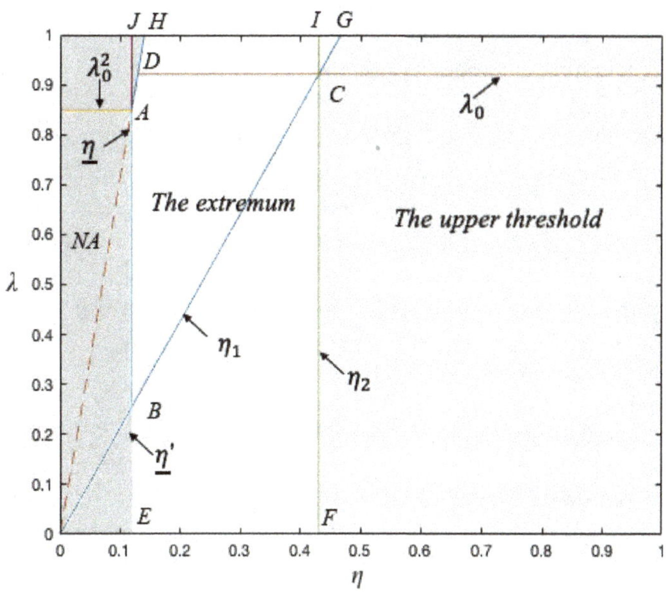


(b)

Fig. 7.1. The region comparisons under (a) PCG and (b) TCF with respect to the risk-averse factor.

In these regions, the supplier with higher risk aversion will set their optimal wholesale prices at the extreme point, while a relatively optimistic supplier will choose the upper limit to obtain the retailer's total income. Therefore, the extreme value area under PCG is smaller than that under TCF. In other words, the upper threshold of the PCG group is larger than the TCF group. This is because when the guarantee coefficient is less than the threshold, even if the supplier tends to avoid risks, the supplier's guarantee risk is within an acceptable range. Therefore, he is more likely to set the wholesale price at the upper limit under PCG instead of TCF.

When $\lambda > \lambda_0$, the guaranteed ratio is large, the extreme value interval under PCG is slightly larger than the extreme value interval under TCF (that is, the area DCGH in Fig. 7.1(a) is greater than the area DCIH in Fig. 7.1(b)). Therefore, in order to avoid guarantee risks, the supplier is more inclined to set the wholesale price at an extreme value instead of setting it at an upper threshold. This illustrates how the guarantee coefficient and risk aversion indicators affect the supplier's wholesale price strategy.

## 7.4. Comparative Analysis

In this section, we aim to establish further managerial insights by comparing the optimal decisions under the two financing strategies obtained in Sec. 7.3, assuming that the uncertain demand $y$ follows a uniform distribution $[0, u]$. To avoid trivial and tedious scenarios, we only consider the situations that $\eta$ is greater than $\max\{\underline{\eta}, \underline{\eta}'\}$.

Comparing the optimal profits and utilities of two members under the two strategies, we can obtain the following results.

**Proposition 7.3.** *Comparing the optimal performances of the chain members under PCG and TCF, we have the following properties:*

(1) *With regard to the optimal expected profit of the retailer:*
   (i) *if* $\lambda < \lambda_0$ *and* $\max\{\underline{\eta}, \underline{\eta}'\} < \eta < \max\{\eta_1, \eta_2\}$, *then* $E(\pi_r^{P^*}) < E(\pi_r^{T*})$;
   (ii) *if* $\lambda_0 \leq \lambda \leq 1$ *and* $\max\{\underline{\eta}, \underline{\eta}'\} < \eta < \max\{\eta_1, \eta_2\}$, *then* $E(\pi_r^{P^*}) > E(\pi_r^{T*})$;
   (iii) *for any* $\lambda$, *if* $\eta \geq \max\{\eta_1, \eta_2\}$, *then* $E(\pi_r^{P^*}) = E(\pi_r^{T*})$.

(2) *With regard to the optimal utility of the supplier:*
   (i) *if* $\lambda < \lambda_0^2$ *and* $\underline{\eta}' < \eta \leq \eta_1$ *or* $\lambda < \lambda_2$ *and* $\eta_1 \leq \eta < \eta_2$, *or* $\lambda < \lambda_3$ *and* $\eta \geq \eta_2$, *then* $\mathrm{CVaR}(\pi_s^{P^*}) > \mathrm{CVaR}(\pi_s^{T*})$;
   (ii) *otherwise* $\mathrm{CVaR}(\pi_s^{P^*}) \leq \mathrm{CVaR}(\pi_s^{T*})$, *where*

$$\lambda_0 = \frac{c(1+R^P)+p}{(1+R^P)(c+p)}, \quad \eta_1 = \frac{\lambda p(1+R^P)}{2(c+p+cR^P)}, \quad \eta_2 = \frac{p}{2(c+p)},$$

$$\lambda_2 = \frac{4\eta[cp(1+R^P) - \eta(c+p)^2(1+R^P) + p^2]}{p^2(1+R^P)},$$

$$\lambda_3 = \frac{1+R^P-4\eta R^P}{1+R^P}.$$

Proposition 7.3(1) indicates that when the supplier tends to be risk-averse, if the supplier's credit guarantee coefficient is relatively large, the optimal expected profit of the retailer under PCG is greater than that under TCF, and vice versa. Proposition 7.3(2) suggests that the supplier has different preferences compared to the retailer. To illustrate this more clearly, Figs. 7.2(a) and 7.2(b) contrast two members' expected profits or utilities through the numerical analysis and the input data is the same as above.

As Corollary 7.1 indicated, the supplier's optimal wholesale price increases in his risk-averse factor, and the supplier's financial risk increases in his guarantee coefficient. Figure 7.2(a) shows that when the guarantee coefficient $\lambda > \lambda_0$, which means the supplier bears higher risk, the risk-averse supplier will set a relatively lower wholesale price to attract the retailer under PCG than TCF. Therefore, in this region, the retailer enjoys a relatively lower wholesale price and a higher order quantity, therefore PCG is a better choice. On the contrary, when the supplier's guarantee percentage is not large enough (i.e., corresponding to the shaded area in Fig. 7.2(a)), a TCF contract is the better choice for the retailer.

In addition, when the supplier tends to be risk-neutral, the optimal expected profits of the retailer are the same under both strategies, which are equal to zero. The reason is that under both PCG and TCF, the retailer has no capital endowment and the supplier shoulders both financing risk and production cost. The supplier's utility increases in his wholesale price and as long as the retailer prefers to stay in the game, the supplier has incentives to increase his wholesale

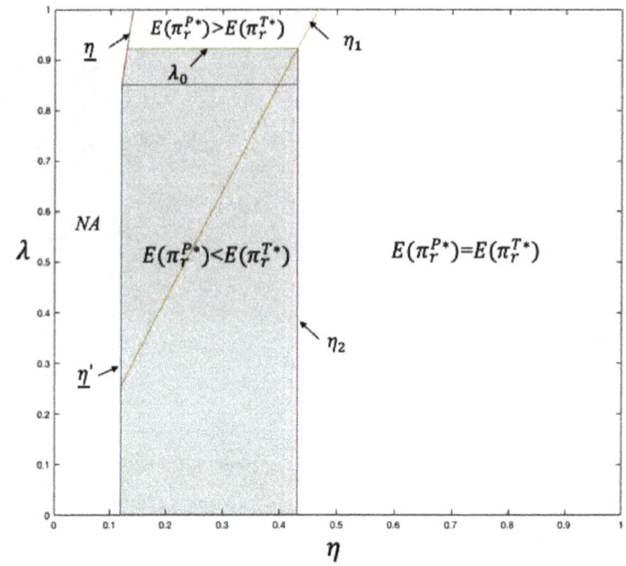


(a)

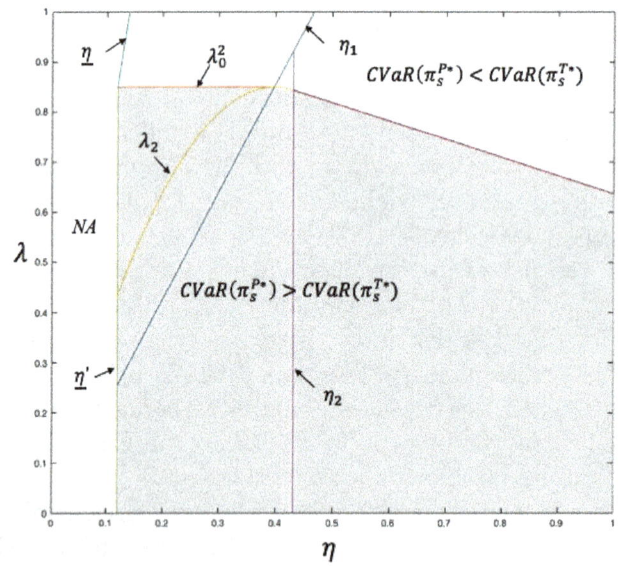


(b)

Fig. 7.2. Optimal utilities comparison of the retailer and the supplier. (a) Retailer's optimal expected profit and (b) supplier's optimal CVaR performance.

price to the upper threshold value in order to seize the retailer's total profit. Here we assume that the retailer is a Pareto player, therefore, the optimal wholesale price is equal to the upper threshold value, which results in the retailer obtaining no profit. Moreover, as shown in Fig. 7.2(a), the region that the retailer prefers TCF is much greater than that of PCG. This is because under TCF, the supplier provides both financing and operational functions to the retailer, therefore the supplier shoulders larger financial risk from the retailer; whereas under PCG, because the supplier only undertakes partial risks of the retailer, the retailer will prefer PCG only when the guarantee coefficient is higher than certain threshold value.

Proposition 7.3(2) shows that when the supplier does not give very high guarantee percentage to the retailer (i.e., corresponding to the shaded region in Fig. 7.2(b)), the utility of the supplier under PCG is greater than that under TCF and vice versa. In particular, in the boundaries, the utility of the supplier under PCG is equal to that under TCF, and the shaded region boundaries consist of three parts: the first is when the supplier's risk-averse factor is lower than $\eta_1$, and the guarantee threshold is $\lambda_0^2$; the second is when $\eta_1 < \eta < \eta_2$, the guarantee threshold is $\lambda_2$; and the third is when $\eta > \eta_2$, the guarantee threshold is $\lambda_3$. The managerial insights behind this are that under TCF, the supplier only obtains the minimum threshold between retailer's revenue and her loan, while under PCG, the supplier can fully obtain his operational revenue and shoulders partial guarantee risk. Therefore, when the guaranteed proportion is not very high, the supplier prefers PCG rather than TCF. However, when the guaranteed proportion is sufficiently high (exceeding the threshold values in the boundary), TCF is the better choice for the supplier. In addition, when the supplier tends to be risk-neutral, we can see the threshold $\lambda_3$ decreases, which means that the region of TCF becomes larger. This reflects the fact that the relatively optimistic supplier can afford to bear greater risks, and the acceptance region of TCF is expanded.

From Proposition 7.3(1) and (2), we can find that there is a region in which the optimal performance of both the supplier and retailer under TCF is higher than that under PCG. Figure 7.3

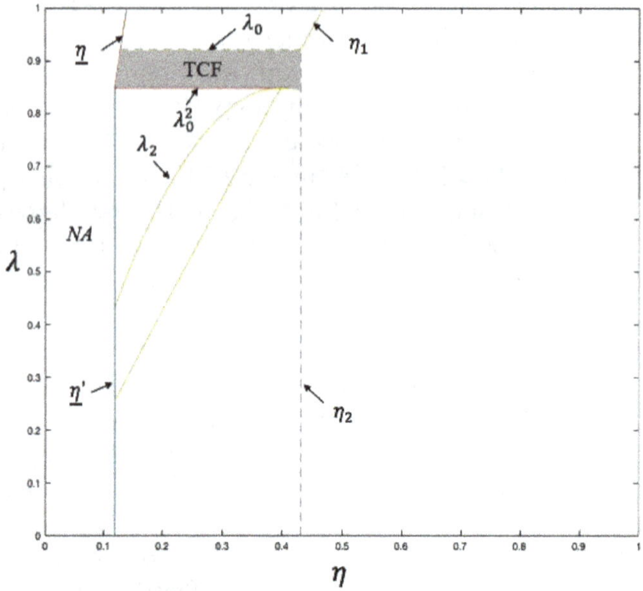


Fig. 7.3. Preference of two financing strategies in the space of $\eta$ and $\lambda$.

summarizes the relative preference of the two financing strategies in the two-dimension space of the risk-averse indicator and the credit guarantee coefficient. The shaded area indicates the region in which the optimal performance of both the supplier and retailer under TCF is higher than PCG.

The phenomenon may be explained as follows. The supplier is more powerful than the downstream retailer and acts as the leader in the Stackelberg game. Note that the supplier's risk is increasing in the guaranteed proportion under PCG. As long as the guaranteed proportion is below the threshold level he will choose PCG, otherwise he selects TCF. However, as a follower, the retailer would prefer PCG if the guaranteed proportion is sufficiently large. Thus, in general, two members in the supply chain cannot achieve win–win outcomes. Nevertheless, in Fig. 7.3, we can see there is a region where both members can achieve better expected profits or utility under TCF. The implication is that when the retailer negotiates with the more risk-averse supplier, she can consciously guide the supplier to choose the guaranteed proportion within this region, which is win–win situation for both parties.

## 7.5. Extension to the Dual-Channel Case with a Risk-Averse Supplier

In this section, we discuss the extension of the model to the dual-channel situation. Suppose the supplier has an online direct channel and an offline channel through the retailer to distribute products. We assume that the supplier is risk-averse, and we adopt the CVaR method to measure the chain members' risk-averse attitudes. The supplier has sufficient capital and offers a trade credit contract to the capital-constrained retailer, which means the retailer could make a delayed payment to the supplier at the end of the period.

Consistent with common practices, the products are homogenous through both the online and offline channel. The unit prices of the online channel and retail channel are $p_o$ and $p_r$. The unit cost of products through dual-channel is different, that is, the unit cost of online channel is lower than that of offline channel ($c_r$), which is $c_o < c_r$. The initial capital of the retailer is $K$. To model the competition between the supplier and the retailer, the time sequence of decision-making is assumed as follows: First, the supplier publishes his wholesale price, and then the retailer decides her offline retail price, after that the supplier decides his online direct price. In this way, the supplier acts more like a vendor and compete vertically with the retailer (Matsui, 2017).

Without loss of generality, we assume the demand of the market to be one, the proportion of the online demand is $\alpha$, and the offline part is $1-\alpha$. The demand is negatively related to the sales price of its own channel and positively related to the price of the other channel. We use $\beta$ to characterize the substitution coefficient between the offline and online channel, where the subscript $o$ and $r$ indicates the online channel and the retail channel. Thus, the demands of dual-channel are given as follows:

$$q_o = \alpha - p_o + \beta(p_r - p_o) + y,$$
$$q_r = 1 - \alpha - p_r + \beta(p_o - p_r) + y,$$

where $y$ represents the random part of the demand. Let $E(\pi_r)$ be the retailer's expected profit, which can be given by

$$E(\pi_r) = (p_r - w)q_r \quad \text{subject to } c_r q_r < K.$$

The supplier's profit optimization problem can be formulized as follows:

$$\max E(\pi_s) = (p_o - c_o)q_o + (w - c_r)q_r.$$

In order to take into account the supplier's risk-averse attitude, the CVaR metric can be used. Then, the supplier's objective function can be defined as follows:

$$\text{CVaR}_\eta(\pi_s) = \max\left\{v - \frac{1}{\eta}E[v - \pi_s]^+\right\}.$$

The detailed analysis in terms of the equilibrium solutions can be done by following the steps in Sec. 7.3. However, it is more challenging because the supplier has to make both decisions in terms of wholesale price and online sale price.

## 7.6. Conclusion

This chapter studies a supply chain system composed of a risk-averse supplier and retailer. The CVaR risk criterion is used to measure the degree of risk aversion of the supply chain members. Two financing strategies (PCG and TCF) are considered in the context supply chain management. The optimal equilibrium solutions under PCG and TCF are obtained, and the sensitivity of the optimal decisions to some parameters is analyzed. Under the assumption that the demand is uniform distributed, we found that the supply chain is feasible only when the supplier's risk aversion degree is within a certain interval, and the intervals under PCG and TCF strategies are different (here feasible means that both the supplier and the retailer are profitable). We have also obtained the analytical results of the preference to two financing strategies, which can be characterized by several switching curves in the two-dimensional space of the credit guarantee coefficient and risk aversion degree. Comparing the two financing strategies, when examining the impact of the supplier's risk aversion attitude and the credit guarantee coefficient, the two participants usually have different preferences to PCG and TCF financing strategies. However, there is a region where the optimal performance under TCF is higher than the optimal performance under PCG, which indicates that TCF is the better financing strategy for the supplier and the retailer in this region. In addition, we discussed how the model can be extended to the dual-channel situations.

Further research can be conducted in the following areas. In practice, the guarantee ratio may be related to the guarantor's attitude toward risk. Honohan (2010) proposed that in order to retain a certain risk, it may not be less than 20%. However, there is no specific research in the literature to quantify the relationship between the guarantee coefficient and the risk aversion factor. Therefore, it is worth further discussion. Secondly, other financing strategies such as green credit financing are an emerging phenomenon (An *et al.*, 2021). Integrating green credit financing strategies into supply chain management deserves more research. Thirdly, treating the bank interest rate as an endogenous decision variable is another interesting research direction.

## References

An, S., Li, B., Song, D., & Chen, X. (2021). Green credit financing versus trade credit financing in a supply chain with carbon emission limits. *European Journal of Operational Research*, 292(1), pp. 125–142.

Beck, T., Klapper, L. F., & Mendoza, J. C. (2010). The typology of partial credit guarantee funds around the world. *Journal of Financial Stability*, 6(1), pp. 10–25.

Buzacott, J. A., & Zhang, R. Q. (2004). Inventory management with asset-based financing. *Management Science*, 50(9), pp. 1274–1292.

Cai, G., Chen, X., & Xiao, Z. (2014). The roles of bank and trade credits: Theoretical analysis and empirical evidence. *Production & Operations Management*, 23(4), pp. 583–598.

Chen, X. (2015). A model of trade credit in a capital-constrained distribution channel. *International Journal of Production Economics*, 159(C), pp. 347–357.

Chen, Z., Li, Y., & Zhang, J. (2016). The bank–firm relationship: Helping or grabbing? *International Review of Economics & Finance*, 42, pp. 385–403.

Fisher, M., & Raman, A. (1996). Reducing the cost of demand uncertainty through accurate response to early sales. *Operations Research*, 44(1), pp. 87–99.

Honohan, P. (2010). Partial credit guarantees: Principles and practice. *Journal of Financial Stability*, 6(1), pp. 1–9.

Hussain, J., Millman, C., & Matlay, H. (2006). SME financing in the UK and in China: A comparative perspective. *Journal of Small Business & Enterprise Development*, 13(4), pp. 584–599.

Jaffee, D. M., & Russell, T. (1976). Imperfect information, uncertainty, and credit rationing. *Quarterly Journal of Economics*, 90(4), pp. 651–666.

Jing, B., Chen, X., & Cai, G. (2012). Equilibrium financing in a distribution channel with capital constraint. *Production & Operations Management*, 21(6), pp. 1090–1101.

Kouvelis, P., & Zhao, W. (2012). Financing the newsvendor: supplier vs. bank, and the structure of optimal trade credit contracts. *Operations Research*, 60(3), pp. 566–580.

Li, B., An, S., & Song, D. (2018). Selection of financing strategies with a risk-averse supplier in a capital-constrained supply chain. *Transportation Research Part E: Logistics and Transportation Review*, 118, pp. 163–183.

Matsui, K. (2017). When should a manufacturer set its direct price and wholesale price in dual-channel supply chains. *European Journal of Operational Research*, 258(2), pp. 501–511.

Rajan, R. G., & Zingales, L. (1995). What do we know about capital structure? Some evidence from international data. *Journal of Finance*, 50(5), pp. 1421–1460.

Rockafellar, R. T., & Uryasev, S. (2000). Optimization of conditional value-at-risk. *Journal of Risk*, 29(1), pp. 1071–1074.

Rockafellar, R. T., & Uryasev, S. (2002). Conditional value-at-risk for general loss distributions. *Journal of Banking & Finance*, 26(7), pp. 1443–1471.

Yan, N., Sun, B., Zhang, H., & Liu, C. (2016). A partial credit guarantee contract in a capital-constrained supply chain: Financing equilibrium and coordinating strategy. *International Journal of Production Economics*, 173, pp. 122–133.

© 2022 World Scientific Publishing Europe Ltd.
https://doi.org/10.1142/9781800610408_0008

# Chapter 8

# Pricing and Order Quantity Decisions in Dual-Channel Supply Chain with a Risk-Averse Retailer Under Demand Asymmetric Information

**Qinghua Li*** **and Bo Li†**

*College of Management and Economics, Tianjin University, China*

**liqinghua123123@126.com*

*†libo0410@tju.edu.cn*

## 8.1. Introduction

The rapid development of information technology enables manufacturers to establish their own online channels to compete with traditional retailers. At present, the combination of traditional retail channels and direct sales channels, that is, dual-channel supply chains, has become the main operating mode for many brand manufacturers (Arya *et al.*, 2007, Karray, 2014). Facing the manufacturer's encroachment, retailers regard the manufacturers' online channels as threats that may harm their profits. Therefore, channel conflicts occur (Liu and Zhang, 2006). In the case of fierce competition between the two channels, retailers may exhibit risk-averse behavior. This risk aversion will affect chain members' decision-making and even affect the profit of the whole supply chain.

Another important phenomenon in supply chain is the information asymmetricity regarding the market. In general, retailers have an advantage in collecting market data via direct interaction with customers and the ability to predict market demand (Huang *et al.*, 2018; Shang *et al.*, 2016). Therefore, retailers can analyze market demand fluctuations and changes more accurately than manufacturers (Feng *et al.*, 2015; Li *et al.*, 2013; Li *et al.*, 2016).

However, due to the online channel insertion from manufacturers, new online channels pose a great threat to retailers' long-term monopoly in the retail market. Retailers with risk-averse behavior may deliberately distort their order quantity which they send to the manufacturer. This leads to information asymmetry among supply chain members. In other words, manufacturers may receive distorted market information, which may cause manufacturers to make wrong decisions in their online channels.

This chapter considers a dual-channel supply chain with a risk-neutral manufacturer (he) and a risk-averse retailer (she). The manufacturer sells the product to the retailer through the traditional retail channel; meanwhile, the manufacturer also has his own online channel to sell homogeneous product directly to consumers. The market demand information is uncertain, but the retailer can predict market demand more accurately than the manufacturer. It is assumed that market demand size takes two types, high and low, and at each type the demand follows a truncated normal distribution. Specifically, this chapter attempts to answer the following questions:

(1) How does the manufacturer identify the actual type of market size to organize production and determine the production quantity in his online channel?
(2) How will the manufacturer and the retailer make the decisions such as wholesale pricing and order quantity in dual-channel supply chain under asymmetric information?
(3) How does the retailer's risk aversion and the manufacturer's unit direct sales cost affect the quantity decisions and the profit or utility of both parties?

The rest of the chapter is organized as follows. Section 8.2 formulates the problem into a Stackelberg game model. Sections 8.3 and 8.4 analyze the model and establish analytical results for three scenarios: the benchmark scenario without the manufacturer's encroachment, the manufacturer's encroachment under symmetric information, and the manufacturer's encroachment under asymmetric information. Finally, a summary is provided in Sec. 8.5.

## 8.2. Model Description

Consider a dual-channel supply chain consisting of a manufacturer (he) and a traditional retailer (she), in which the manufacturer introduces an online channel by himself and sells homogeneous products to consumers through the retailer and his own online channels. In the production and sales process, the manufacturer is the leader and is risk-neutral, while the retailer is the follower, and has risk aversion behavior. We suppose that both agents adopt the make-to-order strategy. The consumer's demand is assumed to be a linear function (Gümüş, 2014),

$$P = a - Q, \tag{8.1}$$

where the parameter $a$ represents the potential market size, $P$ and $Q$ represent the market clearing price and the total quantity of the product deployed for sale, respectively.

To simplify the calculation, the manufacturer's production cost is standardized to be zero, and the retailer's unit cost of sales is also assumed to be zero (Li *et al.*, 2013). Because the retailer usually has a deeper understanding of consumer preferences and more direct contact with consumers, the retailer has some advantages in the retailing business. To reflect the advantages of retailers relative to the manufacturer, we denote $c$ as the per-unit selling cost incurred to the manufacturer when the product is sold by the manufacturer to consumers via the online channel, where $c > 0$.

Let the potential market size ($a$) be an ex ante and random variable. The market size is assumed to have two types, $a_H$ and $a_L$, which differ only in the probability distribution of demand. Firstly, the retailer predicts the market demand, and then the retailer sends her order to the manufacturer. Note that the manufacturer just has prior knowledge regarding the market size. Thus, the demand signal is represented by $i$ to capture the uncertainty of market demand.

The signal can be high ($i = H$), with probability $\lambda \in (0,1)$) or low ($i = L$), with probability $1 - \lambda$. The demand conditional on $i$ is a non-negative random variable $a_i$, and it's cumulative distribution $F_i(\cdot)$ is strictly increased over $R^+$ and probability density function is denoted as $f_i(\cdot)$. A high value signal means a larger random demand $a_H$, and the demand distribution for a $a_H$ type has the first-order stochastic dominance over the demand distribution for a $a_L$ type, i.e., $F_L(a) > F_H(a)$ for all $a \in R^+$. Let $\bar{F}_i(\cdot) = 1 - F_i(\cdot)$. We further assumed that the demand distribution is a truncated normal distribution; that is, for all $a_i \in R^+$, $a_H \sim N(\mu_H, \sigma^2)$, $a_L \sim N(\mu_L, \sigma^2)$ and $\mu_H > \mu_L$ (Feng *et al.*, 2014; Karray, 2014). Although both the manufacturer and the retailer know the prior distribution of the signal and the conditional distributions of the random demand, the true market size (high or low) can only be predicted exactly by retailer. For the manufacturer, the market size will be judged just from the retailer's order quantity. In addition, two parties know all information in the models.

To measure the retailer's risk-averse behavior, we adopt the mean–variance method. That is, $E(U_R) = E(\Pi_R) - k\sqrt{\mathrm{Var}(\Pi_R)}$ is utilized as the expected utility of the retailer, where $k > 0$ is a parameter representing the retailer's risk-averse degree. As the parameter $k$ increases, the retailer becomes more risk-averse. $E(\Pi_R)$, $\mathrm{Var}(\Pi_R)$ are the mean and the variance of the retailer's profit $\Pi_R$ (Xu *et al.*, 2014).

## 8.3. Manufacturer's Encroachment Under Symmetric Information

In this section, we first consider a benchmark case without the manufacturer's encroachment, then consider the case with the manufacturer's encroachment under symmetric information. That is, the benchmark is a single supply chain in which the manufacturer doesn't open his online channel. Thus, the game timeline in our model is defined as: the manufacturer makes his wholesale price $w$ firstly, and then according to her prediction about the market size, the retailer with risk-averse behavior sets her order quantity $q_R$ to maximize her own profit. Last, the manufacturer selects the inventory quantity $q_M$ of the product in his online channel. Thus, the market clearing price is $P_i = E[a_i - (q_R + q_M)]$, $i \in \{H, L\}$.

### 8.3.1. Benchmark case without manufacturer's encroachment

In this benchmark case, the manufacturer only distributes the product from the traditional retail channel, and the retailer is risk-averse. Then, given the wholesale price $w$ and the market size $a_i$, $i \in \{H, L\}$, the retailer will decide the order quantity as

$$\max_{q_R} E[U_{R,i}], \quad i \in \{H, L\}. \tag{8.2}$$

Corresponding to the two market sizes (high and low), the retailer's expected utilities are given by

$$E[U_{R,H}] = [\mu_H - q_R(w;H) - w]q_R(w;H) - k\sigma q_R(w;H),$$
$$E[U_{R,L}] = [\mu_L - q_R(w;L) - w]q_R(w;L) - k\sigma q_R(w;L).$$

From the first-order condition, the retailer's optimal quantity for each type of market size $a_i$, $i \in \{H, L\}$ is

$$q_R^N(w;i) = (\mu_i - w - k\sigma)/2, \quad i \in \{H, L\}. \tag{8.3}$$

The manufacturer aims to maximize his expected profit:

$$\max_w E\left[\prod_M\right] = \max_w \left[\lambda w\left(\frac{\mu_H - w - k\sigma}{2}\right) + (1-\lambda)w\left(\frac{\mu_L - w - k\sigma}{2}\right)\right]. \tag{8.4}$$

Then, the manufacturer's optimal wholesale price is given by $w^N = (\mu - k\sigma)/2$, where $\mu = \lambda\mu_H + (1-\lambda)\mu_L$. That is, under the high and the low market, the retailer's order quantities are $q_R^N(i) = (2\mu_i - \mu - k\sigma)/4$.

The retailer's optimal expected utility $U_R^N$ is

$$U_R^N = \frac{(\lambda\mu_H^2 + (1-\lambda)\mu_L^2) - \mu(\mu - k\sigma)}{4} + \frac{(\mu - 3k\sigma)(\mu + k\sigma)}{16} - \frac{1}{2}k\sigma\sqrt{4(\lambda\mu_H^2 + (1-\lambda)\mu_L^2) + (\mu + k\sigma)^2 - 4\mu}. \tag{8.5}$$

The manufacturer's optimal expected profit is

$$\prod_M^N = \frac{(\mu - k\sigma)^2}{8}. \tag{8.6}$$

To ensure feasible solution $q_R^N(i) > 0$ and $w > 0$, the condition $0 < k < \frac{2\mu_L - \mu}{\sigma}$, $i \in \{H, L\}$, must be satisfied.

### 8.3.2. The manufacturer encroachment case under symmetric information

In this case, a dual-channel supply chain is considered, where the manufacturer and the retailer have symmetric information. That is, both of them know the true market size. For each market size $a_i$, $i \in \{H, L\}$, through observing the order quantity $q_R$ of the retailer, the optimal direct selling quantity decision of manufacturer can be expressed as

$$\max_{q_M} E\left[\prod_M\right] = \max_{q_M}[\mu_i - q_R - q_M - c]q_M. \tag{8.7}$$

The direct selling quantity can be obtained as $q_M(q_R) = \frac{\mu_i - q_R - c}{2}$. In anticipation of the manufacturer's reaction, for $i \in \{H, L\}$, the retailer chooses her own order quantity based on the following objective:

$$\max_{q_R} E[U_R] = \max_{q_R}\left\{\begin{array}{l}\frac{1}{2}q_R(w;i)(\mu_i - q_R(w;i) + c - 2w) \\ -\frac{1}{4}k\sigma(\mu_i - q_R(w;i) + c - 2w)\end{array}\right\}. \tag{8.8}$$

Then, the retailer's order quantity is $q_R(w;i) = \frac{\mu_i - 2w + c - k\sigma}{2}$, and the manufacturer's direct selling quantity is $q_M(q_R(w;i)) = \frac{\mu_i + 2w - 3c + k\sigma}{4}$.

Further, through maximizing the manufacturer's expected profit, we can obtain the equilibrium wholesale price by

$$\begin{aligned}\max_{q_M} E\left[\prod_M\right] &= \max_w\left\{q_R(w;i)w + \begin{bmatrix}\mu_i - q_R(w;i) \\ -q_M(q_R(w;i)) - c\end{bmatrix} q_M(q_R(w;i))\right\} \\ &= \max_w\left\{\left(\frac{\mu_i - 2w + c - k\sigma}{2}\right)w + \left(\frac{\mu_i + 2w - 3c + k\sigma}{4}\right)^2\right\}.\end{aligned} \tag{8.9}$$

The optimal solutions are as follows (where the superscript SI indicates the case of symmetric information of market size):

$$w^{SI}(i) = \frac{3\mu_i - c - k\sigma}{6}, \quad q_R^{SI} = \frac{2c - k\sigma}{3}, \quad q_M^{SI}(i) = \frac{3\mu_i - 5c + k\sigma}{6}.$$

Then, under symmetric information, the manufacturer's optimal expected profit is

$$\prod_M^{SI} = \frac{1}{18}(2c - k\sigma)[3(\lambda\mu_H + (1-\lambda)\mu_L) - c - k\sigma] + \frac{1}{36}\lambda(3\mu_H - 5c + k\sigma)^2 + \frac{1}{36}(1-\lambda)(3\mu_L - 5c + k\sigma)^2. \tag{8.10}$$

The retailer's optimal expected utility under symmetric information is

$$U_R^{\text{SI}} = \frac{1}{9}(c + k\sigma)(2c - k\sigma) - \frac{1}{6}k\sigma(c + k\sigma). \tag{8.11}$$

To ensures $q_R^{\text{SI}} > 0$, $q_M^{\text{SI}}(i) \geq 0$, and $w^{SI}(i) > 0$, it is required that $0 < k < \min\{\frac{2c}{\sigma}, \frac{3\mu_L - c}{\sigma}\}$.

## 8.4. Manufacturer's Encroachment Under Asymmetric Information

Now we consider the circumstance that the manufacturer knows the prior knowledge about the market size, but the market size can only be judged based on the retailer's order quantity. We assume that the sales quantities are positive for the traditional channel and the online channel to make the problem non-trivial.

Let $a_{j(q_R)}$ denote the market size that needs to be determined by the manufacturer after observing the retailer's optimal quantity $q_R$. Given the wholesale price $w$, there exists a threshold of the order quantity $q'_R(w)$. The manufacturer believes that it is a high market size if the retailer's order quantity satisfies $q_R > q'_R(w)$, otherwise it is low. That is,

$$j(q_R) = \begin{cases} H & \text{if } q_R > q'_R(w), \\ L & \text{if } q_R \leq q'_R(w). \end{cases} \tag{8.12}$$

After receiving the retailer's order quantity $q_R$, the manufacturer makes the quantity decision $q_M$ in the online channel by optimizing the following objective:

$$\max_{q_M}[\mu_{j(q_R)} - q_R - q_M(q_R) - c]q_M(q_R), \tag{8.13}$$

It follows that the optimal selling quantity in the online channel is given by

$$q_M(q_R) = \frac{\mu_{j(q_R)} - q_R - c}{2}. \tag{8.14}$$

Given the wholesale price $w$ and the manufacturer's response function in Eq. (8.14), the expected profit function of the retailer is

$$E\left[\prod_R\right] = \left[\mu_i - \frac{1}{2}\mu_{j(q_R)} - \frac{1}{2}q_R(w,i) + \frac{c}{2} - w\right] q_R(w,i). \tag{8.15}$$

The retailer determines her retail quantity $q_R$ by maximizing its expected utility. Her expected utility function is given as follows:

$$E[U_R] = \begin{cases} \lambda\left[\dfrac{\mu_H - q_R(w,H) + c}{2} - w\right] q_R(w,H) \\ \quad + (1-\lambda)\left[\dfrac{\mu_L - q_R(w,L) + c}{2} - w\right] q_R(w,L) \\ \quad - \dfrac{k\sigma}{2}\sqrt{\lambda q_R(w,H)^2 + (1-\lambda)q_R(w,L)^2}, & i = j(q_R), \\ \lambda\left[\mu_H - \dfrac{\mu_L + q_R(w,H) - c}{2} - w\right] q_R(w,H) \\ \quad + (1-\lambda)\left[\mu_L - \dfrac{\mu_H + q_R(w,L) - c}{2} - w\right] q_R(w,L) \\ \quad - \dfrac{\sqrt{5}}{2}k\sigma\sqrt{\lambda q_R(w,H)^2 + (1-\lambda)q_R(w,L)^2}, & i \neq j(q_R). \end{cases} \tag{8.16}$$

Let $q_R^{AI}(i)$ denote the optimal solution of the problem (8.16). Therefore, the objective function is to maximize the expected utility $E[U_R]$.

Under asymmetric information, let $V_{ij}(q_R)$ denote the retailer's expected utility, that is $V_{ij}(q_R) = E[U_R]$.

When $\lambda = 1$, the market size is always high. Thus,

$$\frac{\partial V_{ij}(q_R)}{\partial q_R(w,H)} = \begin{cases} \dfrac{\mu_H - 2w + c}{2} - q_R(w,H) \\ \quad -\dfrac{1}{2}k\sigma, & i = j(q_R) = H, \\ \mu_H - q_R(w,H) - \dfrac{\mu_L - c}{2} \\ \quad -w - \dfrac{\sqrt{5}}{2}k\sigma, & i = H, j = L. \end{cases} \tag{8.17}$$

Similarly, when $\lambda = 0$, the market size is always low. Thus,

$$\frac{\partial V_{ij}(q_R)}{\partial q_R(w,L)} = \begin{cases} \dfrac{\mu_L - 2w + c}{2} - q_R(w,L) \\ \quad -\dfrac{1}{2}k\sigma, & i = j(q_R) = L, \\ \mu_L - q_R(w,L) - \dfrac{\mu_H - c}{2} \\ \quad -w - \dfrac{\sqrt{5}}{2}k\sigma, & i = L, j = H. \end{cases} \tag{8.18}$$

We can verify that the utility function in (8.16) is a concave function, and there is a unique solution $q_R$ to maximize the utility. Then, retailer's optimal order quantity is

$$q_R(w,i) = \begin{cases} \dfrac{\mu_i - 2w + c - k\sigma}{2}, & i = j(q_R), \\ \left(\dfrac{2\mu_i - \mu_j - 2w + c - \sqrt{5}k\sigma}{2}\right)^+, & i \neq j(q_R). \end{cases} \tag{8.19}$$

where $i \in \{H, L\}$, $(g)^+ = \max\{g, 0\}$.

**Lemma 8.1.** *The utility function $V_{ij}(q_R)$, $\forall i, j \in \{H, L\}$, is concave in $q_R$. The optimal decisions of the retailer are as follows:*

(1) *When demand information is symmetric, the retailer's order quantity is*

$$q_R(w,i) = \left(\frac{\mu_i - 2w + c - k\sigma}{2}\right)^+, \quad i = j,\ \forall i, j \in \{H, L\}. \tag{8.20}$$

(2) *When the demand information is asymmetric, the retailer's order quantity is*

$$q_R(w,i) = \left(\frac{2\mu_i - \mu_j - 2w + c - \sqrt{5}k\sigma}{2}\right)^+, \quad i \neq j(q_R),$$
$$\forall i, j \in \{H, L\}. \tag{8.21}$$

From Lemma 8.1, we can see that under symmetric information, if the retailer does not have risk-averse behavior ($k = 0$), then $q_R(w,i) = (\frac{\mu_i - 2w + c}{2})^+$, $i = j$, $\forall i, j \in \{H, L\}$. When the retailer has risk-averse behavior ($k > 0$), if $0 < k < \frac{\mu_i - 2w + c}{\sigma}$, then $q_R(w,i) > 0$. If $k \geq \frac{\mu_i - 2w + c}{\sigma}$, then $q_R(w, a_i) = 0$. Under asymmetric information, when the retailer does not have risk-averse behavior, ($k = 0$), we have $q_R(w,i) = (\frac{2\mu_i - \mu_j - 2w + c}{2})^+$, $i \neq j$, $\forall i, j \in \{H, L\}$. The retailer tends to order less quantity if she is more risk-averse.

In addition, according to Eq. (8.15), we find that for a given order quantity, the retailer will be better off if the manufacturer believes that the market size is low. When the retailer takes risk-averse behavior, there is a lower order quantity $q_R(w)$. This happens because the retailer has incentive to distort the ordering knowledge and induce the manufacturer to believe there is a low size market. In this circumstance, the manufacturer may not accurately predict the market size.

Given the retailer's order quantity $q_R$, we assume that the real market size is $i$, but the manufacturer believes the true market size is $j(q_R)$.

Thus, for each market size $a_i$, $i \in \{H, L\}$ and given the wholesale price $w$, if $j(q_R(w,i)) = i$, there exists a threshold $q'_R(w)$ such that $q_R(w,H) > q'_R(w)$ and $q_R(w,L) \leq q'_R(w)$.

**Lemma 8.2.** *If the retailer has risk-averse behavior, for any given positive ordering quantity $q_R$ and $V_{HL}(q_R) > V_{HH}(q_R)$, then there exists one threshold $\bar{q}_R(w)$, and $\bar{q}_R(w) < \frac{2\mu_H - \mu_L - 2w + c - \sqrt{5}k\sigma}{2}$, such that*

$$V_{HL}(\bar{q}_R(w)) = V_{HH}\left(\frac{\mu_H - 2w + c - k\sigma}{2}\right),$$

*where*

$$\bar{q}_R(w) = \frac{1}{2}(2\mu_H - \mu_L - 2w + c - k\sigma) - \frac{1}{2}\sqrt{B},$$
$$B = (\mu_H - \mu_L)(3\mu_H - \mu_L - 4w + 2c - 2k\sigma).$$

From Lemma 8.2, we can find when $q_R < \bar{q}_R(w)$ is satisfied, we have $V_{HL}(q_R) < V_{HH}(\frac{\mu_H - 2w + c - k\sigma}{2})$. When $\bar{q}_R(w) < q_R < \frac{\mu_H - 2w + c - k\sigma}{2}$, we have $V_{HL}(q_R) > V_{HH}(\frac{\mu_H - 2w + c - k\sigma}{2})$.

Furthermore, let $\bar{w} = \frac{1}{4}(3\mu_L - \mu_H + 2c - 2k\sigma)$. If $w \le \bar{w}$, then $\bar{q}_R(w) \le (\frac{\mu_L - 2w + c - k\sigma}{2})^+$; if $w > \bar{w}$, then $\bar{q}_R(w) > (\frac{\mu_L - 2w + c - k\sigma}{2})^+$.

Based on the result in Lemma 8.2, Proposition 8.1 gives a unique perfect Bayesian separating equilibrium.

**Proposition 8.1.** *When the market size information is asymmetric, there exists a unique perfect Bayesian separating equilibrium.*

(1) *The retailer's order quantity is*

$$q_R(w, H) = \left(\frac{\mu_H - 2w + c - k\sigma}{2}\right)^+,$$

$$q_R(w, L) = q_R'(w) = \min\left\{\left(\frac{\mu_L - 2w + c - k\sigma}{2}\right)^+, \bar{q}_R(w)\right\}.$$

(2) *The manufacturer's direct selling quantity is*

$$q_M(w, i) = \frac{\mu_{j(q_R)} - q_R(w, i) - c}{2}.$$

In Proposition 8.1(1), to ensure $q_R(w, H), q_R(w, L) \ge 0$, when $w \ge \frac{\mu_i + c - k\sigma}{2}$, we found that retailer will not order anything for every market size, and the manufacturer will not benefit from it. Hence, in the following discussion, we only consider the situations under the condition $w < \frac{\mu_i + c - k\sigma}{2}$.

Furthermore, the manufacturer's wholesale pricing decision is discussed as follows:

$$\max \boldsymbol{E}\{wq_R(w, i) + [\boldsymbol{a}_i - q_R(w, i) - q_M(q_R(w, i)) - c]q_M(q_R(w, i))\}. \tag{8.22}$$

According to (8.22), the manufacturer's expected profit is as follows ($NS$ denotes natural separating, i.e., with no distortion)

$$E\left[\prod_M(w)\right] = \begin{cases} w\left[\lambda\left(\dfrac{\mu_H - 2w + c - k\sigma}{2}\right)\right. \\ \left.+(1-\lambda)\left(\dfrac{\mu_L - 2w + c - k\sigma}{2}\right)\right] \\ +\lambda\left(\dfrac{\mu_H + 2w - 3c + k\sigma}{4}\right)^2 \\ +(1-\lambda)\left(\dfrac{\mu_L + 2w - 3c + k\sigma}{4}\right)^2, & w \geq \bar{w}, \\ w\left[\lambda\left(\dfrac{\mu_H - 2w + c - k\sigma}{2}\right) + (1-\lambda)\bar{q}_R(w)\right] \\ +\lambda\left(\dfrac{\mu_H + 2w - 3c + k\sigma}{4}\right)^2 \\ +(1-\lambda)\left(\dfrac{\mu_L - \bar{q}_R(w) - c}{2}\right)^2, & w < \bar{w}. \end{cases} \tag{8.23}$$

Solving Eq. (8.23) is non-trivial. Under the high market size and the low market size, when the manufacturer chooses to introduce a online channel, the following proposition gives the solution to (8.23). For any value of $k$, correspondingly, the ranges of $c$ are provided, and the feasible scope can be divided into three regions.

First, we define the threshold $\bar{c}(\lambda)$ of the manufacturer's per-unit selling cost to ensure that the manufacturer's direct selling quantity under the low market size reaches zero. At this time, we define

$$b = \min\left\{\frac{3(1+2\lambda)(\mu_H - \mu_L) + 4k\sigma}{8},\ 3\mu - k\sigma,\ \frac{2k\sigma + 3\mu_L + 3\mu}{10},\ \bar{c}(\lambda)\right\}.$$

Then, the three regions are defined as follows:

- Region $R_1$:

$$c \in \left(\max\left\{\frac{-3\sqrt{\lambda}(\mu_H - \mu_L) + 2k\sigma}{4}, \frac{k\sigma}{2}\right\},\right.$$
$$\left.\min\left\{\frac{3\sqrt{\lambda}(\mu_H - \mu_L) + 2k\sigma}{4},\ 3\mu_H - k\sigma, \frac{3\mu_H + k\sigma}{5}\right\}\right).$$

- Region $R_2$:

$$c \in \left( \max\left\{ \frac{2k\sigma_H + 3\lambda(\mu_H - \mu_L)}{4}, \ \frac{3\sqrt{\lambda}(\mu_H - \mu_L) + 2k\sigma}{4} \right\}, b \right].$$

- Region $R_3$:

$$c \in \left( \max\left\{ \frac{4k\sigma + (6\lambda - 9)(\mu_H - \mu_L)}{8}, \right.\right.$$
$$\left.\left. \min\left\{ \frac{3(1+2\lambda)(\mu_H - \mu_L) + 4k\sigma}{8}, \ \bar{c}(\lambda) \right\} \right\}, \bar{c}(\lambda) \right).$$

The three feasible regions are illustrated in Fig. 8.1, in which the parameters are as follows: $\mu_H = 1.2$, $\mu_L = 1.0$, $\sigma = 0.05$, $c = 0.2$, $k = 0.5$, $w = 0.3$.

**Proposition 8.2.** *Assume that* $a_H$: $N(\mu_H, \sigma^2)$, $a_L$: $N(\mu_L, \sigma^2)$. *For any* $\lambda \in (0,1)$, *the equilibrium solutions are provided as follows:*

(1) *The manufacturer's direct selling quantity is*

$$q_M(q_R(w^{AI}; i)) = \frac{\mu_i - q_R(w^{AI}; i) - c}{2}, \quad \forall i \in \{H, L\}, \ c \in (0, \bar{c}(\lambda)).$$

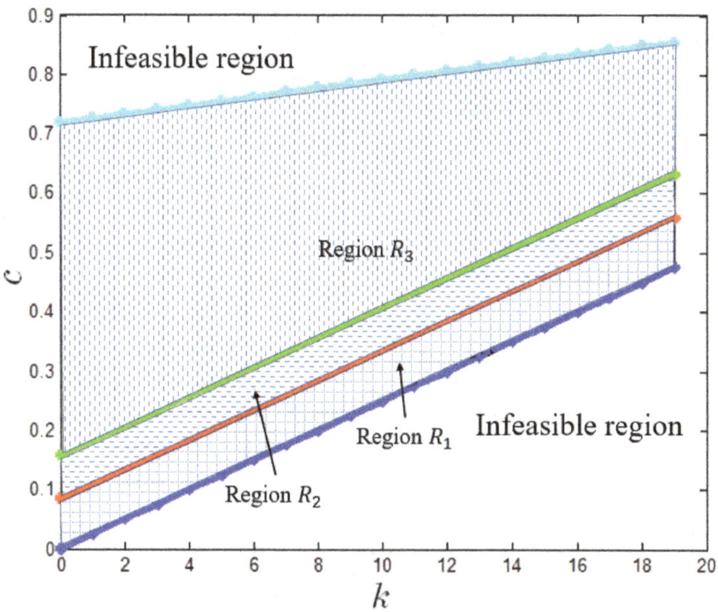


Fig. 8.1. The feasible regions on $c$ and $k$.

(2) *The manufacturer's optimal wholesale price and the retailer's order quantity can be described as follows according to the three regions:*

(i) *in Region* $R_1$, $w^{AI} = \frac{3\mu_H - k\sigma - c}{6}$, $q_R(w^{AI}, H) = \frac{\mu_H - 2w^{AI} + c}{2}$, $q_R(w^{AI}, L) = 0$;

(ii) *in Region* $R_2$, $w^{AI} = \frac{3\mu - k\sigma - c}{6}$, $q_R(w^{AI}, H) = \frac{\mu_H - 2w^{AI} + c}{2}$, $q_R(w^{AI}, L) = \frac{\mu_L - 2w^{AI} + c}{2}$, *where* $\mu = \lambda\mu_H + (1-\lambda)\mu_L$;

(iii) *in Region* $R_3$, $w^{AI} = \min\{w_f, \overline{w}\}$, $q_R(w^{AI}, H) = \frac{\mu_H - 2w^{AI} + c}{2}$, $q_R(w^{AI}, L) = \bar{q}_R(w^{AI})$,

*where* $w_f$ *is the unconstrained maximizer of* (8.16) *with* $q_R(w, L) = \bar{q}_R(w^{AI})$, *and* $w_f > \frac{3\mu - k\sigma - c}{6}$. *Here,* $w_f$ *satisfies the first-order condition:*

$$\lambda(3\mu_H - 6w - c - k\sigma) + (1-\lambda)(\mu_H + 2\mu_L - 6w - c - k\sigma) \times \left(1 - \frac{\sqrt{\mu_H - \mu_L}}{\sqrt{3\mu_H - \mu_L + 2c - 4w - 2k\sigma}}\right) = 0.$$

From Proposition 8.2, we can conclude that the optimal wholesale price $w^{AI} = \min\{w_f, \overline{w}\}$ in Region $R_3$ is larger than that in Region $R_1$ and $R_2$, i.e., $w^{AI} = \frac{3\mu - k\sigma - c}{6}$. In Region $R_1$, the manufacturer's per-unit selling cost $c$ is relatively small. When the manufacturer decides the wholesale price $w$, the retailer's order quantity is positive if and only if the market size is high. Thus, the manufacturer can learn the true market size according to the retailer's order quantity.

Furthermore, in Region $R_2$, the manufacturer's optimal wholesale price induces the retailer to order a positive quantity for both market sizes. We can find that when the selling cost $c$ is intermediate, under the low market size, a natural separating equilibrium exists in which there is no distortion on the retailer's order quantity.

From Proposition 8.2(2), we discover that when the market size is high, there is no distortion on order quantity. Thus, $c$ is relatively large, for instance, in Region $R_3$, when the retailer observes a high market size, she has no incentive to distort a small quantity to cheat the manufacturer. However, when the market size is low, she may distort her order quantity downward to credibly reveal the market size information to the manufacturer. Under the distortion scenario, the optimal wholesale price $w$ must satisfy the condition, i.e., $w_f > \frac{3\mu-c-k\sigma}{6}$, where $\frac{3\mu-c-k\sigma}{6}$ is the wholesale price offered by the manufacturer without distortion.

Note that $c \in (0, \bar{c}(\lambda))$ because under the low market size, the direct quantity of the manufacturer must be positive. For $c > \bar{c}(\lambda)$, regardless of whether the market size is high or low, the direct quantity of the manufacturer may be zero. Therefore, we focus on the situation that manufacturer encroachment always exists.

Next, we will consider the influence of the manufacturer's selling cost and the retailer's risk indicator on the manufacturer's profit and the retailer's utility in the supply chain. Under asymmetric information, we use $\Pi_M^{AI}$ to denote the manufacturer's optimal expected profit with manufacturer encroachment, and $\Pi_M^N$ to denote manufacturer's optimal expected profit without manufacturer encroachment.

**Proposition 8.3.** *Whether the manufacturer is better off or worse off in optimal expected profits will depend on the combination of the cost $c$ and the retailer's risk indicator $k$.*

(1) *In Region $R_1$, there exist two thresholds $g_1$ and $g_2$,*
   - *if $c \le g_1$ or $c \ge g_2$, then $\Pi_M^{AI} - \Pi_M^N > 0$;*
   - *if $g_1 < c < g_2$, then $\Pi_M^{AI} - \Pi_M^N < 0$.*

(2) *In Region $R_2$, there exist two thresholds $h_1$ and $h_2$,*
   - *if $c \ge h_2$ or $0 \le c \le \max\{h_1, 0\}$, then $\Pi_M^{AI} - \Pi_M^N > 0$;*
   - *if $\max\{h_1, 0\} < c < h_2$, then $\Pi_M^{AI} - \Pi_M^N < 0$,*

*where*

$$g_1 = \frac{6\mu + 4\lambda k\sigma - F}{2(4\lambda + 3)}, \quad g_2 = \frac{6\mu + 4\lambda k\sigma + F}{2(4\lambda + 3)},$$

$$h_1 = \frac{3}{56}\left(8\mu + \frac{16}{3}k\sigma\right) - E, \quad h_2 = \frac{3}{56}\left(8\mu + \frac{16}{3}k\sigma\right) + E,$$

$$E = \frac{3}{14}\sqrt{4\left(\mu + \frac{2}{3}k\sigma\right)^2 - \frac{7}{3}\left(\lambda\mu_H^2 + (1-\lambda)\mu_L^2 + \mu^2 + \frac{2}{3}k\sigma(6\mu - k\sigma)\right)},$$

$$F = \sqrt{\begin{array}{l}4(3\mu + 2\lambda k\sigma)^2 - 2(4\lambda + 3)(6\mu k\sigma + (2\lambda - 3)k^2\sigma^2 - 3\mu^2 \\ \quad +6(\lambda\mu_H^2 + (1-\lambda)\mu_L^2)).\end{array}}$$

From Proposition 8.3, we can reveal that when the direct selling cost is very small or relatively large in Region $R_1$, the manufacturer is better off in expected profit by his encroachment. However, when the direct selling cost is in the middle range, the encroachment of the manufacturer will reduce the expected profit. The same conclusion also appears in Region $R_2$. Because the direct selling cost is lower in Region $R_1$ and Region $R_2$, the manufacturer is more willing to open his direct channel.

However, from Proposition 8.3, we can conclude that the manufacturer is not always better off by his encroachment. In Region $R_1$, if the retailer does not place an order when the market size is low, then the manufacturer will bear a loss. However, in Region $R_2$, the situation faced by manufacturers is mainly similar to the situation studied by Arya *et al.* (2007). The retailer tends to order a positive and different quantity for each market size, rather than deliberately distorting it. The encroachment of the manufacturer not only brings new demand, but also gives the manufacturer the ability to control sales prices in the retail market, thereby alleviate double marginalization.

Due to manufacturer encroachment, the retailer will lose the monopoly power in retail market, and this may lead to a lower wholesale price. As revealed in Li *et al.* (2013) and Arya *et al.* (2007), manufacturer encroachment can benefit or hurt the retailer depending on the manufacturer's direct selling cost.

In the following proposition, under asymmetric information, we give a similar result regarding the retailer's utility.

**Proposition 8.4.** *Assume that* $a_H$: $N(\mu_H, \sigma^2), a_L$: $N(\mu_L, \sigma^2)$ *and* $\lambda \in (0,1)$, *whether the utility of the retailer is better off or worse off by manufacturer encroachment in Region* $R_1$ *and Region* $R_2$ *depends on the combined conditions of* $c$ *and* $k$. *That is, there exists a threshold* $c_R(\lambda)$ *such that the retailer is worse off in the expected utility by manufacturer encroachment when the manufacturer's per-unit selling cost*

$$c \in \left(\max\left\{\frac{-3\sqrt{\lambda}(\mu_H - \mu_L) + 2k\sigma}{4}, \frac{k\sigma}{2}\right\},\ c_R(\lambda)\right)$$

*and the retailer is better off when* $c \in (c_R(\lambda), b)$.

Proposition 8.4 shows that for a given $k$, there exists a threshold $c_R(\lambda)$ regarding the manufacturer's direct selling cost. That is, given the risk-averse degree $k$, when the manufacturer's selling cost $c$ is lower than this threshold, the retailer's utility is worse off, because she will lose her monopoly in the downstream market under the encroachment of the manufacturer. On the contrary, when the cost of sales is over the threshold, the retailer obtains the large utility provided by the manufacturer at a lower wholesale price. The benefits of the decrease in wholesale prices will outweigh the losses caused by the reduction in demand under the invaders of the manufacturer. We can observe that the critical value largely depends on the degree of risk aversion.

As the above, we have analyzed the scenarios that the manufacturer has a relatively small or intermediate selling cost $c$ in Region $R_1$ and Region $R_2$, where when retailers observe a higher market size, they have no incentive to deliberately distort the number of orders and induce manufacturers to believe that the market is smaller. However, the optimal wholesale price $w^{AI} = \min\{w_f, \overline{w}\}$ in Region $R_3$ is larger than the optimal wholesale prices in Region $R_1$ and $R_2$, i.e., $w^{AI} = \frac{3\mu-k\sigma-c}{6}$. When the cost of sales is large, the manufacturer will set a large optimal wholesale price, so the retailer may pretend to observe a low market. When the market size is low, the retailer will distort its order volume downward. If distortions occur, the profits of manufacturers and the utility of retailers will change dramatically.

Note that there is a complex implicit equation of the optimal wholesale price of the manufacturer in Region $R_3$. It is technically challenging to obtain the necessary and sufficient conditions for its solution. When the manufacturer chooses to invade the traditional retail market, it will bring pros and cons to retailers.

In fact, after observing a higher market size in the case of information symmetry, the retailer has no incentive to distort the quantity. However, in the case of information asymmetry, the retailer has an incentive to reduce orders, which makes the manufacturer believe that the market is small and thus reduces the sales through online channel.

When the distortion occurs, the retailer's optimal order quantity is increasing at a slower rate as $w$ decreases with order distortion compared with the scenario without distortion. Because $w \geq \bar{w}$,

$|\frac{dq_R(w;L)}{dw}| = 1$; but when $w < \bar{w}$, $|\frac{dq_R(w;L)}{dw}| < 1$. That is, when the market size is low, the retailer's optimal order quantity has stronger sensitivity if there is no distortion ($w \geq \bar{w}$) than that with order distortion ($w < \bar{w}$). For a certain range of $w$, when the actual market size is low, the price elasticity of the retailer's order quantity will decrease.

## 8.5. Conclusion

In this chapter, a dual-channel supply chain which is composed of a risk-neutral manufacturer and a risk-averse retailer is investigated. The retailer has more private information about the real market size, which enables her to predict the market size more accurately than the manufacturer. This gives rise to the phenomenon of information asymmetry. We examine the influences of the manufacturer's encroachment, the information asymmetry and the retailer's risk aversion on two agents' decisions and utility functions. We show that in such a setting, the encroachment can cause the retailer's downward distortion regarding her order quantity after observing a low market size, the manufacturer may make mistakes when judging the market size based on the retailer's order quantity. Manufacturers may increase the wholesale price, thereby amplifying double marginalization. These findings complement existing research results, which show that when two companies have the same information, the manufacturer's encroachment reduces double marginalization (Li *et al.*, 2013). We study the impacts of the retailer's risk-averse behavior and the manufacturer's cost on the order quantity decisions, the profits and utilities of the members in the supply chain. In addition, we provide the feasible regions which are determined by the manufacturer's per-unit selling cost and the retailer's risk-averse degree.

In addition, the following findings have been established. Firstly, for manufacturers, we achieve a unique perfect Bayes separation equilibrium to accurately judge whether the market size is high or low. According to the retailer's order quantity under different demand scenarios, including Benchmark without the manufacturer's encroachment, the manufacturer's encroachment under symmetric information and the manufacturer's encroachment under asymmetric information, the retailer's risk aversion behavior is considered, and the equilibrium results are obtained. Secondly, three feasible regions are characterized by the manufacturer's cost and the retailer's risk aversion behavior, under which the retailer's optimal order quantity and the manufacturer's optimal direct sales quantity are obtained.

## References

Arya, A., Mittendorf, B., & Sappington, D. E. M. (2007). The bright side of supplier encroachment. *Marketing Science*, 26(5), pp. 651–659.

Feng, Q., Lai, G., & Lu, L. X. (2015). Dynamic bargaining in a supply chain with asymmetric demand information. *Management Science*, 61(2), pp. 301–315.

Gümüş, M. (2014). With or without forecast sharing: Competition and credibility under information asymmetry. *Production and Operations Management*, 23(10), pp. 1732–1747.

Huang, S., Guan, X., & Chen, Y. J. (2018). Retailer information sharing with supplier encroachment. *Production and Operations Management*, 27(6), pp. 1133–1147.

Karray, S. (2015). Modeling brand advertising with heterogeneous consumer response: Channel implications. *Annals of Operations Research*, 233, pp. 181–199.

Li, Q., Li, B., Chen, P., & Hou, P. (2017). Dual-channel supply chain decisions under asymmetric information with a risk-averse retailer. *Annals of Operations Research*, 257(1–2), pp. 423–447.

Li, Z., Gilbert, S., & Lai, G. (2013). Supplier encroachment under asymmetric information. *Management Science*, 60(2), pp. 449–462.

Liu, Y., & Zhang, Z. J. (2006). Research note-the benefits of personalized pricing in a channel. *Marketing Science*, 25(1), pp. 97–105.

Shang, W. X., Ha, A. Y., & Tong, S. (2016). Information sharing in a supply chain with a common retailer. *Management Science*, 62(1), pp. 245–263.

© 2022 World Scientific Publishing Europe Ltd.
https://doi.org/10.1142/9781800610408_0009

# Chapter 9

# Contracting and Pricing in a Dual-Channel Supply Chain with a Risk-Averse Retailer Under Cost Information Asymmetry

**Ping Chen*** **and Bo Li**†

*College of Management and Economics, Tianjin University, China*

* *bingling.0815@163.com*

† *libo0410@tju.edu.com*

## 9.1. Introduction

More and more manufacturers distribute their products not only through the offline retail channels but also through their own online channels. Through introducing their online channels, the manufacturers can expand their market size, gain more market demand information from marketing activities, and directly provide the service to consumers (Chiang *et al.*, 2003; Li *et al.*, 2013, 2015). This gives rise to fierce competition and channel conflict between the manufacturer and the retailer in the dual-channel supply chain environment. Such a phenomenon is called "manufacturer encroachment" (Chen *et al.*, 2017; Li *et al.*, 2013).

It has been evident that manufacturer encroachment has a significant influence on retailers in the traditional channel, as they believe that the cannibalization effect in the dual-channel supply chain will be bound to happen (Li *et al.*, 2013, 2015). Under this case, the long-term cooperative relationship among channel members will be undermined, and their profits will be hurt (Yan and Pei, 2012, 2015). Moreover, with the development of IT, through adopting information exchange technologies, like Electronic Data Interchange or the Internet, etc., the players in dual-channel supply chain can easily communicate with each other. However, because of the intense online and offline channel competition, the information distortion may unavoidably occur. That is to say, some players may consciously send the distorted information to his partner and mislead the other players to make poor decisions. Thus, there may exist information asymmetry between the upstream player and the downstream player.

In addition, noting the effect of manufacturer encroachment and uncertain demand, the retailer may take risk-averse behavior. When the manufacturer encroaches with the online channel, he will expand his demand share which may belong to the retailer originally. As a result, the retailer has the feeling of a large threat. Thus, she may make decisions showing risk-averse behavior. Tsay and Agrawal (2004) revealed that risk sensitivity played an important role in the channel members' decision-making in supply chains. In fact, many results have demonstrated that the risk-averse behavior of members has significant influence on the decisions (Artzner *et al.*, 1997; Li *et al.*, 2014).

This chapter analyzes the supply chain systems by explicitly considering the manufacturer's production cost information asymmetry. Four situations are examined, i.e., the manufacturer opens an online channel to compete with the retail channel or not, and the manufacturer keeps his production cost information private or not. The manufacturer is assumed to be risk-neutral, and the retailer is assumed to be risk-averse, which will be measured using CVaR.

To model the production cost information asymmetry, we further assume that the manufacturer's production cost taking two types (a high type and a low type), which is privately known to him. The retailer provides a menu of contracts to the manufacturer. We will address the following questions:

(1) When all of four cases are compared, which strategy, opening an online channel or keeping cost information private, will give the manufacturer more profit?
(2) When we consider the retailer's risk-averse behavior, how will it impact the decisions of the members in the supply chain?
(3) How will some important parameters affect the optimal contracts and their profits? Such as the risk-averse level of the retailer, the channel power of the two members and the manufacturer's high production cost.

The remainder of this chapter is organized as follows. In Sec. 9.2, model description is introduced, including the notations, and assumptions. The perfect production cost information cases are presented in Sec. 9.3, including with/without manufacturer encroachment. Further, the asymmetric production cost information cases with or without the manufacturer encroachment are analyzed in Sec. 9.4. A comparison and numerical analysis are performed in Sec. 9.5. Finally, the conclusion and the future directions are summarized in Sec. 9.6.

## 9.2. Model Description

In this chapter, a supplier encroachment problem is considered with a risk-neutral manufacturer and a risk-averse retailer. The manufacturer with his own online channel produces a perishable product and sells it to customers through online and offline channels. We assume that the risk-averse retailer will face a newsvendor problem and make the decision on the order quantity of the product placed to the manufacturer. The CVaR method is selected to measure the retailer's risk-averse behavior. The manufacturer chooses a make-to-order policy in his online channel. That is, the manufacturer adopts a mixed strategy of make-to-order for the online channel and make-to-stock for the independent traditional channel (Carr and Duenyas, 2000; Iravani *et al.*, 2012; Köber and Heinecke, 2012).

Further, only one sales season is considered. Because we just consider the perishable product, to simplify the model, surplus value of the products at the end of the sales period is assumed to be zero. The manufacturer has private information about his product cost $c_k$ for each unit, where $k \in (L, H)$, that is, $c_k$ may be either high ($c_H$) with probability $\delta$ or low ($c_L$) with probability $1 - \delta$. The retailer cannot observe $k$ and only knows the probabilities of the two types of production cost at the time of placing product order.

The principal-agent theory is utilized to handle the above information asymmetry case. We assume that the retailer is powerful, acting as a principal, and the upstream manufacturer is an agent. The retailer will offer the manufacturer a menu of contracts to encourage the manufacturer to uncover his real production cost information. After the manufacturer selects a contract, the retailer may infer the production cost state from the manufacturer's selection, and the manufacturer cooperates with the retailer only in his retail channel.

The timeline of events is as follows: First, a menu of contracts $(w_k, q_k)_{k\in\{L,H\}}$ proposed by the retailer will be provided to the manufacturer, where $w_k$ is the wholesale price and $q_k$ is the order quantity. Second, the manufacturer selects one of contracts from the menu according to his real production cost state. Third, when observing the manufacturer's selection of the contracts, the retailer can better estimate the production cost of the manufacturer and determine her retail price in the traditional channel. Furthermore, the manufacturer sets the price for his online channel based on the retail price. Finally, the market is realized along with both members' profits in the supply chain.

As we assume that the retailer is the principal and is more powerful than the manufacturer, it is reasonable that the retailer offers a contract menu so that the manufacturer can gain only reservation profit and the retailer herself can obtain all the remaining profits in the supply chain. Özer and Raz (2011) studied a similar problem where the upstream supplier as the agent had private production cost information, while the downstream buyer was a principal. The buyer provided a menu of two-part pricing contracts, including a wholesale price and a fixed payment. Therefore, in this chapter, without a loss of generality, we also normalize the manufacturer's reservation profit to be zero.

In order to address the research questions, we assume that the manufacturer may have options to share his production cost information with the retailer and not to encroach the market. By comparing all these cases, we can obtain the value of introducing an online channel and keeping information private for the manufacturer as well as the influence it brings to the retailer.

The main notations are given as follows:

| Notations | Definitions |
|---|---|
| $i$ | $i = 1, 2$, where $i = 1$ presents the retail channel and $i = 2$ presents the online channel |
| $k$ | the index of the production cost state, $k = L, H$, where $L$ means low cost and $H$ means high cost |
| $D$ | the basic demand in the market |
| $D_i$ | the product demand via channel $i$ |
| $\xi$ | a random variable with support over $[-U, U]$ with a probability density function $\varphi(\cdot)$ and a cumulative distribution function $\Phi(\cdot)$ |
| $\bar{D}$ | the stochastic demand in the market, $\bar{D}$=$D + \xi$ |
| $\gamma_i$ | the price sensitivity of channel $i$ |
| $\gamma$ | the price sensitivity of the retail channel under single-channel structure |
| $\alpha$ | the cross-channel price sensitivity, where $\gamma_i \geq \alpha$ |
| $\theta$ | the proportion of market share in the traditional channel |
| $c_k$ | the per-unit production cost under the cost state $k$ |
| $\delta$ | the manufacturer's production cost is high with probability $\delta$ |
| $\eta$ | the retailer's risk-averse indicator, which is common knowledge |
| $T$ | a subscript to denote the player, where $T = r, m$, and $r$ representing the retailer, $m$ representing the manufacturer |
| $B$ | the index of information state, $B = P, A$, where $P$ is for perfect information, $A$ is for asymmetric information |
| $J$ | the index of distribution strategy, $J = S, D$, where $S$ is a single-channel, $D$ is a dual-channel with manufacturer encroachment |
| $\pi_T^{BJ}$ | the profit of player $T$ under information state $B$ and distribution strategy $J$ |
| $w_k^{BJ}$ | the optimal wholesale price with cost state $k$ under situation $BJ$ |
| ${q_k}^{BJ}$ | the optimal order quantity with cost state $k$ under situation $BJ$ |
| $p_{ik}^{BJ}$ | the optimal price per-unit of the product sold using channel $i$ with cost state $k$ under situation $BJ$ |

Table 9.1. Four different scenarios.

| Scenarios | Encroachment (Dual channel) | No encroachment (Single channel) |
|---|---|---|
| Cost information private(asymmetry) | AD | AS |
| Cost information share(symmetry) | PD | PS |

Four scenarios are considered according to the combination of the index of the information state between both members and the index of the manufacturer's distribution strategy as shown in Table 9.1.

## 9.3. Under Perfect Cost Information Case

In this section, we focus on two scenarios with perfect cost information. That is, the manufacturer and the retailer both know the cost of the manufacturer $c_k$ perfectly, $k = H, L$.

### 9.3.1. With manufacturer encroachment

First, we consider the case in which the manufacturer introduces one online channel to sell his product besides the traditional retail channel. To solve this problem, the market demands on both channels are elicited (Li *et al.*, 2014), the demand functions of the two channels are given by

$$D_1 = \theta \bar{D} - \gamma_1 p_1 + \alpha p_2, \tag{9.1}$$

$$D_2 = (1-\theta)\bar{D} - \gamma_2 p_2 + \alpha p_1, \tag{9.2}$$

where $\gamma_i \geq \alpha$ indicates that the impact of the price on its own channel is larger than that on the other channel (Mukhopadhyay *et al.*, 2008). Then, the manufacturer's expected profit function under cost state $k$ is

$$\begin{aligned} E[\pi_{mk}] &= E[(w_k - c_k)q_k + (p_{2k} - c_k)D_{2k}] \\ &= (w_k - c_k)q_k + (p_{2k} - c_k)[(1-\theta)D - \gamma_2 p_{2k} + \alpha p_{1k}], \end{aligned} \tag{9.3}$$

where $k \in \{L, H\}$.

Denote $(\cdot)^+ = \max(\cdot, 0)$, then $\min(q, D_1) = q - (q - D_1)^+$. The traditional retailer's profit function under cost state $k$ is

$$\begin{aligned}\pi_{rk} &= p_{1k}\min(q_k, D_{1k}) - w_k q_k \\ &= (p_{1k} - w_k)q_k - p_{1k}\{q_k - [\theta\bar{D} - \gamma_1 p_{1k} + \alpha p_{2k}]\}^+. \quad (9.4)\end{aligned}$$

Because the retailer is risk-averse, the CVaR method is adopted to measure her risk-averse level. We assume that $\pi_{rk}$ is the profit function of the retailer with the order quantity $q_k$ and the random demand $D_{1k}$ under cost state $k$, let $v^\eta(\pi_{rk})$ be the $\eta$-quantile of $\pi_{rk}$, where $\eta$ ($\eta \in (0, 1]$) is a confidence indicator specified by the decision-maker to attain a certain level of profit $v$. Similar to previous chapters, we have the following equivalent equation (Rockafellar and Uryasev, 2000):

$$\mathrm{CVaR}^\eta(\pi_{rk}) = \max_{v \in R}\left\{v + \frac{1}{\eta}E[\min(\pi_{rk} - v, 0)]\right\}. \quad (9.5)$$

Therefore, under cost state $k$, the traditional retailer's profit expectation function with CVaR measure is

$$\mathrm{CVaR}^\eta(\pi_{rk}) = \begin{cases} (p_{1k} - w_k)q_k - \dfrac{p_{1k}}{\eta}\theta\displaystyle\int_{-U}^{\frac{q_{1k}+\gamma_1 p_{1k} - \alpha p_{2k}}{\theta} - D}\Phi(\xi)d\xi, & q_k \le Q, \\ -wq_k + p_{1k}\theta\Phi^{-1}(\eta) + \theta p_{1k}D - p_{1k}(\gamma_1 p_{1k} - \alpha p_{2k}) & \\ -\dfrac{p_{1k}}{\eta}\theta\displaystyle\int_{-U}^{\Phi^{-1}(\eta)}\Phi(\xi)d\xi, & q_k > Q, \end{cases} \quad (9.6)$$

where $Q = \theta D - \gamma_1 p_{1k} + \alpha p_{2k} + \theta\Phi^{-1}(\eta)$ and $k \in \{L, H\}$.

Further, under full information, if the manufacturer introduces an online channel, we can apply the backward induction method to solve this problem. When the manufacturer selects the contract, his online selling price under full information is determined by formula (9.3) as follows:

$$p_{2k}^{PD} = \frac{(1-\theta)D + \alpha p_{1k} + \gamma_2 c_k}{2\gamma_2}. \quad (9.7)$$

Thus, the retailer's decision problem can be simplified as follows:

$$\max_{q_k,p_{1k},w_k} \ \mathrm{CVaR}(\pi_r)$$

$$= (p_{1k} - w_k)q_k - \frac{\theta p_{1k}}{\eta} \int_{-U}^{\frac{q_k+\gamma_1 p_{1k}-\alpha p_{2k}^{PD}}{\theta}-D} \Phi(\xi)d\xi, \quad (9.8)$$

$$\text{subject to} \quad (w_k - c_k)q_k \geq 0, \quad (9.9)$$

where inequality (9.9) represents individual rationality constraints.

**Proposition 9.1.** *Under a dual-channel supply chain with perfect cost information $c_k, k = H, L$, the retailer's optimal contracts $(q_k^{PD}, w_k^{PD})$ and the optimal selling prices in two channels $p_{ik}^{PD}(i = 1, 2)$ are given as follows:*

$$q_k^{PD} = \theta\Phi^{-1}\left(\frac{\eta}{p_{1k}^{PD}}(p_{1k}^{PD} - c_k)\right) + \theta D - \gamma_1 p_{1k}^{PD} + \alpha p_{2k}^{PD},$$

$$w_k^{PD} = c_k, \quad p_{2k}^{PD} = \frac{(1-\theta)D + \alpha p_{1k}^{PD} + \gamma_2 c_k}{2\gamma_2}.$$

*Here, $p_{1k}^{PD}$ satisfies the following equation:*

$$2\gamma_2\theta\Phi^{-1}\left(\frac{\eta}{p_{1k}^{PD}}(p_{1k}^{PD} - c_k)\right)$$
$$+ \alpha D + (2\gamma_2 - \alpha)\theta D + (\alpha^2 - 4\gamma_1\gamma_2)p_{1k}^{PD} + (2\gamma_1\gamma_2 + \gamma_2\alpha)c_k$$
$$- \frac{2\gamma_2\theta}{\eta}\int_{-U}^{\Phi^{-1}\left(\frac{\eta}{p_{1k}^{PD}}(p_{1k}^{PD}-c_k)\right)} \Phi(\xi)d\xi = 0, \quad k \in \{L, H\}.$$

Based on the results in Proposition 9.1, the manufacturer's and the retailer's expected profits can also be obtained:

$$\begin{aligned}\pi_m^{PD} &= \delta[(w_H^{PD} - c_H)q_H^{PD} + (p_{2H}^{PD} - c_H)[(1-\theta)D - \gamma_2 p_{2H}^{PD} + \alpha p_{1H}^{PD}]] \\ &\quad + (1-\delta)[(w_L^{PD} - c_L)q_L^{PD} + (p_{2L}^{PD} - c_L)[(1-\theta)D - \gamma_2 p_{2L}^{PD} \\ &\quad + \alpha p_{1L}^{PD}]] \\ &= \delta(p_{2H}^{PD} - c_H)[(1-\theta)D - \gamma_2 p_{2H}^{PD} + \alpha p_{1H}^{PD}] \\ &\quad + (1-\delta)(p_{2L}^{PD} - c_L)[(1-\theta)D - \gamma_2 p_{2L}^{PD} + \alpha p_{1L}^{PD}],\end{aligned}$$

$$\pi_r^{PD} = \delta\left[(p_{1H}^{PD} - c_H)q_H^{PD} - p_{1H}^{PD}\theta\int_{-U}^{\frac{q_H^{PD}+\gamma_1 p_{1H}^{PD}-\alpha p_{2H}^{PD}}{\theta}-D}\Phi(\xi)d\xi\right]$$
$$+(1-\delta)\left[(p_{1L}^{PD} - c_L)q_L^{PD} - p_{1L}^{PD}\theta\int_{-U}^{\frac{q_L^{PD}+\gamma_1 p_{1L}^{PD}-\alpha p_{2L}^{PD}}{\theta}-D}\Phi(\xi)d\xi\right].$$

In Proposition 9.1, when $w_k^{PD} = c_k$, it is easy to infer that the manufacturer has no profit in the retailer's traditional channel when he shares his cost information with the retailer. That is, the retailer will grab all of the profit in the traditional channel. However, when the manufacturer selects to encroach the channel, he can gain profit in the online channel.

### 9.3.2. Without manufacturer encroachment

Next, we will consider the case under which the manufacturer selects not to introduce an online channel. Thus, it means that the manufacturer does not need to make the decision on product selling price and that his connection with the retailer is just the contract, consisting of the wholesale price and the order quantity.

Under this case, the demand function of the retailer in a single channel will be

$$D_1 = \bar{D} - \gamma p_1, \tag{9.10}$$

where $\gamma < \gamma_1$ indicates that the demand on a traditional channel is less sensitive to price if there is no competition from other channels.

Then, the retailer's decision problem under full cost information is simplified as follows:

$$\max_{q_k, p_{1k}, w_k} \text{CVaR}(\pi_r)$$
$$= (p_{1k} - w_k)q_k - \frac{p_{1k}}{\eta}\int_{-U}^{q_k+\gamma p_{1k}-D}\Phi(\xi)d\xi, \tag{9.11}$$
$$\text{subject to} \quad (w_k - c_k)q_k \geq 0. \tag{9.12}$$

Similarly, the optimal solutions can be easily obtained under this case.

**Proposition 9.2.** *Under a traditional single-channel with perfect information on the production cost $c_k, k = H, L$, the retailer's optimal contracts $(q_k^{PS}, w_k^{PS})$ and her retail selling price $p_{1k}^{PS}$ are given as follows:*

$$q_k^{PS} = \Phi^{-1}\left(\frac{\eta}{p_{1k}^{PS}}(p_{1k}^{PS} - c_k)\right) + D - \gamma p_{1k}^{PS}, \quad w_k^{PS} = c_k.$$

*Here, $p_{1k}^{PS}$ satisfies the following equation:*

$$\Phi^{-1}\left(\frac{\eta}{p_{1k}^{PS}}(p_{1k}^{PS} - c_k)\right) + D - 2\gamma p_{1k}^{PS} + \gamma c_k$$
$$-\frac{1}{\eta}\int_{-U}^{\Phi^{-1}\left(\frac{\eta}{p_{1k}^{PS}}(p_{1k}^{PS} - c_k)\right)} \Phi(\xi)d\xi = 0, \quad k \in \{L, H\}.$$

From Proposition 9.2, we can find that Scenario PS is the simplest situation, because there is only one traditional channel and no incentive mechanism.

Thus, both parties' expected profits can be gained as

$$\pi_m^{PS} = \delta(w_H^{PS} - c_H)q_H^{PS} + (1-\delta)(w_L^{PS} - c_L)q_L^{PS} = 0,$$
$$\pi_r^{PS} = \delta\left[(p_{1H}^{PS} - c_H)q_H^{PS} - p_{1H}^{PS}\int_{-U}^{q_H^{PS} + \gamma p_{1H}^{PS} - D} \Phi(\xi)d\xi\right]$$
$$+(1-\delta)\left[(p_{1L}^{PS} - c_L)q_L^{PS} - p_{1L}^{AS}\int_{-U}^{q_L^{PS} + \gamma p_{1L}^{PS} - D} \Phi(\xi)d\xi\right].$$

Shown in Proposition 9.2, when the manufacturer selects to share his cost state with the retailer and not to encroach the channel, he will gain zero profit. The reason is that the retailer can exploit the shared information of production cost and take the advantage as the principal. Clearly, this simplest scenario (Scenario PS) gives us a benchmark to obtain the manufacturer's value of encroaching and hiding information.

## 9.4. Under Asymmetric Cost Information Case

In this subsection, the more complex scenarios are investigated, that is, the manufacturer has private cost information and may select to encroach in the traditional channel. Then, we will explore how the retailer will design the contract menu to the manufacturer, and how the manufacturer will respond to the retailer's contract.

### 9.4.1. With manufacturer encroachment

Under this case, we will consider manufacturer encroachment under asymmetric cost information. Thus, the retailer (as the principal) will first provide a contract menu to the manufacturer (as the agent), and there exists an optimal menu of contracts, with which the retailer can learn the true production cost information from the manufacturer's selection of the contracts.

Then, the backward induction method is adopted to solve the sequence game. Hence, when the manufacturer selects to encroach, through choosing the contract and observing the retail price, his online selling price is solved by

$$\max_{p_{2k}}(p_{2k} - c_k)[(1-\theta)D - \gamma_2 p_{2k} + \alpha p_{1k}], \tag{9.13}$$

which yields the manufacturer's optimal online selling price

$$p_{2k}^{AD} = \frac{(1-\theta)D + \alpha p_{1k} + \gamma_2 c_k}{2\gamma_2}. \tag{9.14}$$

Notice that the manufacturer's online selling price is a function of both the retailer's retail price and the production cost of the manufacturer. Obviously, when the retailer proposes the contracts, she should consider how the manufacturer's subsequent incentive to encroach will affect her optimal decision. As a result, the retailer's contract design problem with manufacturer encroachment can be formulated as follows:

$$\begin{aligned}\max_{q_k, p_{1k}, w_k}\ & \mathrm{CVaR}(\pi_r)\\ =\ & \delta\left[(p_{1H} - w_H)\,q_H - \frac{\theta p_{1H}}{\eta}\int_{-U}^{\frac{q_H + \gamma_1 p_{1H} - \alpha p_{2H}^{AD}}{\theta} - D} \Phi(\xi)d\xi\right]\\ &+ (1-\delta)\left[(p_{1L} - w_L)q_L - \frac{\theta p_{1L}}{\eta}\int_{-U}^{\frac{q_L + \gamma_1 p_{1L} - \alpha p_{2L}^{AD}}{\theta} - D} \Phi(\xi)\, d\xi\right],\end{aligned} \tag{9.15}$$

subject to

$$(w_H - c_H)q_H \geq 0, \tag{9.16}$$

$$(w_L - c_L)q_L \geq 0, \tag{9.17}$$

$$(w_H - c_H)q_H \geq (w_L - c_H)q_L, \tag{9.18}$$

$$(w_L - c_L)q_L \geq (w_H - c_L)q_H, \tag{9.19}$$

where inequalities (9.16) and (9.17) are individual rationality constraints to guarantee that the manufacturer will distribute his product in the traditional channel when his expected profit exceeds the reservation profit. While inequalities (9.18) and (9.19) are incentive compatibility constraints to ensure that the manufacturer will not select the contract which is opposite to his true cost state. Thus, the following proposition is proposed.

**Proposition 9.3.** *Under manufacturer encroachment with asymmetric production cost information* $c_k, k = H, L$, *the retailer's optimal contracts* $(q_k^{AD}, w_k^{AD})$ *and the optimal selling prices* $p_{ik}^{AD}$ *are given as follows*:

(1) *If the manufacturer's cost is at the high state, then*

$$q_H^{AD} = \theta\Phi^{-1}\left(\frac{\eta}{\delta p_{1H}^{AD}}(\delta p_{1H}^{AD} - N)\right) + \theta D - \gamma_1 p_{1H}^{AD} + \alpha p_{2H}^{AD},$$

$$w_H^{AD} = c_H, p_{2H}^{AD} = \frac{(1-\theta)\,D + \alpha p_{1H}^{AD} + \gamma_2 c_H}{2\gamma_2},$$

*and* $p_{1H}^{AD}$ *satisfies the following equation*:

$$\begin{aligned}
&2\gamma_2\delta\theta\Phi^{-1}\left(\frac{\eta}{\delta p_{1H}^{AD}}(\delta p_{1H}^{AD} - N)\right) + \delta\alpha D + (2\gamma_2 - \alpha)\delta\theta D \\
&\quad + (\delta\alpha^2 - 4\gamma_1\gamma_2\delta)p_{1H}^{AD} + (2\gamma_1\gamma_2 + \gamma_2\delta\alpha)c_H + 2\gamma_1\gamma_2(\delta - 1)c_L \\
&\quad - \frac{2\gamma_2\theta\delta}{\eta}\int_{-U}^{\Phi^{-1}\left(\frac{\eta}{\delta p_{1H}^{AD}}(\delta p_{1H}^{AD} - N)\right)} \Phi(\xi)d\xi = 0.
\end{aligned}$$

(2) *If the manufacturer's cost is at the low state, then*

$$q_L^{AD} = \theta\Phi^{-1}\left(\frac{\eta}{p_{1L}^{AD}}(p_{1L}^{AD} - c_L)\right) + \theta D - \gamma_1 p_{1L}^{AD} + \alpha p_{2L}^{AD},$$

$$w_L^{AD} = c_L + \frac{q_H^{AD}}{q_L^{AD}}(c_H - c_L), \quad p_{2L}^{AD} = \frac{(1-\theta)D + \alpha p_{1L}^{AD} + \gamma_2 c_L}{2\gamma_2},$$

*and* $p_{1L}^{AD}$ *satisfies the following equation:*

$$\begin{aligned}
&2\gamma_2\theta\Phi^{-1}\left(\frac{\eta}{p_{1L}^{AD}}(p_{1L}^{AD} - c_L)\right) + \alpha D + (2\gamma_2 - \alpha)\theta D \\
&\quad + (\alpha^2 - 4\gamma_1\gamma_2)p_{1L}^{AD} + (2\gamma_1\gamma_2 + \gamma_2\alpha)c_L \\
&\quad - \frac{2\gamma_1\theta}{\eta}\int_{-U}^{\Phi^{-1}\left(\frac{\eta}{p_{1L}^{AD}}(p_{1L}^{AD} - c_L)\right)} \Phi(\xi)d\xi = 0,
\end{aligned}$$

*where* $N = \delta c_L + c_H - c_L$.

It follows that the manufacturer's expected profit is

$$\begin{aligned}
\pi_m^{AD} &= \delta\{(w_H^{AD} - c_H)\, q_H^{AD} + (p_{2H}^{AD} - c_H)\,[(1-\theta)\,D - \gamma_2 p_{2H}^{AD} \\
&\quad + \alpha p_{1H}^{AD}]\} + (1-\delta)\,\{(w_L^{AD} - c_L)\, q_L^{AD} + (p_{2L}^{AD} - c_L) \\
&\quad \times [(1-\theta)\,D - \gamma_2 p_{2L}^{AD} + \alpha p_{1L}^{AD}]\} \\
&= \delta(p_{2H}^{AD} - c_H)[(1-\theta)D - \gamma_2 p_{2H}^{AD} + \alpha p_{1H}^{AD}] \\
&\quad + (1-\delta)\{(c_H - c_L)q_H^{AD} + (p_{2L}^{AD} - c_L)[(1-\theta)D \\
&\quad - \gamma_2 p_{2L}^{AD} + \alpha p_{1L}^{AD}]\}.
\end{aligned}$$

The retailer's expected profit is

$$\begin{aligned}
\pi_r^{AD} &= \delta\{(p_{1H}^{AD} - w_H^{AD})q_H^{AD} + p_{1H}^{AD} E[q_H^{AD} - \theta\bar{D} + \gamma_1 p_{1H}^{AD} - \alpha p_{2H}^{AD}]^+\} \\
&\quad + (1-\delta)\{(p_{1L}^{AD} - w_L^{AD})q_L^{AD} \\
&\quad + p_{1L}^{AD} E[q_L^{AD} - \theta\bar{D} + \gamma_1 p_{1L}^{AD} - \alpha p_{2L}^{AD}]^+\}
\end{aligned}$$

$$
\begin{aligned}
&= \delta\left[(p_{1H}^{AD} - c_H)q_H^{AD} - p_{1H}^{AD}\theta\int_{-U}^{\frac{q_H^{AD}+\gamma_1 p_{1H}^{AD}-\alpha p_{2H}^{AD}}{\theta}-D}\Phi(\xi)d\xi\right]\\
&\quad + (1-\delta)\\
&\quad \times\left[(p_{1L}^{AD} - w_L^{AD})q_L^{AD} - p_{1L}^{AD}\theta\int_{-U}^{\frac{q_L^{AD}+\gamma_1 p_{1L}^{AD}-\alpha p_{2L}^{AD}}{\theta}-D}\Phi(\xi)d\xi\right].
\end{aligned}
$$

From Proposition 9.3, when $w_H^{AD} = c_H$ and $w_L^{AD} = c_L + \frac{q_H^{AD}}{q_L^{AD}}(c_H - c_L) > c_L$, it can be seen that if the manufacturer's cost state is high, then he will obtain the least profit in his traditional channel, which is the reservation profit. But, if his cost state is low, at this time, his wholesale price is larger than the cost, and he can gain a profit exceeding the reservation profit, which is called information rent. However, how large the information rent is we don't know, neither do we know the value of adding a new online channel.

In addition, through comparing the scenarios AD with PD, we can obtain the information value to the manufacturer under the dual channel, i.e., $\Delta\pi_m^{AD-PD} = \pi_m^{AD} - \pi_m^{PD}$, and the disadvantage it brings to the retailer $\Delta\pi_r^{AD-PD} = \pi_r^{AD} - \pi_r^{PD}$. Moreover, we can also define that the manufacturer's channel value under information symmetry is $\Delta\pi_m^{PD-PS} = \pi_m^{PD} - \pi_m^{PS}$, and the retailer's corresponding channel disadvantage is $\Delta\pi_r^{PD-PS} = \pi_r^{PD} - \pi_r^{PS}$. We will discuss these points in Sec. 9.5.

### 9.4.2. Without manufacturer encroachment

Further, we suppose that the manufacturer will select not to introduce an online channel. Then, in this case, the demand function in the market under a single-channel is given in formula (9.10).

Therefore, when only a single traditional channel exists, we can formulate the retailer's decision problem under asymmetric cost information as follows:

$$
\max_{q_k, p_{1k}, w_k} CVaR(\pi_r) = \delta\left[(p_{1H} - w_H)q_H - \frac{p_{1H}}{\eta}\int_{-U}^{q_H+\gamma p_{1H}-D}\Phi(\xi)d\xi\right]
$$

$$
\begin{aligned}
&+ (1-\delta)\left[(p_{1L} - w_L)q_L \right.\\
&\left. - \frac{p_{1L}}{\eta}\int_{-U}^{q_L+\gamma p_{1L}-D} \Phi(\xi)d\xi\right],
\end{aligned} \tag{9.20}
$$

subject to

$$(w_H - c_H)q_H \geq 0, \tag{9.21}$$

$$(w_L - c_L)q_L \geq 0, \tag{9.22}$$

$$(w_H - c_H)q_H \geq (w_L - c_H)q_L, \tag{9.23}$$

$$(w_L - c_L)q_L \geq (w_H - c_L)q_H. \tag{9.24}$$

Through solving the above problem, Proposition 9.4 is given.

**Proposition 9.4.** *Under no manufacturer encroachment with asymmetric production cost information $c_k, k = H, L$, the retailer's optimal contracts $(q_k^{AS}, w_k^{AS})$ and the optimal selling prices $p_{1k}^{AS}$ are given as follows:*

(1) *If the manufacturer's cost is at the high state, then*

$$q_H^{AS} = \Phi^{-1}\left(\frac{\eta}{\delta p_{1H}^{AS}}(\delta p_{1H}^{AS} - N)\right) + D - \gamma p_{1H}^{AS}, \quad w_H^{AS} = c_H,$$

*and $p_{1H}^{AS}$ satisfies the following equation:*

$$
\begin{aligned}
&\delta\Phi^{-1}\left(\frac{\eta}{\delta p_{1H}^{AS}}(\delta p_{1H}^{AS} - N)\right)\\
&\quad + \delta D - 2\delta\gamma p_{1H}^{AS} + \gamma N - \frac{\delta}{\eta}\int_{-U}^{\Phi^{-1}\left(\frac{\eta}{\delta p_{1H}^{AS}}(\delta p_{1H}^{AS} - N)\right)} \Phi(\xi)d\xi = 0.
\end{aligned}
$$

(2) *If the manufacturer's cost is at the low state, then*

$$
\begin{aligned}
q_L^{AS} &= \Phi^{-1}\left(\frac{\eta}{p_{1L}^{AS}}(p_{1L}^{AS} - c_L)\right)\\
&\quad + D - \gamma p_{1L}^{AS}, \quad w_L^{AS} = c_L + \frac{q_H^{AS}}{q_L^{AS}}(c_H - c_L),
\end{aligned}
$$

*and* $p_{1L}^{AS}$ *satisfies the following equation:*

$$\Phi^{-1}\left(\frac{\eta}{p_{1L}^{AS}}(p_{1L}^{AS}-c_L)\right) + D - 2\gamma p_{1L}^{AS} + \gamma c_L - \frac{1}{\eta}\int_{-U}^{\Phi^{-1}\left(\frac{\eta}{p_{1L}^{AS}}(p_{1L}^{AS}-c_L)\right)} \Phi(\xi)d\xi = 0,$$

*where* $N = \delta c_L + c_H - c_L$.

Similarly, the manufacturer's and the retailer's expected profits are as follows:

$$\begin{aligned}
\pi_m^{AS} &= \delta(w_H^{AS} - c_H)q_H^{AS} + (1-\delta)(w_L^{AS} - c_L)q_L^{AS} \\
&= (1-\delta)(c_H - c_L)q_H^{AS}, \\
\pi_r^{AS} &= \delta[(p_{1H}^{AS} - w_H^{AS})q_H^{AS} + p_{1H}^{AS}E[q_H^{AS} - \bar{D} + \gamma p_{1H}^{AS}]^+] \\
&\quad + (1-\delta)[(p_{1L}^{AS} - w_L^{AS})q_L^{AS} \\
&\quad + p_{1L}^{AS}E[q_L^{AS} - \bar{D} + \gamma p_{1L}^{AS}]^+] \\
&= \delta[(p_{1H}^{AS} - c_H)q_H^{AS} - p_{1H}^{AS}\int_{-U}^{q_H^{AS}+\gamma p_{1H}^{AS}-D} \Phi(\xi)d\xi] \\
&\quad + (1-\delta)\left[(p_{1L}^{AS} - w_L^{AS})q_L^{AS} - p_{1L}^{AS}\int_{-U}^{q_L^{AS}+\gamma p_{1L}^{AS}-D} \Phi(\xi)d\xi\right].
\end{aligned}$$

Under the cost information asymmetry, Proposition 9.4 exhibits the equilibrium solutions in single-channel structure, thus the information rent between two agents still exists in this scenario. However, if the manufacturer's cost is at the high state, then he also gains no profit. The reason is that his profit just comes from the sales in the retail channel and we assume that his reservation profit is zero.

Through comparing the scenarios AD with AS, we can obtain the manufacturer's channel value under information asymmetry, that is, $\Delta\pi_m^{AD-AS} = \pi_m^{AD} - \pi_m^{AS}$, and the retailer's channel disadvantage $\Delta\pi_r^{AD-AS} = \pi_r^{AD} - \pi_r^{AS}$. Meanwhile, the manufacturer's information value can be defined under the single-channel, i.e., $\Delta\pi_m^{AS-PS} = \pi_m^{AS} - \pi_m^{PS}$, and the retailer's corresponding information disadvantage is $\Delta\pi_r^{AS-PS} = \pi_r^{AS} - \pi_r^{PS}$.

Finally, combining the consideration of the manufacturer encroachment and asymmetric information, the manufacturer's total value of combining encroaching and hiding information can be summed, i.e.,

$$\begin{aligned}\Delta\pi_m^{AD-PS} &= \pi_m^{AD} - \pi_m^{PS} \\ &= \Delta\pi_m^{AD-AS} + \Delta\pi_m^{AS-PS} = \Delta\pi_m^{AD-PD} + \Delta\pi_m^{PD-PS},\end{aligned}$$

and the total impact they bring to the retailer is

$$\begin{aligned}\Delta\pi_r^{AD-PS} &= \pi_r^{AD} - \pi_r^{PS} \\ &= \Delta\pi_r^{AD-AS} + \Delta\pi_r^{AS-PS} = \Delta\pi_r^{AD-PD} + \Delta\pi_r^{PD-PS}.\end{aligned}$$

## 9.5. Discussion and Numerical Analysis

In this subsection, the optimal contracts and selling prices are compared under different situations. Furthermore, we also investigate the sensitivities of results with respect to some important factors, that is, how members' optimal decisions and profits are affected by the manufacturer's production cost $c_H$, the retailer's risk-averse indicator $\eta$, and her channel power $\theta$.

First, the following results will be obtained by comparing the optimal solutions under different scenarios.

**Proposition 9.5.** *Comparing the perfect cost information scenarios with the asymmetric cost information scenarios, there exist the following results.*

(1) *When the manufacturer selects to encroach the channel, there are*

$$q_L^{PD} = q_L^{AD}, \quad p_{1L}^{PD} = p_{1L}^{AD}, \quad p_{2L}^{PD} = p_{2L}^{AD},$$
$$w_L^{PD} < w_L^{AD}, \quad w_H^{PD} = w_H^{AD}.$$

(2) *When the manufacturer chooses not to encroach the channel, there are*

$$q_L^{PS} = q_L^{AS}, \quad p_{1L}^{PS} = p_{1L}^{AS}, \quad w_L^{PS} < w_L^{AS}, \quad w_H^{PS} = w_H^{AS}.$$

Proposition 9.5 finds that no matter whether the manufacturer chooses to encroach the traditional channel, the retailer's order quantities and selling prices under perfect cost information are equal to those under asymmetric information if the cost state is low. But, when the cost state of the manufacturer is high, the wholesale prices under asymmetric and symmetric information are identical. On the contrary, when his cost state is low under asymmetric information, the manufacturer will charge a higher wholesale price. It means that the manufacturer benefits from keeping his cost information private, as the retailer has to pay information rent to reveal the manufacturer's exact production cost.

Because the expressions of the retail prices are complex, the optimal contracts and the selling prices are difficult to compare analytically under the high cost state, and so do the players' profits. Thus, the numerical experiments will be performed to discuss the comparison.

Here, in order to make the experiments more tractable, we assume that demand uncertainty follows a uniform distribution. The parameters are assumed to be: $D = 300$, $U = 30$, $\gamma_1 = 0.8$, $\gamma_2 = 0.8$, $\gamma = 0.6$, $\alpha = 0.3$, and $\delta = 0.5$.

### 9.5.1. The impacts of the retailer's risk-averse indicator

First, we examine how both players' profits are influenced by the retailer's risk-averse behavior. Let $c_L = 10$, $c_H = 20$, and $\theta = 0.7$. The results are shown in Fig. 9.1.

Figures 9.1(a) and 9.1(b) exhibit the value of keeping information private and online encroaching to the manufacturer (Fig. 9.1(a)), as well as the impacts it may bring to the retailer (Fig. 9.1(b)). We can find that the value can be divided into two parts: information value (denoted as Rhombus and Triangle lines) and channel value (denoted as Circle and Square lines). From Fig. 9.1(a), the manufacturer's channel value is substantially higher than information value. This reflects that the newly added online channel can produce much more profit than the information rent.

On the contrary, the manufacturer's cost information and distribution strategies have negative influences on the retailer's profit performance, which can also be separated into two portions: information

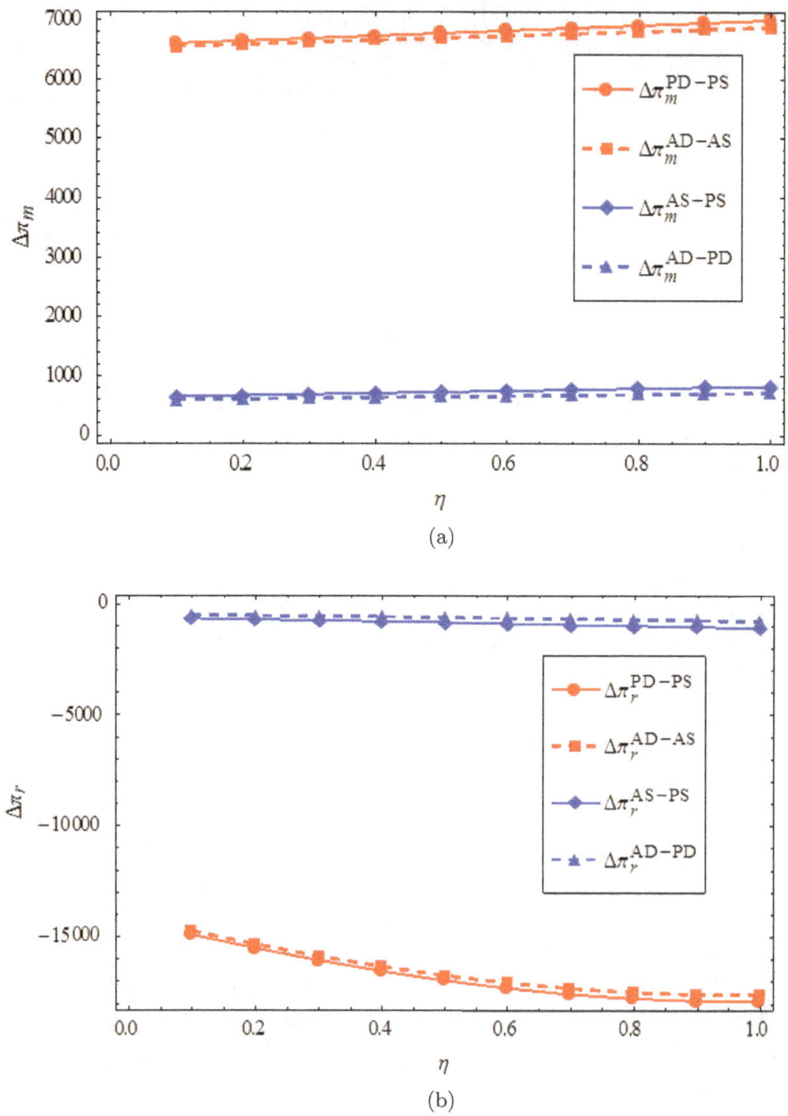


Fig. 9.1. Impacts of the risk-averse indicator on both agents' profits. (a) For the manufacturer and (b) for the retailer.

disadvantage (denoted as Rhombus and Triangle lines) and channel disadvantage (represented as Circle and Square lines) in Fig. 9.1(b). The value of cost information and channel encroachment to the manufacturer is slowly increasing as the retailer becomes less risk-averse, whereas their negative impact on the retailer is decreasing. We find that the channel value to the manufacturer cannot offset the channel disadvantage to the retailer, which appears to be interesting. The reason for this may be that the manufacturer encroachment seriously exacerbates the double marginalization effect between both players. This phenomenon implies that the manufacturer will prefer to introduce an online channel, because the newly added channel can greatly change his passive position as an agent in the traditional channel. Besides, when negotiating with the retailer, the cost information asymmetry obviously provides the manufacturer with more benefits.

### 9.5.2. The impact of the retailer's channel power

Next, we investigate the impacts of the retailer's channel power $\theta$ on two players' profit differences $\Delta\pi_T$. Similarly, let $c_L = 10$, $c_H = 20$ and $\eta = 0.7$. Figure 9.2 shows the results.

In Fig. 9.2(a), we can also see that introducing an online channel is significantly beneficial to the manufacturer, especially when the retailer's channel power is relatively low. That is, if he encroaches the traditional channel, then he has nothing to lose although the retailer is dominating the market. For the retailer, shown in Fig. 9.2(b), her channel disadvantage is decreasing with the increase of her market share. But, the retailer can never achieve the same profit as that under the single channel, even if $\theta = 1$. That is, even if the demand in the manufacturer's channel is zero, the demand in the retailer's channel will be smaller than that under the single-channel, because the added online channel creates the channel competition.

### 9.5.3. The impact of the manufacturer's high production cost

This section evaluates the effect of the manufacturer's production cost $c_H$ on the players' profit differences $\Delta\pi_T$. Particularly, through fixing the low production cost and changing the high production cost, we continue to explore the effects of the production cost to

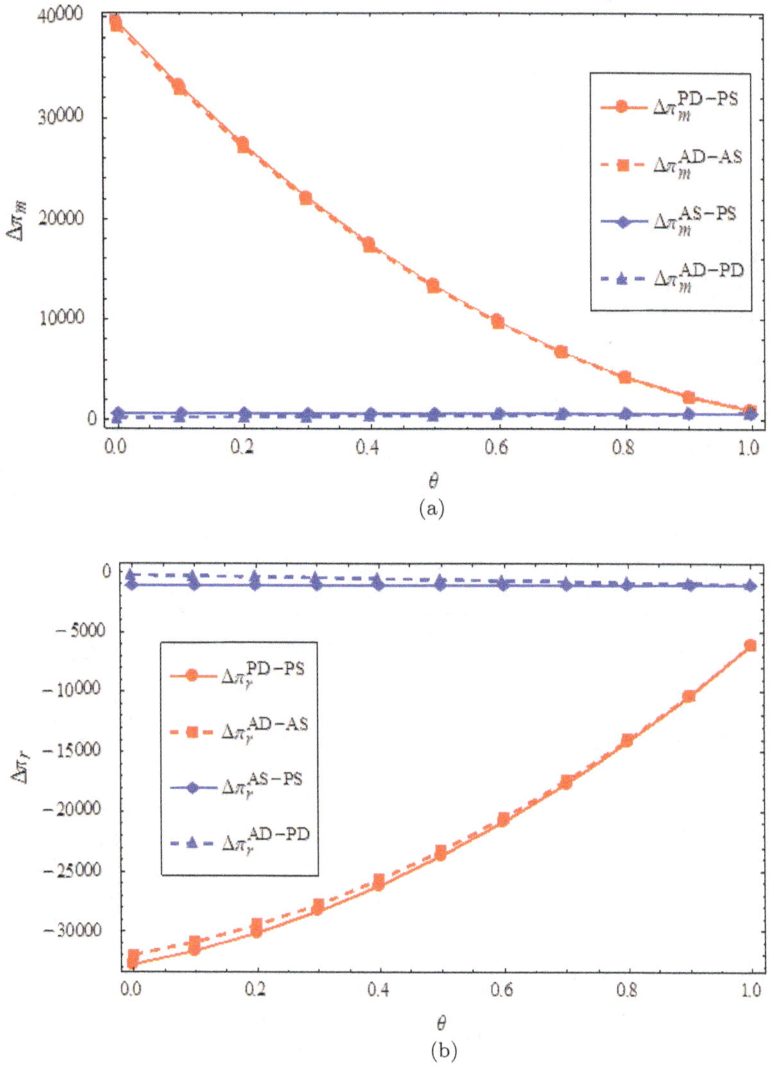


Fig. 9.2. Impacts of the retailer's market share on players' profits. (a) For the manufacturer and (b) for the retailer.

both players in the supply chain. The parameters are set as $\theta = 0.7$, $c_L = 10$, and $\eta = 0.7$. The experiment results are shown in Fig. 9.3.

From Fig. 9.3(a), it can be concluded that the manufacturer's channel value is slowly decreasing, but the information value is increasing as his high production cost increases. For the former

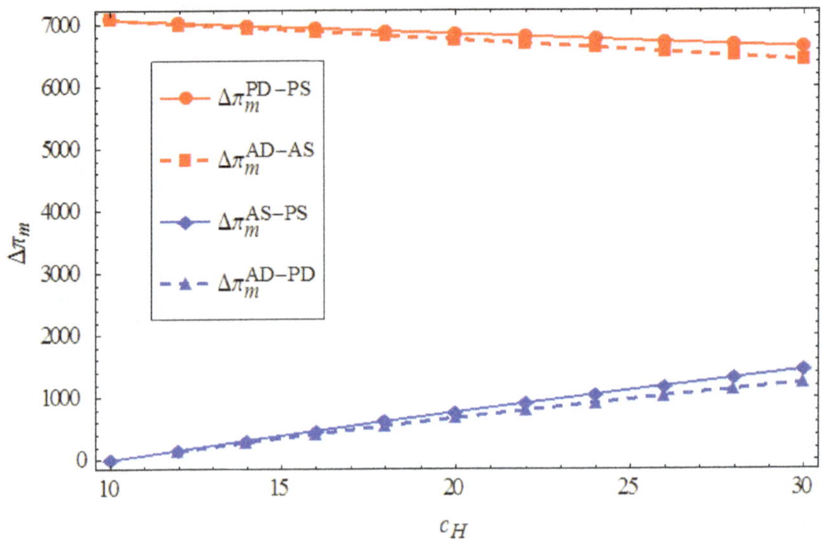


(a)

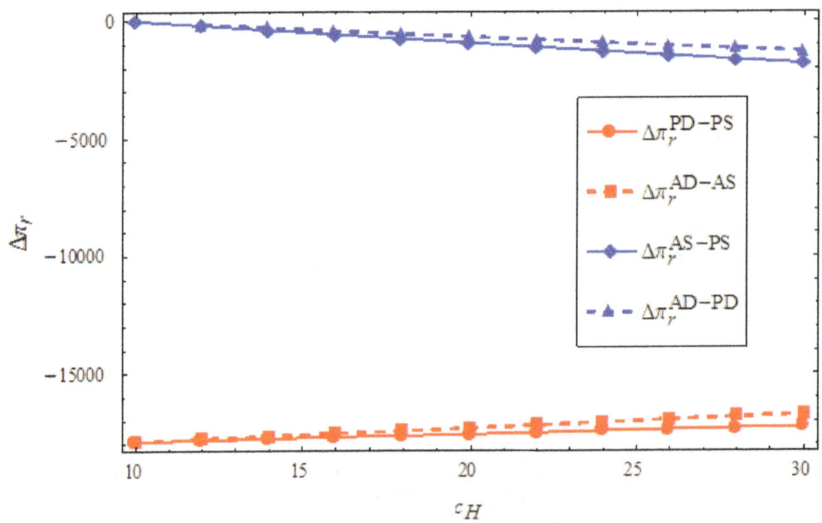


(b)

Fig. 9.3. The impacts of high cost on both players' profits. (a) For the manufacturer and (b) for the retailer.

phenomenon, the reason may be that when he competes with the traditional channel, the higher cost is not beneficial to the manufacturer. The latter phenomenon may reflect the fact that high production cost will enhance the manufacturer's negotiation power when he negotiates the contracts with the retailer under information asymmetry.

Shown in Fig. 9.3(b), for the retailer, her channel disadvantage under information symmetry is more obvious than that under asymmetric cost information. In fact, the retailer's channel disadvantage is decreasing as the manufacturer's high product cost increases. The reason is that the manufacturer's disadvantage resulting from increased production cost is shared between the online channel and the traditional channel. In addition, the retailer's information disadvantage under the dual channel is less significant than that under the single-channel. This may be explained by the fact that the competition between online channel and offline channel harms the players' profits seriously, especially when there exists information asymmetry. We find that the retailer's information disadvantage deteriorates as the increase of the production cost, which can be analyzed through the notion that the manufacturer can achieve much higher information value when the production cost is high.

## 9.6. Conclusion

In this chapter, we studied a supply chain consisting of a risk-neutral manufacturer and a risk-averse retailer facing uncertain demand. The retailer's risk-averse attitude is measured using CVaR method. Four scenarios are designed according to the combination of whether the manufacturer opens an online channel to compete with the retail channel (channel encroachment) and whether the manufacturer shares its production cost information with the retailer (information asymmetry). Under the above four cases, the principal-agent models are built to explore the retailer's optimal contract design and retail pricing decision, and the manufacturer's optimal contract selection and online channel pricing decision (if it is opened).

Through solving the game models, the optimal contracts under four situations are gained. The main conclusions are that whether the manufacturer selects to encroach or not, he can always benefit from keeping his production cost information private. However, it is surprising to notice that for the manufacturer, the information value is much less than channel value. In addition, three sets of numerical experiments are performed to gain more managerial insights by analyzing the impact of the retailer's risk-averse level, the channel power and the manufacturer's high production cost on both players' profits.

Further research could be done in the following directions. First, the model may be extended to situations where both players have a risk-averse attitude. Second, we assume that the retailer has much more power than the manufacturer, and she is the leader as a principal. In practice, manufacturers could be much more powerful than the retailers. It would be interesting to investigate whether the results such as the manufacturer's channel value is much higher than the information value, still hold for more general situations.

## References

Artzner, P., Delbaen, F., Eber, J. M., & Heath, D. (1997). Thinking coherently. *Risk*, 10(11), pp. 68–71.

Carr, S., & Duenyas, I. (2000). Optimal admission control and sequencing in a make-to-stock/make-to-order production system. *Operations Research*, 48(5), pp. 709–720.

Chen, P., Li, B., Jiang, Y. S., & Hou, P. W. (2017). The impact of manufacturer's direct sales and cost information asymmetry in a dual-channel supply chain with a risk-averse retailer. *International Journal of Electronic Commerce*, 21(1), pp. 47–70.

Chiang, W. K., Chajed, D., & Hess, J. D. (2003). Direct marketing indirect profits: A strategic analysis of dual-channel supply chain design. *Management Science*, 49(1), pp. 1–20.

Iravani, S. M., Liu, T., & Simchi-Levi, D. (2012). Optimal production and admission policies in make-to-stock/make-to-order manufacturing systems. *Production and Operations Management*, 21(2), pp. 224–235.

Köber, J., & Heinecke, G. (2012). Hybrid production strategy between make-to-order and make-to-stock — A case study at a manufacturer of agricultural machinery with volatile and seasonal demand. *Procedia CIRP*, 3, pp. 453–458.

Li, B., Chen, P., Li, Q., & Wang, W. (2014). Dual-channel supply chain pricing decisions with a risk-averse retailer. *International Journal of Production Research*, 52(23), pp. 7132–7147.

Li, Z., Gilbert, S. M., & Lai, G. (2013). Supplier encroachment under asymmetric information. *Management Science*, 60(2), pp. 449–462.

Li, Z., Gilbert, S. M., & Lai, G. (2015). Supplier encroachment as an enhancement or a hindrance to nonlinear pricing. *Production and Operations Management*, 24(1), pp. 89–109.

Mukhopadhyay, S. K., Yao, D. Q., & Yue, X. H. (2008). Information sharing of value-adding retailer in a mixed channel hi tech supply chain. *Journal of Business Research*, 61(9), pp. 950–958.

Özer, Ö., & Raz, G. (2011). Supply chain sourcing under asymmetric information. *Production and Operations Management*, 20(1), pp. 92–115.

Rockafellar, R. T., & Uryasev, S. (2000). Optimization of conditional value-at-risk. *Journal of Risk*, 2, pp. 21–41.

Yan, R., & Pei, Z. (2012). Incentive-compatible information sharing by dual-channel retailers. *International Journal of Electronic Commerce*, 17(2), pp. 127–157.

Yan, R., & Pei, Z. (2015). The strategic value of cooperative advertising in the dual-channel competition. *International Journal of Electronic Commerce*, 19(3), pp. 118–143.

© 2022 World Scientific Publishing Europe Ltd.
https://doi.org/10.1142/9781800610408_0010

# Chapter 10

# Pricing Decisions in Two Competing Channels with a Risk-Averse Capacity-Constrained Carrier

**Wei Zheng**[*,‡], **Bo Li**[*,§], **and Dong-Ping Song**[†,¶]

[*] *College of Management and Economics, Tianjin University, China*
[†] *School of Management, University of Liverpool, Liverpool, UK*
[‡] *zhengw@tju.edu.cn*
[§] *libo0410@tju.edu.cn*
[¶] *Dongping.Song@liverpool.ac.uk*

## 10.1. Introduction

Maritime transportation plays a central role in today's economy because there is no effective alternative way to transport large-scale goods over long distances. According to Lloyds Marine Intelligence Unit (Mandryk, 2009), about 60% of international trade by value were carried by sea; among the maritime transport sectors, 52% of cargoes by value were carried by container ships. Container transportation has experienced rapid growth in the past 20 years. The size of the largest container ship has increased from 8000 TEU (twenty-foot equivalent unit) in 2000 to 23,964 TEU in 2020. Container liner shipping can be seen as a capital-intensive industry with a long investment cycle (Fransoo and Lee, 2013). A modern container ship usually costs more than $100 million and takes several years to build. Container ships regularly sail according to a published schedule. In order to comply with the schedule, even if the container ship is under-loaded, it still has to leave the port. Today, global shipping companies usually provide similar shipping services every week, such as Asia–Europe route, trans-Pacific route, or trans-Atlantic route, although individual shipping services may differ in terms of ports of call. The capital-intensive nature associated with the demand for scheduled shipping services leads to fierce competition among shipping companies. Low service differentiation in liner shipping means that competition is mainly based on cost or freight rate (Lee and Song, 2017). In addition, seasonal variations of the shrinking market and fluctuations in fuel prices have also promoted volatilities in freight rates. For example, Lloyd's List reported that in November 2015, freight rates slumped 40% within a week. Shipping companies face two types of customer demands: long-term contract demand and spot market demand. The long-term demand price is usually a fixed contract price once a year, while the spot market demand price can be dynamically negotiated by the shipping company and the shipper (or freight forwarder) on a daily/weekly basis. Since the 2008 financial crisis, the economic recession and declining trade demand have led to overcapacity in the liner shipping market. The decentralized container shipping market and the continued pursuit of economies of scale by shipping companies (such as purchasing larger and larger vessels) have made the situation worse. In recent years, shippers tend to seek lower freight rates through the spot market (Lee *et al.*, 2015). This has intensified competition among shipping companies and increased the unpredictability of a single shipping company's freight volume. The uncertainty of customer demands has always been one of the main challenges that shipping companies have to deal with in order to survive in the current highly competitive environment.

In addition, the liner service market is perishable in nature, which means that the unused shipping space will lose the opportunity to generate revenue. Thus, in the fiercely competitive and uncertain spot market, it is an urgent balance for shipping companies to find a suitable pricing strategy to maximize revenue. It is understandable that, given the perishable nature of the liner service market, some shipping companies may adopt a risk-averse attitude in their pricing strategies.

This chapter aims to investigate the competition outcome and pricing strategies of shipping companies with uncertain spot market demands considering risk-averse behavior and capacity constraint. Specifically, we consider the competition between two shipping companies: one larger and one smaller. The larger shipping company is risk-neutral with sufficient capacity; while the smaller shipping company is risk-averse with limited shipping capacity. In addition, the smaller shipping company here can be regarded as freight forwarders or non-vessel operating common carriers (NVOCC) who have purchased a certain number of slots from shipping companies. The research questions we would like to address are listed as follows (Zheng *et al.*, 2017):

(1) What are the optimal freight rate strategies and the profits of two carriers when the smaller carrier is risk-averse with uncertain spot market demand?
(2) What is the difference between the two carrier's freight rate strategies? How does the risk attitude influence freight rate strategies and profits?
(3) What are the effects of other parameters, e.g., competition intensity and the spot market price sensitivity, on the decision variables and the profits?

The remainder of this chapter is organized as follows. In Sec. 10.2, we describe the problem and formulate a Nash game model. In Secs. 10.3 and 10.4, we analyze the model, obtain the equilibrium solution, and establish a series of analytical results. In Sec. 10.5, a range of numerical experiments are performed to illustrate the analytical results and explore their validity in more general situations. Finally, conclusions and suggestions for further research are drawn in Sec. 10.6.

## 10.2. Problem Description

Consider a maritime shipping market consisting of two shipping lines, denoted by carrier 1 (he) and carrier 2 (she), who compete with each other for the uncertain spot market demands in a specific shipping service route. Assume that carrier 1 is a larger carrier with sufficient shipping capacity, while carrier 2 is a small one with constrained shipping capacity. In practice, carrier 1 can be regarded as a major shipping company operating multiple strings in a given service route, while carrier 2 can represent the smaller shipping company or the NVOCC. In the spot market, the shipping demands are uncertain and are mainly based on freight rates (i.e., shipping price). This represents the fluctuations in trade volume and shipping prices in the liner shipping industry in recent years. In addition, the service route is limited to a two-location structure, under which two operators offer essentially the same service products. The two-location one product service may be regarded as an approximation to a service route that connects two continents, e.g., a trans-Pacific service route that calls a few ports in China and a few ports in the USA, or a trans-Atlantic service that calls a few ports in North Europe and a few ports in the USA. This chapter focus on the pricing decision-making problem for carriers in an uncertain spot market.

Due to fierce competition in the spot market, the smaller carrier is often at a disadvantage due to limited capacity and are more concerned about losses and operational risks. Therefore, it is rational to assume that carrier 2 may take the risk-averse attitude when she makes her decision. Because of the severe overcapacity in the current shipping environment, large shipping companies are often not limited by shipping capacity. Small shipping companies (such as freight forwarders or NVOCC) are more vulnerable to capacity utilization because they are smaller in size and/or must pay for the purchased space in advance, regardless of whether space is used. Therefore, risk aversion and capacity constraints are important characteristics of small and medium-sized carriers in the container shipping spot market. In addition, the benchmark price (which represents the long-term contracted freight rate) should be considered when making pricing decisions for the spot market.

The notations and parameters in the chapter are defined as follows:

| Notations | Definitions |
|---|---|
| $i$ | $i = 1, 2$, where $i = 1$ represents the larger carrier and $i = 2$ represents the smaller carrier |
| $\xi$ | the forecasted market demand, which is a random variable with the probability density function and the cumulative distribution function $\phi(\cdot), \Phi(\cdot)$, respectively |
| $\theta$ | the fraction of the forecasted market demand occupied by carrier 2, then $(1 - \theta)$ represents the forecasted market demand to be met by carrier 1, where $\theta \in (0,\ 1)$ |
| $\alpha_i$ | the price sensitivity for carrier $i$, $i = 1, 2$ |
| $p_0$ | the shipping price per unit as a benchmark, which can be regarded as the reference freight rate or the long-term contracted price |
| $p_i$ | the shipping price per unit for carrier $i$, which is a decision variable, $i = 1, 2$ |
| $\gamma_i$ | the competition intensity of the price for carrier $i$, $i = 1, 2$ |
| $c_i$ | the shipping cost per unit for carrier $i, i = 1, 2$ |
| $D_i$ | the random demand for carrier $i, i = 1, 2$ |
| $C$ | the shipping capacity of carrier 2 |
| $\pi_i$ | the profit of carrier $i, i = 1, 2$ |
| $\eta$ | the risk-averse indicator of carrier 2, where $0 < \eta \leq 1$ |

We assume that the demand for one carrier' service depends linearly on his/her own price and the rival's price as shown in the following equation:

$$D_1 = (1 - \theta)\xi - \alpha_1(p_1 - p_0) + \gamma_1(p_2 - p_1), \tag{10.1}$$

$$D_2 = \theta\xi - \alpha_2(p_2 - p_0) + \gamma_2(p_1 - p_2). \tag{10.2}$$

The parameter $\theta$ is introduced to represent market shares of two shipping lines in the spot market, which may be determined by factors such as service quality, company size, and reputation. The parameter $\gamma_i$ represents the demand that carrier $i$ attracts from his/her competitor by cutting one unit of price, whereas $\alpha_i + \gamma_i$ indicates the total increased demand when carrier $i$ decreases his/her shipping price by one unit. To simplify the narrative, let $\beta_i = \alpha_i + \gamma_i$, $i = 1, 2$.

Here, some constraints must be satisfied, that is, $D_1 \geq 0$, $D_2 \geq 0$, and $p_i \geq c_i$, $i = 1, 2$. It should be noted that the constraint $p_i \geq c_i$ is not needed if we allow shipping lines to make a loss, e.g., when a shipping line operates a global shipping network, it is acceptable to make a loss for some service products in order to maintain the global supply chain operations.

Since carrier 2 has the finite shipping capacity $C$, he can only generate the revenue from the fulfilled demands constrained by his shipping capacity. The unmet demands are assumed to be lost. Thus, the profits for two carriers can be given by

$$\pi_1 = (p_1 - c_1) \cdot D_1, \tag{10.3}$$

$$\pi_2 = (p_2 - c_2) \cdot \min(C, D_2). \tag{10.4}$$

Denote $(\cdot)^+ = \max(\cdot, 0)$, $\min(C, D_2) = C - (C - D_2)^+$. The carrier 2's profit function can be rewritten as

$$\pi_2 = (p_2 - c_2)C - (p_2 - c_2)(C - D_2)^+. \tag{10.5}$$

To model the risk-averse behavior of carrier 2, in this chapter, we use the CVaR as the criterion to evaluate the risk-averse behavior. Following the arguments in Artzner *et al.* (1997) and Rockafellar and Uryasev (2000), carrier 2's utility under $\eta$-CVaR criterion can be defined as follows:

$$\mathrm{CVaR}^{\eta}(\pi_2) = \max_{v} \left\{ v + \frac{1}{\eta} E[\min(\pi_2 - v, 0)] \right\}, \tag{10.6}$$

where the parameter $\eta$ can be interpreted as a risk-averse indicator taking a value in the interval (0, 1]. As the parameter $\eta$ decreases toward 0, carrier 2 becomes more risk-averse. Now the problem can be formulated as follows:

$$\max_{p_1 > c_1} E(\pi_1) \quad \text{and} \quad \max_{p_2 > c_2} \mathrm{CVaR}^{\eta}(\pi_2).$$

## 10.3. Optimal Pricing Strategies for Competing Shipping Lines

In this section, we aim to derive the optimal pricing strategy for risk-neutral carrier 1 and risk-averse carrier 2 at the Nash equilibrium state.

The equilibrium solution can be found by using the first-order method. First, we need to analyze $\text{CVaR}^{\eta}(\pi_2)$.

$$\text{CVaR}^{\eta}(\pi_2) = \max_{v} \left\{ v + \frac{1}{\eta} E[\min(\pi_2 - v, 0)] \right\}, \tag{10.7}$$

which can be rewritten as

$$\text{CVaR}^{\eta}(\pi_2) = \max_{v} \left\{ v + \frac{1}{\eta} E[\min((p_2 - c_2) \cdot \min(D_2, C) - v, 0)] \right\}. \tag{10.8}$$

Thus, we have

$$\begin{aligned} &\text{CVaR}^{\eta}(\pi_2) \\ &= \begin{cases} (p_2 - c_2) \left[ -A_2 + \dfrac{1}{\eta} \displaystyle\int_{-\infty}^{\Phi^{-1}(\eta)} \theta \xi d\Phi(\xi) \right] & \text{if } \theta\Phi^{-1}(\eta) - A_2 \leq C, \\ (p_2 - c_2) \left[ C - \dfrac{C + A_2}{\eta} \Phi\left( \dfrac{C + A_2}{\theta} \right) \right. & \\ \qquad \left. + \dfrac{1}{\eta} \displaystyle\int_{-\infty}^{\frac{C+A_2}{\theta}} \theta \xi d\Phi(\xi) \right] & \text{if } \theta\Phi^{-1}(\eta) - A_2 \geq C. \end{cases} \end{aligned} \tag{10.9}$$

The amount $\theta\Phi^{-1}(\eta) - A_2$ can be regarded as the perceived demand of carrier 2 with the risk-averse indicator $\eta$. Thus, the above equation can be interpreted as follows: when the perceived demand of carrier 2 is less than her carrying capacity, $\text{CVaR}^{\eta}(\pi_2)$ takes the first form, otherwise, it takes the second form.

In our model, the actions of the two carriers are price decisions (i.e., $p_1$ and $p_2$), which take values within closed intervals in the practical context. It is easy to see that the payoff functions of two carriers, $E(\pi_1)$ and $\mathrm{CVaR}^\eta(\pi_2)$, are continuous in both $p_1$ and $p_2$. In addition, we will show that the payoff functions are concave in the player's own price decision in the following.

To further simplify the narrative, let $H_1 = \int_{-\infty}^{+\infty}(1-\theta)xd\Phi(x)$, $H_2 = \frac{1}{\eta}\int_{-\infty}^{\Phi^{-1}(\eta)}\theta xd\Phi(x)$. Now we can obtain the equilibrium solutions by solving the above game model under two cases as follows:

If $\theta\Phi^{-1}(\eta) - A_2 \leq C$, we have

$$p_i^H = \frac{[2\alpha_i\beta_{3-i} + \alpha_{3-i}\gamma_i]\,p_0 + 2\beta_i\beta_{3-i}c_i + \gamma_i\beta_{3-i}c_{3-i} + 2\beta_{3-i}\mathrm{H}_i + \gamma_i\mathrm{H}_{3-i}}{4\beta_i\beta_{3-i} - \gamma_i\gamma_{3-i}},$$
$$i = 1, 2.$$

If $\theta\Phi^{-1}(\eta) - A_2 \geq C$, we have

$$p_1^L = \frac{\alpha_1 p_0 + \gamma_1 p_2^L}{2\beta_1} + \frac{H_1}{2\beta_1} + \frac{c_1}{2},$$

and $p_2^L$ is given implicitly by

$$C - \frac{1}{\eta}\int_{-\infty}^{\mathrm{M}}\theta\Phi(\xi)d\xi - \frac{1}{\eta}(p_2^L - c_2)\beta_2\Phi(\mathrm{M}) = 0,$$

where

$$\mathrm{M} = \frac{\alpha_2(p_2^L - p_0) + C}{\theta} + \frac{p_2^L - c_1}{2\theta} - \frac{\alpha_1(p_0 - p_2^L) + H_1}{2\theta\beta_1}.$$

**Proposition 10.1.** *In the Nash game model, there exists a threshold value $C^*$ for carrier 2's capacity, and the equilibrium solutions are given as follows:*

$$(p_1^*, p_2^*) = \begin{cases} (p_1^L, p_2^L), & \text{if} \quad C \in (0, C^*), \\ (p_1^H, p_2^H), & \text{if} \quad C \in (C^*, +\infty), \end{cases}$$

$$C^* = \theta\Phi^{-1}(\eta) - A_2 = \theta\Phi^{-1}(\eta) - \left[\alpha_2(p_2^H - p_0) - \gamma_2(p_1^H - p_2^H)\right].$$

Further, the optimal profit and utility of two carriers can be obtained. From Proposition 10.1, an interesting point can be observed that there exists a threshold value $C^*$ for carrier 2's shipping capacity, which characterizes the optimal pricing strategy into two forms. When carrier 2's capacity is greater than $C^*$, two carriers are facing a buyer's market and the competition of two carriers is intense. In this situation, they will reduce their prices to grab more customers' orders until reaching an equilibrium by choosing the optimal prices in the form of $p_1^H$, $p_2^H$. We call this situation as high capacity (HC) condition.

If carrier 2's capacity is less than $C^*$, carrier 1 is still facing the buyer's market, whereas carrier 2 is confronting a seller's market. Hence, carrier 2 tends to increase her price to gain more profits. However, because of the risk-averse attitude, even though her capacity is limited, she will not always raise her price. The equilibrium will be reached when two carriers choose the optimal prices in the form of $p_2^L$ and $p_1^L$. We called this situation as low capacity (LC) condition.

Particularly, when both carriers have sufficient shipping capacity, the optimal pricing strategy at Nash equilibrium can only be given by the form under the HC condition. It should be pointed out that the existence of two pricing strategies is the result of capacity constraints. If there is no capacity constraint, we will only have a one equilibrium pricing strategy, which will continuously change with the risk-averse attitude.

However, the combination of the two effects (capacity constraint and risk aversion attitude) is more interesting because the risk-averse attitude will affect the pricing strategies of the two operators. Although the existence of the threshold $C^*$ is the result of capacity constraints, it is a function of the risk-averse indicator $\eta$. On the one hand, the threshold $C^*$ represents the optimal choice of the two pricing strategies based on the current capacity of carrier 2; on the other hand, the formula of the threshold $C^*$ determines how the risk-averse attitude influences such choice at the equilibrium.

**Proposition 10.2.** *Under the HC condition,* (i) *the optimal prices of two carriers are symmetric;* (ii) *the optimal prices for two carriers are increasing in the benchmark shipping price and the cost of each* *carrier*; (iii) *the optimal price decisions under the HC condition is independent of the capacity constraint C.*

In the current shipping environment, overcapacity is severe. Drewry Shipping Consultancy reported that in early November 2016, the total number of idle container ships reached 435, with a total of 1.7 million TEUs, accounting for 9% of the global container ship fleet (Drewry, 2016). This means that in the current shipping market, major shipping lines are having sufficient carrying capacity. The competition between the two major shipping companies, one is risk-neutral, and the other is risk-averse, which is in line with the scenario of Proposition 10.2. Therefore, the results of Proposition 10.2 can provide management insights into the current shipping environment.

In the above analysis, the probability distribution of the market demand is general. No specific type of demand distribution is assumed. This leads to general but complicated forms of the optimal equilibrium outcomes, which makes the theoretical analysis relatively difficult to interpret. To ease the theoretical analysis, in the following we assume that the random demand follows a uniform distribution.

**Proposition 10.3.** *Assuming that the random demand $\xi$ follows a uniform distribution $U(a,b)$, the equilibrium solutions $(p_1^*, p_2^*)$ and the threshold value $C^*$ can be simplified as follows:*

(i) *If $C \in (0, C^*)$, then $p_1^L = \frac{c_1}{2} + \frac{(1-\theta)(a+b)}{4\beta_1} + \frac{\alpha_1 p_0 + \gamma_1 p_2^L}{2\beta_1}$, and $p_2^L$ is given implicitly by the solution of to $K_1 p_2^2 + K_2 p_2 + K_3 = 0$, where*

$$K_1 = \theta F^2 + 2\beta_2 F, \quad K_2 = 2\theta F(T-a) + 2\beta_2(T-a-c_2F),$$
$$K_3 = \theta(T-a)^2 + 2\beta_2 c_2(a-T) - 2\eta C(b-a),$$

*and*

$$F = \frac{2\alpha_2\beta_1 + 2\gamma_2\alpha_1 + \gamma_1\gamma_2}{2\beta_1\theta},$$
$$T = \frac{4C\beta_1 - 4\alpha_2\beta_1 p_0 - \gamma_2\left[2\alpha_1 p_0 + 2\beta_1 c_1 + (1-\theta)(b+a)\right]}{4\beta_1\theta}.$$

(ii) *If* $C \in (C^*, +\infty)$, *then*

$$p_1^H = \frac{\begin{array}{c}2(1-\theta)\beta_2(a+b) + 4\alpha_1\beta_2 p_0 + 2\gamma_1\alpha_2 p_0 + 4\beta_1\beta_2 c_1 \\ +(b-a)\theta\eta\gamma_1 + 2\gamma_1 a\theta + 2\gamma_1\beta_2 c_2\end{array}}{8\beta_1\beta_2 - 2\gamma_1\gamma_2},$$

$$p_2^H = \frac{\begin{array}{c}(1-\theta)\gamma_2(a+b) + 4\beta_1\alpha_2 p_0 + 2\alpha_1\gamma_2 p_0 + 2\beta_1\gamma_2 c_1 \\ +2(b-a)\theta\eta\beta_1 + 4\beta_1 a\theta + 4\beta_1\beta_2 c_2\end{array}}{8\beta_1\beta_2 - 2\gamma_1\gamma_2},$$

*where* $C^* = \theta\Phi^{-1}(\eta) - A_2 = \theta\eta(b-a) + \theta a - [\alpha_2(p_2^H - p_0) - \gamma_2(p_1^H - p_2^H)]$.

**Corollary 10.1.** *Assuming that the carrier 2 is risk-neutral, i.e.,* $\eta = 1$, *and the random demand* $\xi$ *follows a uniform distribution* $U(a,b)$, *then the equilibrium solution* $(p_1^*, p_2^*)$ *and the threshold value* $C^*$ *are given as follows:*

(i) *If* $C \in (0, C^*)$, *then* $p_1^L = \frac{c_1}{2} + \frac{(1-\theta)(a+b)}{4\beta_1} + \frac{\alpha_1 p_0 + \gamma_1 p_2^L}{2\beta_1}$, *and* $p_2^L$ *is given implicitly by the solution of* $K_1 p_2^2 + K_2 p_2 + K_3 = 0$, *where*

$$K_1 = \theta F^2 + 2\beta_2 F, \quad K_2 = 2\theta F(T-a) + 2\beta_2(T - a - c_2 F),$$
$$K_3 = \theta(T-a)^2 + 2\beta_2 c_2(a-T) - 2C(b-a),$$

*and*

$$F = \frac{2\alpha_2\beta_1 + 2\gamma_2\alpha_1 + \gamma_1\gamma_2}{2\beta_1\theta},$$

$$T = \frac{4C\beta_1 - 4\alpha_2\beta_1 p_0 - \gamma_2[2\alpha_1 p_0 + 2\beta_1 c_1 + (1-\theta)(b+a)]}{4\beta_1\theta}.$$

(ii) *If* $C \in (C^*, +\infty)$, *then*

$$p_1^H = \frac{\begin{array}{c}2(1-\theta)\beta_2(a+b) + 4\alpha_1\beta_2 p_0 + 2\gamma_1\alpha_2 p_0 + 4\beta_1\beta_2 c_1 \\ +(b-a)\theta\gamma_1 + 2\gamma_1 a\theta + 2\gamma_1\beta_2 c_2\end{array}}{8\beta_1\beta_2 - 2\gamma_1\gamma_2},$$

$$p_2^H = \frac{\begin{array}{c}(1-\theta)\gamma_2(a+b) + 4\beta_1\alpha_2 p_0 + 2\alpha_1\gamma_2 p_0 \\ +2\beta_1\gamma_2 c_1 + 2(b-a)\theta\beta_1 + 4\beta_1 a\theta + 4\beta_1\beta_2 c_2\end{array}}{8\beta_1\beta_2 - 2\gamma_1\gamma_2},$$

*where* $C^* = \theta\Phi^{-1}(1) - A_2 = \theta(b-a) + \theta a - [\alpha_2(p_2^H - p_0) - \gamma_2(p_1^H - p_2^H)]$.

From Corollary 10.1, we can see that the equilibrium solution can also be characterized by two regimes based on the capacity of the second carrier. However, in the case with a risk-averse carrier 2, an important feature is that the threshold value $C^*$ for carrier 2's shipping capacity is varying in carrier 2's risk preference. We will analyze this point in more detail in the next section.

## 10.4. The Role of Risk Attitude, Capacity, and Competition

Firstly, from Proposition 10.3, the properties of $p_1^*, p_2^*$ with $p_0$ and $\eta$ are given as follows.

**Proposition 10.4.** *Assuming that the random demand* $\xi$ *follows a uniform distribution* $U(a,b)$ *and other parameters are constant. Then two carriers' optimal prices* $p_1^*$ *and* $p_2^*$ *are increasing as carrier* 2's *risk-averse indicator* $\eta$ *increases in* $(0,1]$.

Proposition 10.4 can be explained as follows. When carrier 2 becomes more risk-averse, it tends to lower its prices to attract more customers to make better use of her capacity. Due to the competition between the two carriers, carrier 1 will also respond to price reductions, even though he is risk-neutral. On the other hand, if carrier 2 becomes risk-neutral, the highest possible price of the two carriers will be realized. The profits of the two carriers will subsequently be affected by the risk-averse indicator $\eta$. However, due to the complicated form of the profit functions, it is difficult to analyze the impact analytically. We will use numerical methods to examine the impact of $\eta$ on the profits of the two carriers in later sections.

**Proposition 10.5.** *Assuming that the random demand* $\xi$ *follows a uniform distribution* $U(a,b)$ *and other parameters are constant.*

(i) *Let* $C^*(\eta)$ *denote the threshold value, defined in Proposition* 10.3, *as a function of carrier* 2's *risk-averse indicator* $\eta$. *Then the threshold value* $C^*(\eta)$ *is increasing as* $\eta$ *increases in the interval* $(0,1]$.

(ii) *If carrier 2's capacity $C$ is in the range of $C^*_{\eta=0} < C < C^*_{\eta=1}$, then as carrier 2's risk preference $\eta$ increases to a certain level, it will trigger the switch of two carriers' price strategies from one regime to the other. That is, there is a boundary jump for pricing strategies in response to carrier 2's risk-averse attitude.*

(iii) $C^*(1) - C^*(0) = \theta(b-a)\frac{6\beta_1\beta_2-\gamma_1\gamma_2}{8\beta_1\beta_2-2\gamma_1\gamma_2}$ *is increasing in $\gamma_1$ and $\gamma_2$ (competition intensity parameters), but decreasing in $\alpha_1$ and $\alpha_2$ (price sensitivity parameters).*

Proposition 10.5 shows how the threshold value $C^*$ responds to the change of carrier 2's risk-averse attitude $\eta$. In our model, the threshold value $C^*(\eta)$ can be interpreted as carrier 2's perceived demand when carrier 2 takes the risk-averse preference at a level $\eta$. It is possible that as $\eta$ increases in $(0, 1]$, the corresponding threshold value $C^*(\eta)$ exceeds carrier 2's actual shipping capacity $C$, which means when carrier 2 becomes less risk-averse, her perception about the market demand becomes more optimistic and even over-optimistic. As a result, the operation environment may change from HC condition to LC condition. This implies that carriers' pricing strategies may take different forms (e.g., the price strategies in HC and LC conditions given in Proposition 10.3) as carrier 2's risk-averse attitude changes. Figure 10.1 shows the curve of $C^*(\eta)$ with varying $\eta$ for a specific example. It divides the pricing strategies into two regimes: HC Condition and LC Condition. When carrier 2's capacity is at a moderate level (i.e., in the range of $C^*_{\eta=0} < C < C^*_{\eta=1}$), her price strategy will transform from the HC regime to the LC regime as the risk-averse indicator $\eta$ reaches a certain level (i.e., when $C^*(\eta)$ intersects with $C$). This result will be further illustrated in the numerical experiments.

Proposition 10.5(iii) gives the range of carrier 2's capacity, under which the switch of the pricing strategies is possible when $\eta$ changes. This range of the switching boundary is increasing as the competition intensity parameter ($\gamma_1$ or $\gamma_2$) increases. The implication is that in a more competitive market carrier 2's perceived demand $C^*(\eta)$ tends to be more sensitive to the risk-averse indicator $\eta$, which results in a larger range of capacity for carrier 2, under which the pricing strategy will switch from one regime to the other when the risk-averse indicator changes. On the other hand, the price sensitivity parameter ($\alpha_1$ or $\alpha_2$) has the opposite impact on the range of

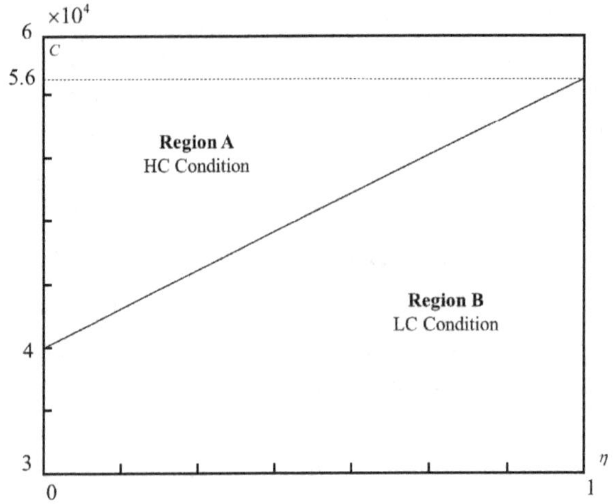


Fig. 10.1. $C^*(\eta)$ with varying $\eta$.

the switching boundary. This may be interpreted as: when a carrier's demand becomes more sensitive to its own price, carrier 2's perceived demand $C^*(\eta)$ tends to be less sensitive to the risk-averse indicator.

Next, we consider the impacts of price sensitivity and competition intensity parameters on the optimal prices. To simplify the analysis, we let the benchmark price $p_0 = 0$. We also assume that the two carriers have the same price sensitivity in the spot market. Let $\alpha = \alpha_1 = \alpha_2$, then we can obtain more specific results as follows:

**Proposition 10.6.** *Assuming that the random demand $\xi$ follows a uniform distribution $U(a, b)$, and $p_0 = 0$, $\alpha = \alpha_1 = \alpha_2$. Suppose both carriers have sufficient shipping capacity, then*

(i) *The prices of two carriers $p_1$ and $p_2$ are decreasing in $\alpha$.*
(ii) *The prices of two carriers $p_1$ and $p_2$ are decreasing in $\gamma_1$ if $2\alpha\gamma_2 c_1 + 4(\alpha + \gamma_2)\alpha c_2 < J$, and increasing in $\gamma_1$ otherwise; where $J = (1-\theta)(a+b)(4\alpha + 3\gamma_2) - 2\alpha[(b-a)\theta\eta + 2a\theta]$.*
(iii) *The prices of two carriers $p_1$ and $p_2$ are decreasing in $\gamma_2$ if $4(\alpha + \gamma_1)\alpha c_1 + 2\alpha\gamma_1 c_2 < I$, and increasing in $\gamma_2$ otherwise; where $I = [(b-a)\theta\eta + 2a\theta](8\alpha + 6\gamma_1)\gamma_1 - 4(1-\theta)(a+b)\alpha\gamma_1$.*
(iv) *Under $\alpha \neq 0$, two carriers' prices are increasing in $\gamma_1$ and $\gamma_2$ if carriers' shipping cost $c_1$ and/or $c_2$ is sufficiently large.*

(v) *Under $\alpha = 0$, two carriers' prices are decreasing in $\gamma_1$ and $\gamma_2$ regardless the values of $c_1$ and $c_2$.*

Proposition 10.6(i) may be interpreted as follows. Since the price sensitivity parameter $\alpha$ represents the degree of demand changes in response to the change of price, increasing price sensitivity parameter from a Nash equilibrium would imply the decrease of demand for both carriers (but in different scales because their optimal prices are different). This causes two carriers to reduce prices in order to reach a new Nash equilibrium. Proposition 10.6(ii) is more interesting and counter-intuitive to some extent. It states that the competition intensity could have either negative impact on two carriers' prices, or positive impact on two carriers' prices. More importantly, Proposition 10.6(ii) provides a necessary and sufficient condition to characterize whether two carriers' optimal prices would be positively or negatively affected by the competition intensity parameter $\gamma_1$ and $\gamma_2$. Specifically, two carriers' optimal prices $p_1$ and $p_2$ are decreasing in $\gamma_1$ if and only if $2\alpha\gamma_2 c_1 + 4(\alpha + \gamma_2)\alpha c_2 < J$; and the optimal prices $p_1$ and $p_2$ are decreasing in $\gamma_2$ if and only if $4(\alpha + \gamma_1)\alpha c_1 + 2\alpha\gamma_1 c_2 < I$. Note that $J$ is decreasing in $\theta$ with $J(\theta = 0) = (a + b)(4\alpha + 3\gamma_2)$ and $J(\theta = 1) = -2\alpha[(b - a)\eta + 2\alpha]$, where $\theta$ represents the market share of carrier 2 and $1 - \theta$ represents the market share of carrier 1. From the above necessary and sufficient conditions, we can observe that when carrier 1 has a large market share (i.e., $\theta \to 0$), it is likely that the condition $2\alpha\gamma_2 c_1 + 4(\alpha + \gamma_2)\alpha c_2 < J$ holds. This implies that carrier 1's competitive intensity $\gamma_1$ could have a negative effect on both carriers' prices when $\theta$ is small. On the other hand, as carrier 1's market share decreases to a certain point (i.e., $\theta$ is increasing), we will certainly know that $2\alpha\gamma_2 c_1 + 4(\alpha + \gamma_2)\alpha c_2 < J$ cannot be satisfied because $J(\theta = 1)$ is negative. Under such circumstance, carrier 1's competitive intensity $\gamma_1$ would have a positive effect on both carriers' prices. From Proposition 10.6(ii), the impact of carrier 2's competitive intensity $\gamma_2$ on the optimal prices can be similarly interpreted in relation to her market share. In addition, Proposition 10.6(iii) reveals that when shipping cost parameter $c_1$ and/or $c_2$ increases to a certain level under the conditions $\alpha \neq 0$, the competition intensity $\gamma_1$ and $\gamma_2$ would have positive impact on both carriers' prices.

Proposition 10.6(iv) considers a scenario that the price sensitivity is negligible (i.e., $\alpha = 0$) whereas the competition intensity is significant (i.e., $\gamma_1 \neq 0$ and $\gamma_2 \neq 0$). In such a scenario the competition intensity $\gamma_1$ and $\gamma_2$ would always have negative impact on both carriers' prices.

It should be noted that the results in Proposition 10.6 are based on the assumptions that $p_0 = 0$, $\alpha = \alpha_1 = \alpha_2$, and both carriers have sufficient shipping capacity. In more general cases, analytical results are difficult to obtain. Numerical methods will be used to explore whether the results can be generalized in the next section.

## 10.5. Numerical Experiments of Model Results

In this section, we further investigate the effects of some system parameters on the profits (or the utility) in more general cases. The following system parameters are set up largely based on Lee *et al.* (2015) and Chen *et al.* (2016). Let $\alpha_1 = 80$, $\alpha_2 = 100$, $\gamma_1 = 40$, $\gamma_2 = 60$, $\theta = 0.3$, $p_0 = 900$. Since carrier 2 is a smaller company, we suppose its operating cost is higher than carrier 1's, that is, $c_1 = 500$, $c_2 = 600$. The uncertain market demand $\xi$ is assumed to follow a uniform distribution $U(a, b)$ with $a = 80000$ and $b = 150000$.

From Proposition 10.5(i), when $\eta$ changes from 0 to 1, the threshold value $C^*(\eta)$ increases from 39806 to 55726. Three cases can be categorized. First, when the capacity of carrier 2 is lower than 39806, no matter what value $\eta$ takes, $C$ is always lower than $C^*$. This case belongs to the *LC condition only*. Second, when the capacity of carrier 2 is higher than 55726, we always have $C > C^*$ regardless the value of $\eta$. This case belongs to the *HC condition only*. Third, when carrier 2's capacity is in the range $(39806, 55726]$, whether this case belongs to HC or LC condition will depend on the value of $\eta$. We can term this case as the *medium capacity (MC) condition*. To compare the influence of carrier 2's capacity on price decisions and profits, we take three levels of carrier 2's capacity as follows: $C^H = 80000$ in the HC condition only category, $C^L = 20000$ in the LC condition only category, and $C^M = 50000$ in the MC condition category.

The results of how the risk aversion indicator of carrier 2 affects the utilities are shown in Fig. 10.2. To save space, we put the results

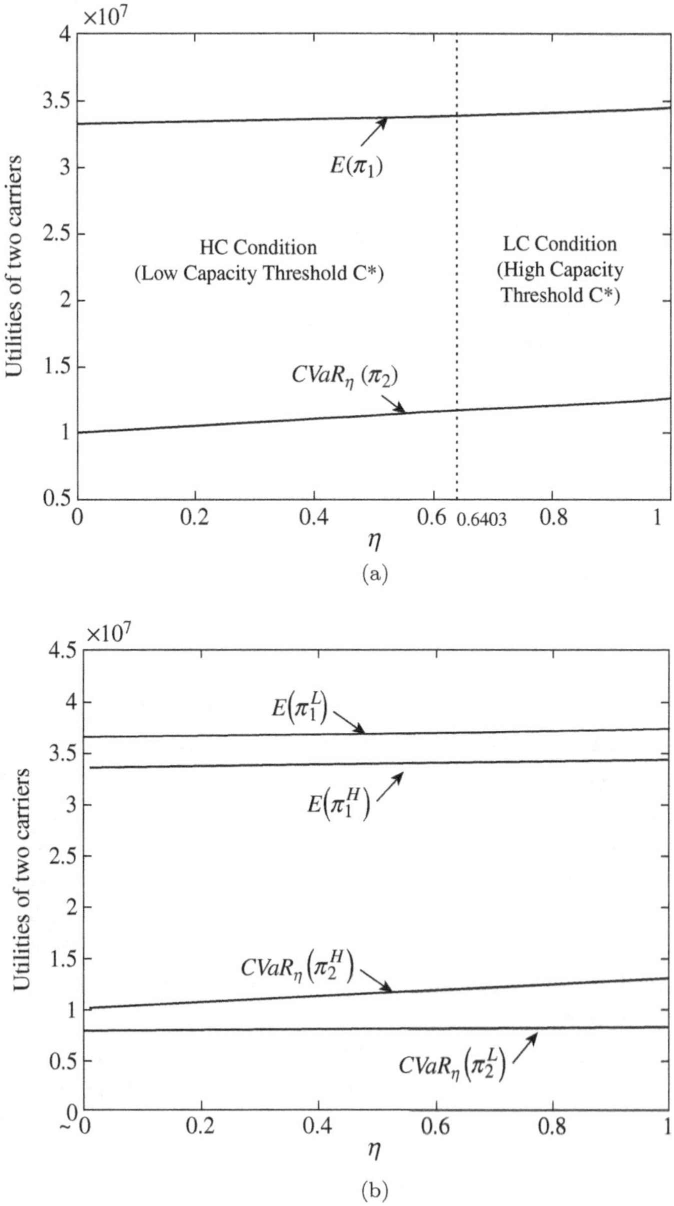


Fig. 10.2. The effects of $\eta$ on the utilities of two companies: (a) HC and LC conditions and (b) MC condition.

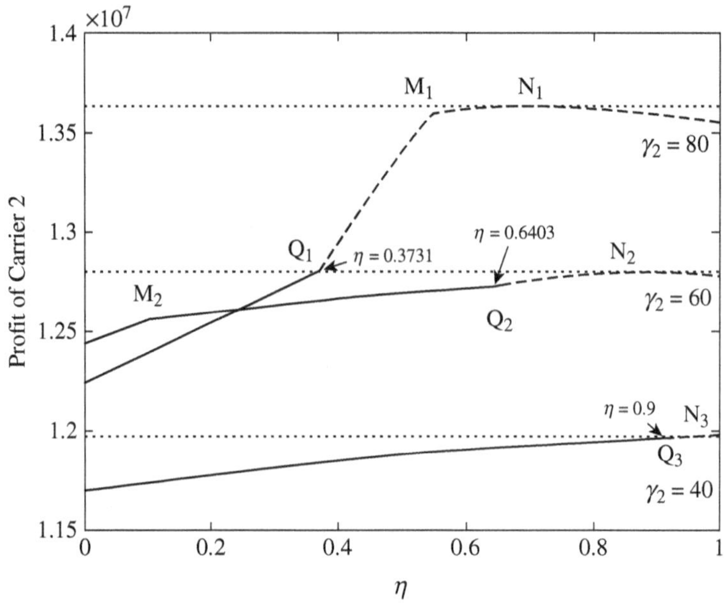


Fig. 10.3. The effects of $\eta$ on the expected profit of carrier 2.

of the HC condition and the LC condition cases on Fig. 10.2(a), and the result of the MC condition on Fig. 10.2(b).

Define $E(\pi_1)$ as carrier 1's utility and $\text{CVaR}(\pi_2)$ as carrier 2's utility. Figure 10.2 shows the utilities of two carriers with varying $\eta$. In general, the utilities in all three cases are increasing as carrier 2 becomes less risk-averse. Now let us examine how the carrier 2's risk-averse indicator influences on carrier 2's expected profit, $E(\pi_2)$. We take the MC condition case as an example. The results are shown in Fig. 10.3 ($\gamma_2 = 60$). The change rate of carrier 2's profit could be quite different for different risk-averse indicators, e.g., there exist at least two points O and Q in Fig. 10.3 ($\gamma_2 = 60$), where the rate changes suddenly. More importantly, it can be seen that carrier 2's expected profit is not necessarily always increasing in $\eta$. This point is intriguing. The implication is that appropriately selecting risk-averse preference would maximize the expected profit.

When there is a single carrier that monopolizes the market, its risk aversion attitude will lead to lower expected profits, thereby providing downside protection for possible losses. When there is a competition in the market, customers are not only affected by the freight rate of one carrier, but also by the price gap between the two carriers. Under the assumption of a risk-neutral attitude, the two carriers will reach Pareto optimal at the equilibrium point and will not unilaterally change their freight rate decisions. However, when one carrier has risk-averse attitude, it tends to choose a lower price, whereas the other risk-neutral carrier will not reduce its price at the same degree (because of its risk-neutral attitude). As a result, the price gap between two carriers increases. The risk-averse carrier can then snatch more demands at the new equilibrium point. In that case, the risk-averse carrier will gain higher profits than before (i.e., when it is risk-neutral). This may be explained by the demand function $D_2 = \theta\xi - \alpha_2(p_2 - p_0) + \gamma_2(p_1 - p_2)$, which will be increasing as the price gap increases particularly in a market with high competitive intensity $\gamma_2$. In our research context, with the increase of risk-averse attitude (i.e., the decrease of $\eta$), the decrease in price will generate additional demand for carrier 2 that could be sufficient to offset the loss caused by the price decrease at the beginning stage. This means that the expected profit of carrier 2 may increase as she changes from being risk-neutral to risk-averse. However, when the risk aversion indicator of carrier 2 reaches a certain point, the loss due to the price decrease will be greater than the gain from additional demand, so its expected profit will drop. Obviously, choosing appropriate risk aversion attitude can help carrier 2 maximize its expected profit.

To further illustrate the combined effect of the competition intensity (assuming $\gamma_2 \geq \gamma_1$) and the risk-averse indicator on carrier 2's expected profit, a few additional examples are shown in Fig. 10.3, in which $\gamma_2$ takes 40 and 80, and carrier 2 takes different risk attitudes. The points denoted by $N_1$, $N_2$ and $N_3$ in Fig. 10.3 represent the maximum expected profit of carrier 2 for the cases $\gamma_2 = 80, 60, 40$, respectively. It can be observed as $\gamma_2$ increases, carrier 2's maximum expected profit will be achieved at a more risk-averse indicator (i.e., smaller $\eta$). This observation is interesting. However, we are not able to establish this relationship analytically due to the complexity of the solutions. More research is required in this direction.

Figure 10.4 shows the utilities with different capacities of carrier 2. Under the LC condition, it can be seen that the utility of

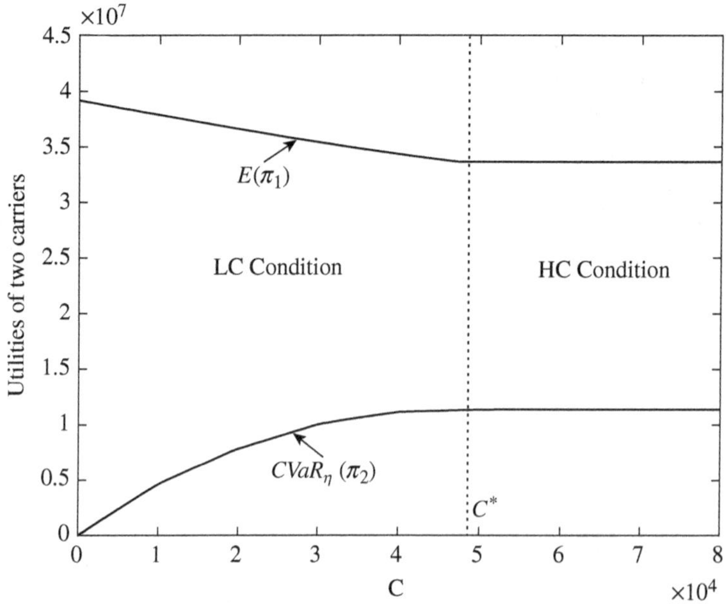


Fig. 10.4. The effects of carrier 2's capacity.

carrier 2 is increasing in $C$, although its price is decreasing. For carrier 1, its utility is reduced in $C$; this is because carrier 2 attracts more demand from carrier 1 by lowering the price far lower than carrier 1. Finally, under HC condition, $C$ has no effect on the utility of the two carriers (because it has no effect on pricing decisions).

## 10.6. Conclusion

The main characteristics of the current liner shipping market are severe overcapacity, fierce price competition, and large demand uncertainty. It is natural that some shipping companies may adopt a risk-averse attitude in their pricing strategies. This chapter considers the pricing strategies of two competing shipping companies facing uncertain demand. The first carrier is risk-neutral with sufficient capacity, while the second carrier is risk-averse with limited capacity. CVaR is used to measure the second carrier's risk-averse attitude. A Nash game model is established to model pricing decisions.

The equilibrium solution is obtained analytically. The results show that the solution takes two forms, which can be determined by the capacity threshold of carrier 2. With the assumption of the random demand following a uniform distribution, we find that when the second carrier becomes more risk-averse, the optimal freight rates of both carriers are decreasing, and the threshold for determining the pricing strategy is also decreasing. Under some conditions (e.g., zero benchmark price, same price sensitivity and sufficient capacity for both carriers), we can prove that the price sensitivity parameter has a negative impact on the prices of the two carriers; and the competition intensity may have a negative or positive impact on the freight rates of both carriers. More importantly, we provide a sufficient and necessary condition to determine whether the optimal freight rates of the two carriers would be positively or negatively affected by the competition intensity parameter.

The model is quite generic and is essentially applicable to other industrial sectors with limited capacity and perishable products. In this sense, it enriches the risk-averse literature in a broader context. However, it should be pointed out that this model has some limitations. The model is relatively simple that only considers the two-location one product service with two shipping lines. In practice, a shipping service route often covers multiple ports. Naturally, a shipping company may offer customers multiple routes (container paths) that share the shipping capacity in the shipping network (Wang *et al.*, 2015). It is possible to take into account the carrier's risk-averse behavior (with respect to the revenue) in a more general shipping network. This problem can be reformulated into stochastic multi-commodity network flow models (in which the expected revenue may be replaced by a CVaR). Some studies have established stochastic programming models to maximize expected profits under uncertain demand or capacity considering network effects (for example, Wang (2016); Wang *et al.* (2017)). These models may be extendable to include risk-averse behaviors. However, one challenging issue is how to determine and split the vessel capacity among different service products when facing uncertain demands. Moreover, two competing channels in this chapter are represented by two carriers. It would be interesting to expand the model to the case with multiple channel members.

## References

Artzner, P., Delbaen, F., Eber, J. M., & Heath, D. (1997). Thinking coherently. *Risk*, 10, pp. 68–71.

Chen, R., Dong, J. X., & Lee, C. Y. (2016). Pricing and competition in a shipping market with waste shipments and empty container repositioning. *Transportation Research Part B: Methodological*, 85, pp. 32–55.

Drewry (2016). Desperately waiting for ship operators. *Container Insight Weekly*, 4th December 2016.

Fransoo, J. C., & Lee, C. Y. (2013). The critical role of ocean container transport in global supply chain performance. *Production and Operations Management*, 22(2), pp. 253–268.

Lee, C. Y. & Song, D. P. (2017). Ocean container transport in global supply chains: Overview and research opportunities. *Transportation Research Part B: Methodological*, 95, pp. 442–474.

Lee, C. Y., Tang, C. S., Yin, R., & An, J. (2015). Fractional price matching policies arising from the ocean freight service industry. *Production and Operations Management*, 24(7), pp. 1118–1134.

Mandryk, W. (2009). Measuring global seaborne trade, *International Maritime Statistics Forum*, New Orleans, 4–6 May 2009.

Rockafellar, R. T., & Uryasev, S. (2000). Optimization of conditional value-at-risk. *Journal of Risk*, 2, pp. 21–42.

Rockafellar, R.T. & Uryasev, S. (2002). Conditional value-at-risk for general loss distributions. *Journal of Banking & Finance*, 26(7), pp. 1443–1471

Sarykalin, S., Serraino, G., & Uryasev, S. (2008).Value-at-risk vs. conditional value-at-risk in risk management and optimization, *Tutorials in Operations Research*. INFORMS, pp. 270–294.

Wang, H., Wang, X., & Zhang, X. (2017). Dynamic resource allocation for intermodal freight transportation with network effects: Approximations and algorithms. *Transportation Research Part B: Methodological*, 99, pp. 83–112.

Wang, X. (2016). Stochastic resource allocation for containerized cargo transportation networks when capacities are uncertain. *Transportation Research Part E: Logistics and Transportation Review*, 93, pp. 334–357.

Zheng, W., Li, B., & Song, D. P. (2017). Effects of risk-aversion on competing shipping lines' pricing strategies with uncertain demands. *Transportation Research Part B: Methodological*, 104, pp. 337–356.

© 2022 World Scientific Publishing Europe Ltd.
https://doi.org/10.1142/9781800610408_bmatter

# Index

## M



## N



## O



## P



## R

CPSIA information can be obtained
at www.ICGtesting.com
Printed in the USA
JSHW031729080921
18553JS00003B/3

9 781800 610392